中華譯學館

莫言題

中华译学倡立倡字与
以中华为根译与学并重
弘扬优秀文化促进中外交流
拓展精神疆域驱动思想创新

丁酉年冬月许钧撰 罗卫东书

中华译学馆·中华翻译家代表性译文库

许 钧 郭国良 / 总主编

林语堂 卷

冯全功 / 编

ZHEJIANG UNIVERSITY PRESS
浙江大学出版社

SELECTIONS OF LIN YUTANG'S TRANSLATION

总　序

　　考察中华文化发展与演变的历史,我们会清楚地看到翻译所起到的特殊作用。梁启超在谈及佛经翻译时曾有过一段很深刻的论述:"凡一民族之文化,其容纳性愈富者,其增展力愈强,此定理也。我民族对于外来文化之容纳性,惟佛学输入时代最能发挥。故不惟思想界生莫大之变化,即文学界亦然。"①

　　今年是五四运动一百周年,以梁启超的这一观点去审视五四运动前后的翻译,我们会有更多的发现。五四运动前后,通过翻译这条开放之路,中国的有识之士得以了解域外的新思潮、新观念,使走出封闭的自我有了可能。在中国,无论是在五四运动这一思想运动中,还是自1978年改革开放以来,翻译活动都显示出了独特的活力。其最重要的意义之一,就在于通过敞开自身,以他者为明镜,进一步解放自己,认识自己,改造自己,丰富自己,恰如周桂笙所言,经由翻译,取人之长,补己之短,收"相互发明之效"②。如果打开视野,以历史发展的眼光,

① 梁启超.翻译文学与佛典//罗新璋.翻译论集.北京:商务印书馆,1984:63.
② 陈福康.中国译学理论史稿.上海:上海外语教育出版社,1992:162.

从精神深处去探寻五四运动前后的翻译,我们会看到,翻译不是盲目的,而是在自觉地、不断地拓展思想的疆界。根据目前所掌握的资料,我们发现,在 20 世纪初,中国对社会主义思潮有着持续不断的译介,而这种译介活动,对社会主义学说、马克思主义思想在中国的传播及其与中国实践的结合具有重要的意义。在我看来,从社会主义思想的翻译,到马克思主义的译介,再到结合中国的社会和革命实践之后中国共产党的诞生,这是一条思想疆域的拓展之路,更是一条马克思主义与中国革命相结合的创造之路。

开放的精神与创造的力量,构成了我们认识翻译、理解翻译的两个基点。在这个意义上,我们可以说,中国的翻译史,就是一部中外文化交流、互学互鉴的历史,也是一部中外思想不断拓展、不断创新、不断丰富的历史。而在这一历史进程中,一位位伟大的翻译家,不仅仅以他们精心阐释、用心传译的文本为国人打开异域的世界,引入新思想、新观念,更以他们的开放性与先锋性,在中外思想、文化、文学交流史上立下了一个个具有引领价值的精神坐标。

对于翻译之功,我们都知道季羡林先生有过精辟的论述。确实如他所言,中华文化之所以能永葆青春,"翻译之为用大矣哉"。中国历史上的每一次翻译高潮,都会生发社会、文化、思想之变。佛经翻译,深刻影响了国人的精神生活,丰富了中国的语言,也拓宽了中国的文学创作之路,在这方面,鸠摩罗什、玄奘功不可没。西学东渐,开辟了新的思想之路;五四运动前后的翻译,更是在思想、语言、文学、文化各个层面产生了革命性的影响。严复的翻译之于思想、林纾的翻译之于文学的作用无须赘言，而鲁迅作为新文化运动的旗手，其翻译动机、翻译立场、翻译选择和翻译方法，与其文学主张、文化革新思想别无二致，其翻译起着先锋性的作用，引导着广大民众掌握新语言、接受新思想、表达自己的精神诉求。这条道路，是通向民主的道路，也是人民大众借助掌握的新语言创造新文化、新思想的道路。

回望中国的翻译历史，陈望道的《共产党宣言》的翻译，傅雷的文学翻译，朱生豪的莎士比亚戏剧翻译……一位位伟大的翻译家创造了经典，更创造了永恒的精神价值。基于这样的认识，浙江大学中华译学馆为弘扬翻译精神，促进中外文明互学互鉴，郑重推出"中华译学馆·中华翻译家代表性译文库"。以我之见，向伟大的翻译家致敬的最好方式莫过于(重)读他们的经典译文，而弘扬翻译家精神的最好方式也莫过于对其进行研究，通过他们的代表性译文进入其精神世界。鉴于此，"中华译学馆·中华翻译家代表性译文库"有着明确的追求：展现中华翻译家的经典译文，塑造中华翻译家的精神形象，深化翻译之本质的认识。该文库为开放性文库，入选对象系为中外文化交流做出了杰出贡献的翻译家，每位翻译家独立成卷。每卷的内容主要分三大部分：一为学术性导言，梳理翻译家的翻译历程，聚焦其翻译思想、译事特点与翻译贡献，并扼要说明译文遴选的原则；二为代表性译文选编，篇幅较长的摘选其中的部分译文；三为翻译家的译事年表。

需要说明的是，为了更加真实地再现翻译家的翻译历程和语言的发展轨迹,我们选编代表性译文时会尽可能保持其历史风貌,原本译文中有些字词的书写、词语的搭配、语句的表达,也许与今日的要求不尽相同,但保留原貌更有助于读者了解彼时的文化,对于历史文献的存留也有特殊的意义。相信读者朋友能理解我们的用心,乐于读到兼具历史价值与新时代意义的翻译珍本。

许　钧

2019 年夏于浙江大学紫金港校区

目　录

第二编　古文小品

第三编　古典诗词

第四编　传奇散文

导　言

一、林语堂的传奇人生

林语堂(1895—1976)是中国现代著名作家、翻译家、语言学家和编辑出版家,在中外文化交流方面做出了杰出贡献,他的存在简直就是一个文化奇迹。

林语堂出生在福建的一个牧师家庭,从小受基督教文化影响,曾应父亲林至诚要求开堂讲道,题目是"把《圣经》像文学来读"①。1912 年,林语堂考入上海圣约翰大学,读遍学校图书馆的藏书,担任学校刊物《约翰声》英文版编辑,并在上面发表了一系列用英文写的学术文章与文学作品。大学毕业后,赴清华学校执教,参与多种教学与指导工作。三年后携妻子赴美国哈佛大学继续深造(通过学分转换获该校硕士学位),后在德国莱比锡大学攻读博士学位。博士毕业后,回国执教于北京大学,任英文及语言学教授。此后又辗转任教于其他高校,如北京女子师范大学、厦门大学、新加坡南洋大学等。

林语堂首先是一位举世闻名的双语作家,一生中创作了大量作品,其英文作品在国内外的影响尤为深远,如英文小说《京华烟云》《风声鹤唳》《朱门》《啼笑皆非》《红牡丹》,英文散文集《吾国与吾民》《生活的艺术》,英

---

① 郑锦怀.林语堂学术年谱.厦门:厦门大学出版社,2018:21.

文传记《苏东坡传》《武则天传》等。其中《吾国与吾民》《生活的艺术》语言优美,内容丰富,一出版就极其畅销,成为西方人了解中国的经典图书。林语堂的小品散文也很有名气,与以鲁迅为代表的作家的政治性小品文不同,林语堂的小品文特征鲜明,强调"独抒性灵和欢愉情怀"①。林语堂的很多小品文是双语的,最开始往往用英文发表,后陆续自译成汉语,尤其是发表在《中国评论周报》的《小评论》栏目中的英文小品文。林语堂的英文作品大多具有介绍中国传统文化的功能,有力地推动了中国文化在英语世界的传播,影响深远。

　　林语堂也是一位举世闻名的翻译家,其翻译与创作互动,被学界称为"创译一体",两者相互交织,界限模糊,开创了中国文化对外传播的"林语堂模式"②。林语堂所著的《老子的智慧》《孔子的智慧》《中国印度之智慧》等英文作品中的翻译成分大于创作成分,不妨视其为翻译作品;所著的《生活的艺术》《吾国与吾民》《苏东坡传》等英文作品中的创作成分大于翻译成分,不妨视其为原创作品。林语堂的代表性译作当属其翻译的清代沈复的《浮生六记》,他对这部作品情有独钟,尤其喜欢书中的女主人公芸,故倾力译出全文。其他典型的译文(集)还有《古文小品译英》《英译重编传奇小说》等。林语堂的翻译成就主要集中在汉译英上,也就是所谓"对西方人讲中国文化"。他在英译汉方面则着力较少。1931 年,他曾翻译出版过萧伯纳的戏剧《卖花女》,其他英译汉的知名作品相对较少。值得一提的是,林语堂一生钟爱《红楼梦》,著有《平心论高鹗》③一书,其创作的《京华烟云》也深受《红楼梦》影响。其实他也翻译过《红楼梦》(编译本),佐藤亮一的《红楼梦》日译本就是根据林语堂编译的《红楼梦》转译而

---

① 　王兆胜.论林语堂的小品散文.宝鸡文理学院学报(社会科学版),2003(4):31.
② 　冯智强,庞秀成.宇宙文章中西合璧,英文著译浑然天成——林语堂"创译一体"的文章学解读.上海翻译,2019(1):11.
③ 　还有的书名为《眼前春色梦中人:林语堂平心论红楼》(陕西师范大学出版社,2007年出版),两者收录的林语堂红学文章大同小异。

来的,只是林语堂的译本未公开出版,手稿现存于日本的一家图书馆。①
林语堂编译的《红楼梦》如能正式出版,相信会成为其最有代表性的译作。

　　林语堂还是一位出色的语言学家、发明家和编辑出版家。林语堂的
博士论文就是研究汉语音韵的,题目为《中国古代音韵学》。他还出版了
《语言学论丛》一书,收录了 30 余篇自己写的语言学文章。除了音韵学,
林语堂的语言研究还有现代方言、新标准韵、辞书编纂、文字改革、汉语拼
音,甚至还有翻译、外语教学及研究信息方面的。② 林语堂痴迷于发明,为
了发明中文打字机几乎倾家荡产,倾注差不多 30 年的心血,终于使得一
台"明快中文打字机"诞生,为电脑中文输入做出了独特的贡献。作为编
辑出版家,林语堂先后创办了《论语》《人间世》《宇宙风》等杂志,他在自己
的译著中也表现出独特的编辑智慧。

　　林语堂也是一名坚定的爱国者,在国内外重要报刊(如《大陆报》《纽
约时报》)上反复呼吁和宣传抗日,鼓舞士气,壮我民心。林语堂的长篇小
说《京华烟云》就是献给抗日志士的,其中的献词被张振玉译为:"全书写
罢泪涔涔,献予奸倭抗日人。不是英雄流热血,神州谁是自由民。"③林语
堂的爱国之心由此也能略窥一斑。

二、林语堂的人生哲学

　　人生哲学在很大程度上是对待人生的态度,就像林语堂所说的"佛教
的否定人生,儒家的正视人生,道家的简化人生"④。林语堂的人生观就像
苏东坡的一样,在很大程度上也是一种混合的人生观,所谓"老庄精神,孔
孟面目",甚至由他创办的两个期刊《论语》和《人间世》的命名也源自孔子
和庄子的作品。这在他创作与翻译的作品中有更明显的表现,如《生活的

①　详见:宋丹.日藏林语堂《红楼梦》英译原稿考论.红楼梦学刊,2016(2):73-116.
②　周祖庠.林语堂与语言学.黑龙江社会科学,2006(4):109-110.
③　林语堂.京华烟云.张振玉,译.沈阳:万卷出版公司,2013.
④　林语堂.苏东坡传.北京:外语教学与研究出版社,2009:XVI-XVII.

艺术》《吾国与吾民》《京华烟云》《老子的智慧》《孔子的智慧》等。林语堂认为，"孔子学说的本质是都市哲学，而道家学说的本质是田野哲学"，前者强调世俗社会，后者强调天地自然，这导致了"林语堂对于孔孟儒家文化和老庄道家文化的双向接受态度，即一面离不开都市文化的现实追求，一面更向往田野自然的回归理想，这成为他文化观、文学观、人生观和审美观的一个相当重要的标尺"。① 所以，中国儒道文化的熏陶，再加上从小接受的基督教文化影响，使得林语堂逐渐形成了一种浑厚、深刻的人生哲学。

对林语堂影响最深、他本人也最着力研究的当属以老庄为代表的道家思想，他那种强调"闲适""性灵""女性""自然"的文学创作思想以及他在对外译介过程中对类似体裁的偏爱与道家哲学也密不可分。正如王兆胜所言，"他终其一生投入了大量时间和精力研讨和翻译道家经典，在其著述中随处可见道家语句，他对道家有着强烈的崇拜之情。林语堂深受道家文化精神的熏染，这包括归于自然和天地大道、柔弱的女性美学、保守主义的价值取向、浪漫优雅的文体风格等方面"②。林语堂对自然的热爱与敬畏不仅因为自然有利于人们克服都市生活对人的异化，还在于自然本身就是生命之本，是自由的象征，博奥之所在，大道之所寄。《道德经》有典型的女性哲学（美学）思想，尤其是女性的柔弱，含蕴着深刻的人生智慧。然而，柔弱并不是软弱，更不是懦弱，就《道德经》第七十八章所言，"天下莫柔弱于水，而攻坚强者莫之能胜，其无以易之"。林语堂对这种柔弱的女性哲学是非常认同的，并且创作了很多类似的女性形象，最典型的就是《京华烟云》中的姚木兰。林语堂的一生或思想就是"一团矛盾"，他"是一个人生的激进主义者，但他更是一个保守主义者"③，后面这种人生态度正是在道家思想的熏陶下形成的。林语堂清新自然、浪漫飘逸、优雅美妙的创作风格也颇受道家思想影响。道家的生活方式在动乱、

① 王兆胜.林语堂与道家文化精神.海南师范大学学报（社会科学版），2008(4):49.
② 王兆胜.林语堂与道家文化精神.海南师范大学学报（社会科学版），2008(4):48.
③ 王兆胜.林语堂与道家文化精神.海南师范大学学报（社会科学版），2008(4):55.

迷惘的年代会给人更多的清醒与向往,也是人类普遍的智慧化生存方式,这也许是林语堂大力宣扬与译介道家哲学的重要原因。

　　针对儒家(伦理)哲学,林语堂取其精华,弃其糟粕,这集中体现在其贴近人生、淡化纲常的人生取舍,并且尤其认可儒家的中庸哲学。他把孔子从圣贤的地位拉向普通人,"还原"孔子在现实生活中的"真实面目",也就是一个活生生的人,有自己的喜怒哀乐和偏爱嗜好。林语堂对儒家入世文化的认可在很大程度上与其信奉的人文主义信条不谋而合,两者都强调人的现世存在与人性尊严,强调修身养性与健全人格,强调人的自我实现与个性化发展。与儒家强调"忠孝节义""仁义礼智信"等伦理生活稍有不同,林语堂的入世或贴近人生更多地表现在倡导"一种更实在、更真实具体、更生活化的人生态度,即更关注人的衣、食、住、行,更关注人的情、理,更关注人的快乐和幸福"①,或者就像他自己说的,"尘世是唯一的天堂"②。林语堂不走极端,"相信中庸之道",强调中和之美,这也是他信奉的生活准则。林语堂特别欣赏清代李密庵的《半半歌》(并对之进行翻译),所谓"看破浮生过半,半之受用无边"。这种不走极端、逍遥自在的人生态度也被称为"半半哲学",不失为儒家中庸观的世俗映照,同时也不乏道家精神的渗透。

　　林语堂从小受基督教文化影响,曾写过《从异教徒到基督徒》一书。综观林语堂的一生,"从最初对基督教文化的朦胧接受,到反叛基督教教义,信奉以儒家为主干的人文主义,最后又回到宗教中去获取一种更为博大幽深的人生理想形态的追求"③,体现出他错综复杂、相互交织的精神信仰与人生哲学。道家、儒家和基督教思想在他身上都有抹不去的痕迹,这也许是他自视为"一团矛盾"的重要原因。

---

① 王兆胜.紧紧贴近人生本相——林语堂的人生哲学.中国文学研究,1997(3):57.

② 林语堂.我这一生——林语堂口述自传.南京:江苏人民出版社,2014:260.

③ 刘勇,杨志.论林语堂的宗教文化思想与文学创作.中国现代文学研究丛刊,2008 (4):129.

三、林语堂的创作思想

林语堂的创作思想是其人生哲学在文学创作中的反映,如果把他的译作也纳入其创作范围的话,林语堂无疑受道家思想和儒家文化的影响最深。林语堂笃信"中国人生就一半道家主义,一半儒家主义"①,他的人生哲学也是在两者之间徘徊,或者说融合了两家哲学思想的精髓,儒道互补,和大多古代文人一样,同样具有"外儒内道"("行为尊孔孟,思想服老庄")的典型特征。所以从深层来看,道家精神在他的论著中表现得更为丰盈,如林语堂反复提倡与称颂的性灵、闲适、柔弱、自然等,都可以在道家哲学中找到根源。

林语堂在其作品中表现的家国意识、家园情怀、仁爱母题、中庸之道以及早期很多积极入世、批评现实的文章大多受儒家思想影响。林语堂对《孔子的智慧》一书的选编和翻译也在很大程度上体现了他对儒家文化的选择与态度。林语堂的"小说三部曲"(《京华烟云》《风声鹤唳》《朱门》)都表现出了强烈的家国意识或家园情怀,其中家是最重要的,也是国之基础,小说人物或被动卷入国之政治,或主动地介入进去,表现出了一种强烈的家国责任感。在动乱失序、内忧外患、民不聊生的特殊年代,如何守护家,如何保卫国,成为林语堂小说的重要主题之一。其实,林语堂对儒家文化并不是全盘接受的,对其不合理的部分(比如压抑人性的"三纲五常""三从四德"等)也会持批判态度。林语堂善于通过对小说中人物形象(如《红牡丹》中的梁牡丹,《朱门》中的杜柔安等)的塑造来建立一种新型的个体人格。首先从人的感官体验入手,肯定人的基本欲望与情感,满足人对幸福与快乐的追求;其次就是在精神层面寻求独立与自由,呼唤一种

---

① 冯智强.中国智慧的跨文化传播——林语堂英文著译研究.青岛:中国海洋大学出版社,2011:53.

平等意识(尤其表现在性别与阶级上)。① 这种新型人格也是林语堂超越传统儒家文化之处,是他倡导的中国人文主义精神的重要载体。不管是对人文主义的倡导,还是对"半半哲学"的偏爱,都是以儒家文化为底色的。

　　林语堂对"抒情哲学"的提倡是儒道互补的结果,这种"抒情哲学"也被其称为"闲适哲学""生活哲学"或"快乐哲学",也就是从中国文化的人文主义精神出发,以人和人生作为哲学和其他一切人文学问的出发点和归宿,强调对人类现实幸福的关怀,同时以真实的人生、人生实践和人生感悟作为哲学和其他一切人文学问立足的基点。② 我们不妨认为这种抒情哲学是林语堂作品的最大特征,也是其创作思想的集中表现。抒情哲学强调一种乐享人生的闲适情怀,关照人的内心世界与精神生活,"以自我为中心,以闲适为格调",注重一种诗意化或艺术化的人生,与道家思想具有更多的相通之处。这种抒情哲学或创作思想在他本人比较推崇的中国文人身上也有明显的表现,如陶渊明、苏东坡、张潮、李笠翁、郑板桥、金圣叹、袁中郎等。沈复的《浮生六记》也是如此,书中所描述的就是林语堂所赞美与向往的生活,虽然其中也不乏悲凉的色彩,但至少那是真实的、艺术化的、苦中寻乐的生活。《生活的艺术》更是其抒情哲学的高度浓缩,《苏东坡传》也是这种思想的重要载体。林语堂大力提倡的幽默也是其抒情哲学的重要特征。幽默与其说是一种文体文风,不如说是一种对待生活的态度,所以幽默还代表着一种生存智慧。要想有幽默,就要有闲适,就要解脱性灵,就要保留一颗童心,就要把人生艺术化。林语堂甚至把幽默追溯到了老庄与孔子,使之闪现出智慧的锋芒。幽默、闲适、性灵共同支撑着林语堂基于抒情哲学的文学创作与翻译。

　　林语堂的"闲适哲学"包括相辅相成的两个层面:一是表现内容上的

---

①　肖百容,马翔.论儒家传统与林语堂小说.湖南大学学报(社会科学版),2017(6):92-93.

②　冯智强.中国智慧的跨文化传播——林语堂英文著译研究.青岛:中国海洋大学出版社,2011:62.

闲适精神；另一是表现形式上的闲适文体。① 所以闲适文体也是林语堂创作精神的重要组成部分，主要表现在把读者视为知己、向读者说真心话的读者意识，显现出一种自然亲切的闲谈语气和清顺自然的语言特征。这种闲适文体在林语堂创作和翻译的小品文中表现得尤为明显。如张潮的《幽梦影》，作品本身就是对话形式，娓娓道来，妙抒胸怀，内容更是闲适的产物。正如作者张潮所言，"人莫乐于闲，非无所事事之谓也。闲则能读书，闲则能游名胜，闲则能交益友，闲则能饮酒，闲则能著书。天下之乐，孰大于是?"②相信林语堂对这种闲暇观或闲适观是有同感的，所以才会翻译《幽梦影》中的绝大部分内容。

四、林语堂的翻译思想

林语堂的翻译思想既可以从他发表的相关论著中得以归纳，又可以从他丰富的翻译实践中得以总结，前者是他本人对翻译本身的理性认识，后者一般是他的翻译观应用于翻译实践的结果。林语堂一生中专门论述翻译的论著不多，其翻译思想仅散见于几篇文章而已，他的翻译实践却异常丰富，所以从他的翻译实践中总结其翻译思想还有待深入挖掘。

林语堂专门论述翻译的文章中影响最大的当属其 1933 年发表的长篇文章《论翻译》，里面很多观点至今仍不乏洞见。在这篇文章中，林语堂提出了忠实、通顺、美的翻译标准，类似于严复的"信达雅"，尤其是前两者。林语堂认为，"忠实就是'信'，通顺就是'达'，至于翻译与艺术文(诗文戏曲)的关系，当然不是'雅'字所能包括"③。所以林语堂提出的这个翻译标准与严复的"信达雅"主要区别就在于美的问题，不妨认为美比雅更有涵盖力，当然他对忠实和通顺的解释也更加深入。忠实是针对原文而

① 冯智强.中国智慧的跨文化传播——林语堂英文著译研究.青岛:中国海洋大学出版社,2011:150.
② 林语堂.古文小品译英.北京:外语教学与研究出版社,2009:457.
③ 林语堂.论翻译//罗新璋.翻译论集.北京:商务印书馆,1984:418.

言的,通顺是针对译文而言的,美则是翻译与艺术文的问题。忠实要求译者对原作者负责,通顺要求对译文读者负责,美则要求对艺术本身负责。林语堂开篇就提出了翻译是一种艺术的观点,认为艺术素来没有成功的捷径,翻译艺术所依赖的"第一是译者对于原文文字上及内容上透彻的了解;第二是译者有相当的国文程度,能写清顺畅达的中文;第三是译事上的训练,译者对于翻译标准及手术的问题有正当的见解"[①]。由此可见,林语堂关于翻译的标准、译者的责任以及译者的素养的观点基本上是一脉相通的。真正的艺术化翻译家,是三者兼备的。

林语堂认为忠实是译者的第一责任,也就是忠实于原文,这里的关键便是如何解释忠实的问题。林语堂首先指出了直译和意译的命名之不妥,提出了字译和句译说,主要针对的是译者对文字的解法与译法,涉及理解与表达两个层面。句译说认为句子是有组织、有结构的东西,有集中的句义作为全句的命脉,强调对句子总体意义的领悟与传达,把字义看成活的、连贯的、不可强为分裂的东西。在翻译过程中,林语堂指出字典意义并不可靠,强调字词的意义在于译者的用法,这与维特根斯坦的意义观不谋而合。正如林语堂所言,"译者所应忠实的,不是原文的零字,乃零字所组者的语意。忠实的第二义,就是译者不但须求达意,并且须以传神为目的。译成须忠实于原文之字神句气与言外之意"[②]。传神主要在于传达字词的"暗示力",强调在情感上使译文读者有动于中。林语堂还强调绝对忠实的不可能性,译者所能做到的只是相对的忠实,或者"比较的忠实",强调对原文整体意义的传达。林语堂提倡的句译说相对字译说而言无疑是一种进步,其对翻译单位的探讨不无启发。在操作层面,句子无疑是最基本、最重要的翻译单位,林语堂的句译说很有道理;但在理论层面,其实也不妨把语篇视为翻译单位,把原文意义的生成放置在更大的层面。译者不但要对原文与原作者负责,还要对译文读者负责,这涉及译文的通

---

① 林语堂.论翻译//罗新璋.翻译论集.北京:商务印书馆,1984:417.
② 林语堂.论翻译//罗新璋.翻译论集.北京:商务印书馆,1984:425.

顺问题,林语堂也将其视为忠实的题中应有之义。通顺涉及表达,也要以句为本位,并且要符合目的语读者的接受心理,其实更多的就是译文读者对目的语用法的心理,这种观点和傅雷、钱锺书等翻译理论家强调对目的语的纯熟运用也非常相似。林语堂认为,(文学)翻译是一种艺术,译者要以爱艺术之心爱翻译,以对待艺术的谨慎不苟之心来对待翻译。林语堂首先强调了艺术文的不可译性,这里的不可译其实也就是绝对忠实的不可能性导致的。其次,林语堂强调了文体风格的传达问题,"说什么"属于内容层面,"怎样说"属于风格层面,在风格传达方面,译者要特别注意与作者创作个性直接相关的"内的体裁"。林语堂最后还借克罗齐的观点强调了"翻译即创作"(不是再创作)的观点。以上便是林语堂《论翻译》中的主要理论观点。由此可见,他提出的忠实、通顺、美的标准并不是虚无缥缈的,而是有具体观点支撑的,尤其是他的句译说、意义观以及读者心理说等。这些观点与其翻译实践也是相通的,两者可以相互印证。

从林语堂的创作与翻译活动中也可以总结出很多有价值的翻译思想,这些翻译思想林语堂本人也许没有明说,但无疑有重要的理论价值。在此不妨选择几种有代表性的思想予以简要论述。首先是林语堂的互文翻译观,"所谓互文翻译就是译者在翻译一部文学作品时广泛参照和利用相关互文资源,在借鉴其他文本的基础上力争产生精品译文"[1],其中的互文资源包括某一文本的现有译文(如果有的话)、对这一文本的研究成果以及其他相关文本或研究资源。林语堂不管是在创作还是翻译中对互文资源都有充分的利用。他在创作中最典型的表现就是把一些相关文本(或文本片段)或隐或显地植入自己的行文,这种现象在《生活的艺术》《吾国与吾民》《苏东坡传》等作品中尤其突出。《京华烟云》对《红楼梦》的互文借鉴也是非常典型的,包括情节设置、人物塑造等,小说还多次借人物之口明确地提到《红楼梦》。他在翻译时对互文资源的利用形式主要包括

---

① 冯全功.论文学翻译中的互文翻译观及其应用——以《红楼梦》复译为例.北京第二外国语学院学报,2015(8):22.

思想的相互印证,如《老子的智慧》《孔子的智慧》中利用了庄子、孟子的论著等;对前人译文的借鉴,尤其是典籍的翻译,如翻译《中庸》时直接使用辜鸿铭的译文,翻译《道德经》时对亚瑟·韦利译文的借用等;对相关研究资源的利用,主要集中在参考前人对典籍的解读上。王少娣在其专著《跨文化视角下的林语堂翻译研究》中也曾以互文视角探讨林语堂的翻译,包括互文性视域下的林语堂东西宗教哲学观、林语堂女性观的互文解析、互文性视域下的林语堂东西融合的审美观等①,读者不妨参考。其次是丰厚翻译观,也就是充分利用注释、文内补偿、前言后记等副文本的翻译理念。这种翻译理念主要是由原文读者和译文读者存在语境视差引起的,所以要补偿相关信息,以便为译文读者提供更有利的解读环境。林语堂的前言是极具研究价值的,里面囊括的内容也非常丰富多样,如《浮生六记》的前言、《老子的智慧》的前言等。林语堂的文内注释也是比较普遍地出现在他的作品中的,不管是加注补偿还是整合补偿,如《京华烟云》中就有很多整合补偿的现象,尤其是对具体文化负载词的处理,如"宋词""木兰""孙悟空"等。丰厚翻译观在很大程度上反映了林语堂高度的读者意识,带有一定的学术性,但更重要的是其跨文化传播的有效性,所以他的译文中很少出现臃肿的信息补偿,往往是适可而止,甚至是点到为止,阅读起来还是很舒服的。最后是创译一体的翻译理念,创作中有翻译,翻译中有创作,反映了其所信奉的翻译信条——"翻译即创作"。林语堂大量的小品文自译也颇能反映这种理念,其中很多对应的篇目在语义甚至是结构层面也很难用"忠实"二字概括。其他如林语堂著译作品中各种变译形式、编辑思想以及由其著译作品引发的无本(根)回译②、瘦身翻译③等翻译现象也值得进一步探索。

——————————

① 王少娣.跨文化视角下的林语堂翻译研究.上海:上海外语教育出版社,2011.
② 王宏印,江慧敏.京华旧事,译坛烟云——*Moment in Peking* 的异语创作与无根回译.外语与外语教学,2012(2):65-69.
③ 冯全功,侯小圆.瘦身翻译之理念与表现——以 *Moment in Peking* 的汉译为例.外语学刊,2017(5):105-110.

五、林语堂的译文赏析

林语堂的语言是精妙的,不管是汉语还是英语,而他的英语水平甚至让英美人士汗颜。他的翻译成就主要集中在汉译英上,包括哲学典籍、古代小品文、古典小说、古典诗词等。清代张潮的《幽梦影》主要是对话体的形式,张潮说句话,众人对之评论,别有风趣,文集本身很好地体现了林语堂的闲适哲学。这里我们主要以林语堂翻译的《幽梦影》为例,来简单印证一下他的翻译思想,同时也稍微领略一下他的英语修养与翻译技巧。

林语堂为《幽梦影》的翻译提供了一个几百个单词的前言,前言对于林语堂的翻译而言是非常重要的副文本。在该前言中,林语堂首先介绍了这种格言或语录体的形式特征,尤其是《幽梦影》中朋友的评论,就像私人谈话,轻松戏谑,亲密无间。随后他介绍了翻译情况:(1)删除了原文的十分之一左右的内容,这些内容涉及中国古典主题,除非有长长的解释,否则西方读者读起来将是一头雾水;(2)书中朋友的评论,删除了一些无趣的;(3)对原文内容进行了重新编排。这三点是非常重要的,体现了林语堂一贯的读者意识和重新编辑的能力。类似的副文本在林语堂的译文中比比皆是,通常是对原文的介绍再加上对自己翻译行为的说明。原文介绍主要是为了扩展一下译文读者的语境视野,翻译说明则主要是解释自己的做法,或出于对译文读者或目的语诗学的考虑,或出于自己独特的审美认识。

林语堂的译文还加入了一些自己的评论,好像他也是张潮的朋友之一,参与了张潮与朋友的对话。林语堂加入的评论与其说是翻译,不如说是创作,体现了他创译一体的翻译理念。这些评论有的是对张潮朋友(包括他的侄子张竹坡)的介绍与评论,有的是对文本内容选择的说明(如译文中选择的清代朱锡绶《幽梦续影》中的一段文字),有的是对相关话题或术语的解释(如"才子""杜鹃""豪友""淡友"等),有的是用苏东坡或其他人的话语对张潮所言的相互印证,有的是对中国特殊文化的解释,有的是对张潮或朋友话语本身的评论与说明等。林语堂的介入很多具有副文本的性质，主要是为了向译文读者提供相关语境信息，也有一些像其他朋友的评论，是对张潮所言的直接评论或引申，更具创作的性质。在此不妨聊举两例予以说明。例如张潮说："凡花色之娇媚者，多不甚香；瓣之千层者，多不结实。甚矣，全才之难也，兼之者其惟莲乎！"在四位朋友的评论之后，林语堂又加了一句："*Yutang*：The lotus grows out of mud, but is uncontaminated by it."[1]显然，这句话出自周敦颐《爱莲说》中的"出淤泥而不染"，凸显了莲之高洁，在很大程度上丰富了其作为"全才"的内涵。再如张潮（号心斋）又说道："读书不难，能用为难；能用不难，能记为难。"洪去芜曰："心斋以能记次于能用之后，想亦苦记性不如耳，世固有能记不能用者。"张竹坡曰："能记固难，能行尤难。"在两人之后，林语堂则评曰："*Yutang*：You both misunderstood Shintsai. He means 'to remember to apply them.'"[2]直接指出了两人对张潮的误解，比加注解释更有趣味。

林语堂充分认识到了英汉之间的语言和诗学差异，转换得体，译文非常地道。《幽梦影》中的"楼上看山，城头看雪，灯前看月，舟中看霞，月下看美人，另是一番情境"被林语堂译为："Things give you a different mood and impression when looked at from a particular place：such as hills seen from a tower, snow seen from the top of a city wall, the moon seen from the lamplight, river haze seen from a boat, and pretty women seen in the moonlight."[3]"有功夫读书，谓之福；有力量济人，谓之福；有学问著述，谓之福；无是非到耳，谓之福；有多闻直谅之友，谓之福"被译为："Blessed are those who have time for reading, money to help others, the learning and ability to write, who are not bothered with gossip and disputes, and who have learned friends frank with

---

① 　林语堂.古文小品译英.北京：外语教学与研究出版社，2009：42.
② 　林语堂.古文小品译英.北京：外语教学与研究出版社，2009：51.
③ 　林语堂.古文小品译英.北京：外语教学与研究出版社，2009：39.

advice."①这两句涉及英汉互译中评述位置的转换,也就是把汉语的"述评"位置(句尾焦点)转换成了英语的"评述"位置(句首焦点),符合英语的表达习惯。

英语书写过程中经常会出现(段落)主题句,后面的内容就是对主题句的阐述,汉语则往往是先分后总,水到渠成,或者一一叙说,靠读者自己去领会。所以有经验的译者在翻译汉语作品时经常会添加一些主题句或者类似主题句的话语,如"一日之计种蕉,一岁之计种竹,十年之计种柳,百年之计种松"被林语堂译为:"In planting trees, so much depends on in how many years you want to see the results. For immediate results, choose bananas; planning for one year, choose bamboos; for ten years, willows; and for a hundred years, pine trees."②这里译文的第一句就是根据原文添加的主题句,颇为自然。此外,汉语的话语重复易构成排比,形成节奏感,英语往往注重替换或省略,该句后面的两个分句就承前省略了动词 choose,遵循了英语的表达习惯。林语堂翻译的《幽梦影》还有很多其他值得欣赏的地方,此不赘述,希望这里的赏析能达到窥一斑而知全豹的目的。

六、林语堂的时代价值

中国文学与文化"走出去"已成为国家战略层面的议题,如何才能真正地"走出去"是当下学界需要深思的。潘文国在为冯智强的专著《中国智慧的跨文化传播——林语堂英文著译研究》写的序中说道:"我一直非常关注林语堂,并始终认为他是一百多年来,向世界介绍中国文化做得最成功的人。"③他的成功经验在哪里? 对当下中国文学与文化"走出去"有

---

① 林语堂.古文小品译英.北京:外语教学与研究出版社,2009:13.
② 林语堂.古文小品译英.北京:外语教学与研究出版社,2009:46.
③ 潘文国.序//冯智强.中国智慧的跨文化传播——林语堂英文著译研究.青岛:中国海洋大学出版社,2011:序1.

何启发？这也许就是林语堂最为显著的时代价值之所在。

首先，在译介过程中要注意译介内容的系统性与典型性。这种系统性与典型性还要与译者本人的喜好和价值取向一致。林语堂译介的道家文化和儒家文化就是代表，尤其是《老子的智慧》和《孔子的智慧》。这两本书各有一个基点，那就是《道德经》和《论语》，然后林语堂围绕这两部著作再添加一些其他典型的相关论著，如《庄子》《孟子》《中庸》等对相关话语进行相互印证，深入、系统地介绍儒道文化。在介绍儒道文化时，林语堂还会通过其他著作，如《生活的艺术》《吾国与吾民》《京华烟云》等，通过具体话语（文章）或人物形象来进一步宣扬或强化儒道文化。林语堂对中国的儒道文化基本上是认同的，或者说是有批判性的认同（尤其是儒家文化），在宣扬道家文化（精神）方面更是不遗余力，这在他选择的古代小品文英译中也有突出的体现。林语堂选择著译这些作品，一方面是想让世界更好地了解中国文化，另一方面也想用中国文化（尤其是道家精神）来拯救西方物质主义泛滥带来的危害。这些著译作品很大程度上也是其信奉的人文主义的载体，强调闲适的生活、女性的柔弱、中庸的原则以及回归自然、守护家园的情怀。这说明对外译介过程中要遵循"有所为有所不为"的原则，注意选择合适的作品在合适的时候系统地推介出去。

其次，要充分发挥编译一体的优势。林语堂是编、译、创，三位一体，样样出色，但并不是所有译者都有创作才能，所以针对翻译而言，要充分发挥编译的优势。这里的编译具有两层主要意义：第一是宏观层面上对相关文本进行整合编辑的能力，如《古文小品译英》《英译重编传奇小说》《孔子的智慧》等，这些书中的编译更侧重编，也就是根据特定目的或原则进行遴选的能力。第二是微观层面上对具体文本的编辑重构的能力。林语堂对很多文本的翻译并不是字对字、句对句的翻译，而是在结构上有所调整，内容上有所增删，如他在《孔子的智慧》中对《论语》的翻译，对其中的内容进行选择性翻译，并且对之进行了重新排列，就连全译的《道德经》也加上了一些章节标题（顺序未打乱）。在《英译重编传奇小说》中对元稹《莺莺传》的翻译，对原文也是经过编辑加工的，甚至还有很多创作的成

分。林语堂自译作品中也有大量类似的编译现象。这种编译在很大程度
上迎合了英语读者的阅读口味以及英语文本的诗学规范,传播效果比较
理想。中国文学与文化博大精深,源远流长,但并不是所有的作品都适合
忠实的全译,有时编译的效果可能会更好。

最后,要具有高度的读者意识与杂合的翻译策略。林语堂的读者意
识是非常强烈的,相对百分之百的文化传真而言,他更注重翻译的传播效
果,其中读者因素是他首要考虑的。林语堂在其《论翻译》中非常强调读
者接受,并把该理念付诸实践。从行文风格而言,林语堂使用的闲适笔调
是读者易于接受的,这种笔调就像和老朋友谈话一样,轻松自然,娓娓道
来。闲适笔调就像一条主线,贯穿在他的著译作品中。从内容选择而言,
林语堂选择翻译的作品也都是读者比较易于接受的,晦涩难懂的不多,如
果文章中有太多令译文读者比较费解的内容(如含有很多文化典故),林语
堂有时也会删除不译。从翻译策略而言,林语堂选择了归化和异化相
结合的杂合翻译策略,在两者之间保持动态平衡,这样既有利于文化传
播,又有利于读者接受。从文本构成而言,林语堂使用了大量的副文本,
包括前言、加注补偿、整合补偿、评论、附录、图片等,这些副文本有利于读
者对译文本身的信息进行有效解读。从读者评价而言,林语堂的翻译作
品也是成功的,包括对其翻译选材、翻译策略以及译文语言风格等方面的
评价。总之,这种读者导向型或读者友好型的译介值得我们借鉴。

七、编选说明

林语堂的时代价值并不限于此,从这位"两脚踏东西文化,一心评宇
宙文章"的文化巨人身上我们需要学习的东西还有很多。他的大量翻译
实践为我们留下了宝贵的精神财富,尤其是他的汉译英作品。在中国文
学与文化"走出去"的大背景下,我们精选了林语堂翻译的中国古典作品,
以飨读者。本书中的英语译文主要参考了外语教学与研究出版社出版的
两套丛书——2009 年版的"林语堂英文作品集"和 2015 年版的"林语堂英

译诗文选",前者包括《老子的智慧》《孔子的智慧》《古文小品译英》《英译重编传奇小说》《浮生六记》,后者包括《诸子百家》《晋唐心印》《东坡笔意》《明清小品(上)》《明清小品(中)》《明清小品(下)》。这些古典作品的中文原文参考了上述丛书以及中国基本古籍库的权威版本等资料。此外,这些原文在不同版本间有一些文字和标点上的差异,至于采取哪个版本,本书中一般参考林语堂的译文,回译过来,哪个版本最相似,就采取哪个版本。同时,本书对于相关译本中的一些排印错误做了修正(如将 congree 修正为 congee),但对于林语堂行文间,特别是不同文章间的一些单词拼写、大小写、译法不一致的情况(例如 Ch. 与 Chapter,virtue 与 Virtue,King 与 Emperor),以及可能因口音不同而导致拼写与实际发音不同(如"邺"拼写为 Nieh)等情况尽量予以保留。林语堂对于中文姓名、地名等的英文拼写,采用的是当时通行的威妥玛-翟理思式拼音,本书中也予以保留。由于林语堂常采取编、译、创一体的方式,许多译文都对原文进行了一定的增删和改动,本书仅在有必要时增加了相关的脚注说明,未在译文与原文有所不同的每一处加以赘述。

本书的代表性译文部分共有四编,分别为"诸子百家""古文小品""古典诗词"和"传奇散文"。由于我们删除了大量副文本信息,尤其是前言与导读部分,并且很多译文本身就是对林语堂译文的二度节选,所以把书中遴选的文章作为研究对象并不见得合适,读者若要做深入研究,则建议读林语堂的原始著译作品。闲暇之际,阅读本书中遴选的原文和对应译文,如果能从中悟得林语堂翻译的一些妙处,受到一些文化熏陶,学到一种处世态度,平添几分闲适情怀,我们的目的也就达到了。

此外,责任编辑董唯女士认真细致,为本书的出版付出了大量精力,在此谨表衷心谢意!

第一编

诸子百家

道德经
Book of Tao

1　道之德
The Character of Tao①

第一章

道可道，非常道；名可名，非常名。无名，天地之始；有名，万物之母。故常无欲，以观其妙；常有欲，以观其徼。此两者，同出而异名，同谓之玄，玄之又玄，众妙之门。

On the Absolute Tao

The Tao that can be told of

　　Is not the Absolute Tao;

The Names that can be given

　　Are not Absolute Names.

---

① 这些小标题是林语堂在《老子的智慧》(*The Wisdom of Laotse*)中根据《道德经》内容添加的，皆由数章构成，小标题用汉语译出。此外，每一章林语堂也都加有标题，如第一章加的标题为"On the Absolute Tao"，此类标题在本书中不再按照字面直译过来，而是采取还原为"第一章"的做法。——编者注

The Nameless is the origin of Heaven and Earth；

The Named is the Mother of All Things.

Therefore：

Oftentimes, one strips oneself of passion

 In order to see the Secret of Life；

Oftentimes, one regards life with passion

 In order to see its manifest forms.

These two (the Secret and its manifestations)

 Are (in their nature) the same；

They are given different names

 When they become manifest.

They may both be called the Cosmic Mystery；[1]

Reaching from the Mystery into the Deeper Mystery

Is the Gate to the Secret[2] of All life.

第二章

天下皆知美之为美,斯恶已;皆知善之为善,斯不善已。故有无相生,难易相成,长短相较[3],高下相倾,音声相和,前后相随。是以圣人处无为之事,行不言之教,万物作焉而不辞,生而不有,为而不恃,功成而弗居。夫唯弗居,是以不去。

---

[1] *Hsuän*—This word is the equivalent of "mystic" and "mysticism." Taoism is also known as the *Hsuänchiao*, or "Mystic Religion."——译者注。由于本书绝大多数注释(包括脚注和文中注)为译者林语堂本人的注释,下文凡是译者注,不再单独标出,其他如编者注则标出,特此说明。——编者注

[2] *Miao* may also be translated as "Essence"; it means "the wonderful," "the ultimate," "the logically unknowable," "the quintessence," or "esoteric truth."

[3] 此处的"长短相较",有些版本为"长短相形"。《道德经》的断句也很复杂,其中的标点符号,本书综合各版本之长,时参己见,不足为训。本书其他一些作品也有类似情况,后不赘述。——编者注

The Rise of Relative Opposites

When the people of the Earth all know beauty as beauty,

There arises (the recognition of) ugliness.

When the people of the Earth all know the good as good,

There arises (the recognition of) evil.

Therefore:

Being and non-being interdepend in growth;

Difficult and easy interdepend in completion;

Long and short interdepend in contrast;

High and low interdepend in position;

Tones and voice interdepend in harmony;

Front and behind interdepend in company.

Therefore the Sage:

Manages affairs without action;

Preaches the doctrine without words;

All things take their rise, but he does not turn away from them;

He gives them life, but does not take possession of them;

He acts, but does not appropriate;

Accomplishes, but claims no credit.

It is because he lays claim to no credit

That the credit cannot be taken away from him.

第三章

不尚贤,使民不争;不贵难得之货,使民不为盗;不见可欲,使民心不乱。是以圣人之治,虚其心,实其腹;弱其志,强其骨。常使民无知无欲,使夫知者不敢为也。为无为,则无不治。

Action Without Deeds

Exalt not the wise,①

 So that the people shall not scheme and contend;

Prize not rare objects,

 So that the people shall not steal;

Shut out from sight the things of desire,

 So that the people's hearts shall not be disturbed.

Therefore in the government of the Sage:

 He keeps empty their hearts,②

 Makes full their bellies,

 Discourages their ambitions,

 Strengthens their frames;

So that the people may be innocent of knowledge and desires.

And the cunning ones shall not presume to interfere.③

 By action without deeds

 May all live in peace.

第四章

道冲,而用之或不盈,渊兮,似万物之宗。挫其锐,解其纷,和其光,同其尘。湛兮,似或存。吾不知谁之子,象帝之先。

---

① Exalting the wise in government is a typical Confucian idea.

② "Empty-heart" in the Chinese language means "open-mindedness," or "humility," a sign of the cultured gentleman. Sometimes used to mean "passivity." Throughout Laotse's book, "empty" and "full" are used as meaning "humility" and "pride" respectively.

③ *Wei*, "to act," frequently used in this book to denote "interfere." *Wu-wei*, or "inaction" practically means non-interference, for it is the exact equivalent of laissez-faire.

The Character of Tao

Tao is a hollow vessel,

　　And its use is inexhaustible!

Fathomless!

　　Like the fountain head of all things.

　　Its sharp edges rounded off,

　　Its tangles untied,

　　Its light tempered,

　　Its turmoil submerged,

Yet dark like deep water it seems to remain.

　　I do not know whose Son it is,

　　An image of what existed before God.

第五章

天地不仁,以万物为刍狗;圣人不仁,以百姓为刍狗。天地之间,其犹橐籥乎! 虚而不屈,动而愈出。多言数穷,不如守中。

Nature

Nature is unkind:

　　It treats the creation like sacrificial straw-dogs.

The Sage is unkind:

　　He treats the people like sacrificial straw-dogs. [1]

How the universe is like a bellows!

　　Empty, yet it gives a supply that never fails;

　　The more it is worked, the more it brings forth.

---

[1]　The doctrine of naturalism, the Sage reaching the impartiality and often the stolid indifference of Nature.

By many words is wit exhausted.

Rather, therefore, hold to the core. ①

第六章

谷神不死,是谓玄牝,玄牝之门,是谓天地根。绵绵若存,用之不勤。

The Spirit of the Valley

The Spirit of the Valley② never dies.

It is called the Mystic Female. ③

 The Door of the Mystic Female

 Is the root of Heaven and Earth.

 Continuously, continuously,

 It seems to remain.

 Draw upon it

 And it serves you with ease. ④

2 道之训

The Lessons of Tao

第七章

天长地久。天地所以能长且久者,以其不自生,故能长生。是以圣人后其身而身先,外其身而身存。非以其无私邪?故能成其私。

Living for Others

The universe is everlasting.

---

① Center, the original nature of man. "Hold to the core" is an important Taoist tenet.

② The Valley, like the bellows, is a symbol of Taoistic "emptiness."

③ The principle of *yin*, the negative, the receptive, the quiescent.

④ He who makes use of nature's laws accomplishes results "without labor."

The reason the universe is everlasting

    Is that it does not live for Self. ①

Therefore it can long endure.

Therefore the Sage puts himself last,

    And finds himself in the foremost place;

Regards his body as accidental,

    And his body is thereby preserved.

Is it not because he does not live for Self

That his Self is realized?

第八章

上善若水。水善利万物而不争,处众人之所恶,故几于道。居善地,心善渊,与善仁,言善信,政善治,事善能,动善时。夫唯不争,故无尤。

Water

The best of men is like water;

    Water benefits all things

    And does not compete with them.

It dwells in (the lowly) places that all disdain—

    Wherein it comes near to the Tao.

In his dwelling, (the Sage) loves the (lowly) earth;

In his heart, he loves what is profound;

In his relations with others, he loves kindness;

In his words, he loves sincerity;

In government, he loves peace;

In business affairs, he loves ability;

---

① Gives life to others through its transformations.

In his actions, he loves choosing the right time.

    It is because he does not contend

    That he is without reproach.

第九章

持而盈之,不如其已;揣而锐之,不可长保;金玉满堂,莫之能守;富贵
而骄,自遗其咎。功成身退,天之道。

The Danger of Overwhelming Success

Stretch (a bow) to the very full,

    And you will wish you had stopped in time.

Temper (a sword-edge) to its very sharpest,

    And the edge will not last long.

When gold and jade fill your hall,

    You will not be able to keep them safe.

To be proud with wealth and honor

    Is to sow the seeds of one's own downfall.

Retire when your work is done,

    Such is Heaven's way. ①

第十章

载营魄抱一,能无离乎？专气致柔,能如婴儿乎？涤除玄览,能无疵
乎？爱民治国,能无为乎？天门开阖,能为雌乎？明白四达,能无知乎？
生之畜之,生而不有,为而不恃,长而不宰,是谓玄德。

Embracing the One

In embracing the One② with your soul,

---

①   The whole chapter is rhymed.

②   Important phrase in Taoism.

Can you never forsake the Tao?

In controlling your vital force to achieve gentleness,

Can you become like the new-born child?[①]

In cleansing and purifying your Mystic vision,

Can you strive after perfection?

In loving the people and governing the kingdom,

Can you rule without interference?

In opening and shutting the Gate of Heaven,

Can you play the part of the Female?[②]

In comprehending all knowledge,

Can you renounce the mind?[③]

To give birth, to nourish,

To give birth without taking possession,

To act without appropriating,

To be chief among men without managing them—

This is the Mystic Virtue.

第十一章

三十辐共一毂,当其无,有车之用。埏埴以为器,当其无,有器之用。凿户牖以为室,当其无,有室之用。故有之以为利,无之以为用。

The Utility of Not-Being

Thirty spokes unite around the nave;

From their not-being (loss of their individuality)

---

① The babe as symbol of innocence, a common imagery found also in Chuangtse; sometimes the imagery of the "new-born calf" is used.

② The *Yin*, the receptive, the passive, the quiet. "The Door of the Mystic Female is the root of Heaven and Earth," see Ch. 6.

③ This section is rhymed throughout.

Arises the utility of the wheel.

Mold clay into a vessel;

　From its not-being (in the vessel's hollow)

　Arises the utility of the vessel.

Cut out doors and windows in the house (-wall),

　From their not-being (empty space) arises the utility of the

　　house.

Therefore by the existence of the things we profit.

And by the non-existence of things we are served.

第十二章

五色令人目盲,五音令人耳聋,五味令人口爽,驰骋畋猎令人心发狂,难得之货令人行妨。是以圣人为腹不为目,故去彼取此。

The Senses

The five colors blind the eyes of man;

The five musical notes deafen the ears of man;

The five flavors dull the taste of man;

Horse-racing, hunting and chasing madden the minds of man;

Rare, valuable goods keep their owners awake at night. [1]

Therefore the Sage:

　Provides for the belly and not for the eye. [2]

　Hence, he rejects one and accepts the other.

---

[1]　Lit. "Keep one on one's guard."

[2]　"Belly" here refers to the inner self, the unconscious, the instinctive; the "eye" refers to the external self or the sensuous world.

第十三章

宠辱若惊,贵大患若身。何谓宠辱若惊? 宠为上,辱为下①,得之若惊,失之若惊,是谓宠辱若惊。何谓贵大患若身? 吾所以有大患者,为吾有身,及吾无身,吾有何患? 故贵以身为天下,若可寄天下;爱以身为天下,若可托天下。

Praise and Blame

Favor and disgrace cause one dismay;

What we value and what we fear are within our Self.

What does this mean:

"Favor and disgrace cause one dismay?"

Those who receive a favor from above

    Are dismayed when they receive it,

    And dismayed when they lose it.

What does this mean:

"What we value and what we fear② are within our Self?"

We have fears because we have a self. ③

When we do not regard that self as self,

What have we to fear?

Therefore he who values the world as his self

    May then be entrusted with the government of the world;

And he who loves the world as his self—

    The world may then be entrusted to his care.

---

① 此处的"宠为上,辱为下"有些版本为"宠为下",很难判断译者采用了哪个版本。——编者注

② Interpreted as life and death. The text of Chuangtse confirms this interpretation.

③ Lit. "body."

3　道之法

The Imitation of Tao

第十四章

视之不见,名曰夷;听之不闻,名曰希;搏之不得,名曰微。此三者,不可致诘,故混而为一。其上不皦,其下不昧。绳绳不可名,复归于无物。是谓无状之状,无物之象。是谓惚恍,迎之不见其首,随之不见其后。执古之道,以御今之有,能知古始,是谓道纪。

Prehistoric Origins

Looked at, but cannot be seen—

　　That is called the Invisible (*yi*).

Listened to, but cannot be heard—

　　That is called the Inaudible (*hsi*).

Grasped at, but cannot be touched—

　　That is called the Intangible (*wei*)①.

These three elude all our inquiries

And hence blend and become One.

Not by its rising, is there light,

Nor by its sinking, is there darkness.

　　Unceasing, continuous,

　　It cannot be defined,

And reverts again to the realm of nothingness.

That is why it is called the Form of the Formless,

The Image of nothingness.

---

①　Jesuit scholars consider these three words (in ancient Chinese pronounced nearly like *i-hi-vei*) an interesting coincidence with the Hebrew word "*Jahve*."

That is why it is called the Elusive:

Meet it and you do not see its face;

Follow it and you do not see its back.

He who holds fast to the Tao of old

In order to manage the affairs of Now

Is able to know the Primeval Beginnings

Which are the continuity[1] of Tao.

第十五章

古之善为道者,微妙玄通,深不可识。夫唯不可识,故强为之容。豫兮若冬涉川,犹兮若畏四邻,俨兮其若客,涣兮若冰之将释,敦兮其若朴,旷兮其若谷,浑兮其若浊。孰能浊以静之徐清? 孰能安以久动之徐生? 保此道者不欲盈。夫唯不盈,故能蔽而新成[2]。

The Wise Ones of Old

The wise ones[3] of old had subtle wisdom and depth of
understanding,

So profound that they could not be understood.

And because they could not be understood,

Perforce must they be so described:

Cautious, like crossing a wintry stream,

Irresolute, like one fearing danger all around,

Grave, like one acting as guest,

Self-effacing, like ice beginning to melt,

---

[1] *Chi*, a word meaning "main body of tradition," "system" and also "discipline."

[2] 有的版本为"故能弊不新成"。——编者注

[3] Another ancient text, the "rulers."

Genuine[1], like a piece of undressed wood[2],

Open-minded, like a valley,

And mixing freely[3], like murky water.

Who can find repose in a muddy world?

By lying still, it becomes clear.

Who can maintain his calm for long?

By activity, it comes back to life.

He who embraces this Tao

Guards against being over-full.

Because he guards against being over-full[4],

He is beyond wearing out and renewal.

第十六章

致虚极,守静笃。万物并作,吾以观复。夫物芸芸,各复归其根。归根曰静,是谓复命。复命曰常,知常曰明。不知常,妄作凶。知常容,容乃公,公乃王,王乃天,天乃道,道乃久,没身不殆。

Knowing the Eternal Law

Attain the utmost in Passivity,

Hold firm to the basis of Quietude.

The myriad things take shape and rise to activity,

---

[1] *Tun*, "thickness," like solid furniture, associated with the original simplicity of man, in opposition to "thinness," associated with cunning, over-refinement and sophistication.

[2] *P'u*, important Taoist idea, the uncarved, the unembellished, the natural goodness and honesty of man. Generally used to mean simplicity, plainness of heart and living.

[3] *Hun*, "muddled," "mixing freely," therefore "easygoing," "not particular." Taoist wisdom: a wise man should appear like a fool.

[4] Self-satisfaction, conceit.

But I watch them fall back to their repose.

    Like vegetation that luxuriantly grows

But returns to the root (soil) from which it springs.

To return to the root is Repose;

    It is called going back to one's Destiny.

Going back to one's Destiny is to find the Eternal Law. [1]

    To know the Eternal Law is Enlightenment.

And not to know the Eternal Law

    Is to court disaster.

He who knows the Eternal Law is tolerant;

Being tolerant, he is impartial;

Being impartial, he is kingly; [2]

Being kingly, he is in accord with Nature; [3]

Being in accord with Nature, he is in accord with Tao;

Being in accord with Tao, he is eternal,

And his whole life is preserved from harm.

第十七章

太上,下知有之;其次,亲而誉之;其次,畏之;其次,侮之。信不足焉,有不信焉。悠兮其贵言。功成事遂,百姓皆谓我自然。

---

[1] *Ch'ang*, the "constant," the law of growth and decay, of necessary alteration of opposites, can be interpreted as the "universal law of nature," or the "inner law of man," the true self (*hsingming chih ch'ang*), the two being identical in their nature.

[2] *Wang*; a possible translation is "cosmopolitan," i. e., regarding the world as one.

[3] *T'ien*, heaven or nature. Both *t'ien* here and Tao in the next line are clearly used as adjectives; hence the translation "in accord with." *T'ien* very commonly means "nature," or "natural."

Rulers

Of the best rulers

 The people (only) know[①] that they exist;

The next best they love and praise;

The next they fear;

And the next they revile.

 When they do not command the people's faith,

 Some will lose faith in them,

 And then they resort to oaths!

But (of the best) when their task is accomplished, their work done,

The people all remark, "We have done it ourselves."

第十八章

大道废,有仁义;智慧出,有大伪;六亲不和,有孝慈;国家昏乱,有忠臣。

The Decline of Tao

On the decline of the great Tao,

 The doctrine of "humanity" and "justice"[②] arose.

When knowledge and cleverness appeared,

 Great hypocrisy followed in its wake.

When the six relationships no longer lived at peace,

 There was (praise of) "kind parents" and "filial sons."

When a country fell into chaos and misrule,

 There was (praise of) "loyal ministers."

---

① Some texts read: "The people do *not* know."

② Essential Confucian doctrine, usually translated (badly) as "benevolence" and "righteousness."

第十九章

绝圣弃智,民利百倍;绝仁弃义,民复孝慈;绝巧弃利,盗贼无有。此三者以为文不足,故令有所属,见素抱朴,少私寡欲。

Realize the Simple Self

Banish wisdom, discard knowledge,

    And the people shall profit a hundredfold;

Banish "humanity," discard "justice,"

    And the people shall recover love of their kin;

Banish cunning, discard "utility,"

    And the thieves and brigands shall disappear.

As these three touch the externals and are inadequate,

    The people have need of what they can depend upon:

    Reveal thy simple self,[①]

    Embrace thy original nature,

    Check thy selfishness,

    Curtail thy desires. [②]

第二十章

绝学无忧。唯之与阿,相去几何? 善之与恶,相去若何? 人之所畏,不可不畏。荒兮其未央哉! 众人熙熙,如享太牢,如春登台。我独泊兮其未兆,如婴儿之未孩。傫傫兮,若无所归。众人皆有余,而我独若遗。我愚人之心也哉! 沌沌兮! 俗人昭昭,我独昏昏;俗人察察,我独闷闷。澹

---

①   *Su*, the unadorned, uncultured, the innate quality, simple self; originally "plain silk background" as opposed to superimposed colored drawings; hence the expression to "reveal," "realize," *su*.

②   The eight characters in these four lines sum up practical Taoist teachings.

兮其若海,飂兮若无止。众人皆有以,而我独顽似鄙。我独异于人,而贵食母。

The World and I

Banish learning and vexations end.

Between "Ah!" and "Ough!"①

    How much difference is there?

Between "good" and "evil"

    How much difference is there?

That which men fear

    Is indeed to be feared;

But, alas, distant yet is the dawn (of awakening)!

The people of the world are merry-making,

    As if partaking of the sacrificial feasts,

    As if mounting the terrace in spring;

I alone am mild, like one unemployed,

    Like a new-born babe that cannot yet smile,

    Unattached, like one without a home.

The people of the world have enough and to spare,

But I am like one left out,

    My heart must be that of a fool,

    Being muddled, nebulous!

The vulgar are knowing, luminous;

    I alone am dull, confused.

The vulgar are clever, self-assured;

    I alone, depressed.

Patient as the sea,

---

① *Wei* and *o*. "*O*" is an utterance of disapproval.

Adrift, seemingly aimless.

The people of the world all have a purpose;

I alone appear stubborn and uncouth.

I alone differ from the other people,

And value drawing sustenance from the Mother. [1]

第二十一章

孔德之容,惟道是从。道之为物,惟恍惟惚。惚兮恍兮,其中有象;恍兮惚兮,其中有物。窈兮冥兮,其中有精;其精甚真,其中有信。自古及今,其名不去,以阅众甫。吾何以知众甫之状哉? 以此。

Manifestations of Tao

The marks of great Character[2]

Follow alone from the Tao.

The thing that is called Tao

Is elusive, evasive.

Evasive, elusive,

Yet latent in it are forms.

Elusive, evasive,

Yet latent in it are objects.

Dark and dim,

Yet latent in it is the life-force.

The life-force being very true,

Latent in it are evidences.

From the days of old till now

---

[1] Imagery of the sucking child, symbolizing drawing power from Mother Nature.

[2] *Teh* as manifestation of Tao, or Tao embodied, the moral principle, tr. by Waley as "power."

Its Named (manifested forms) have never ceased,

By which we may view the Father of All Things.

How do I know the shape of Father of All things?

Through these!①

第二十二章

曲则全,枉则直,洼则盈,敝则新,少则得,多则惑。是以圣人抱一,为天下式。不自见,故明;不自是,故彰;不自伐,故有功;不自矜,故长。夫唯不争,故天下莫能与之争。古之所谓曲则全者,岂虚言哉!诚全而归之。

Futility of Contention

To yield is to be preserved whole.

To be bent is to become straight.

To be hollow is to be filled.

To be tattered is to be renewed.

To be in want is to possess.

To have plenty is to be confused.

Therefore the Sage embraces the One,②

And becomes the model of the world.

He does not reveal himself,

And is therefore luminous.③

He does not justify himself,

And is therefore far-famed.

————————————

① Manifested forms.

② The Absolute, to which transient attributes revert.

③ *Ming* with two meanings, "clear" (bright, sterling) and "clear-sighted" (wise, discerning).

He does not boast of himself,

　And therefore people give him credit.

He does not pride himself,

　And is therefore the chief among men.

It is because he does not contend

That no one in the world can contend against him.

Is it not indeed true, as the ancients say,

　"To yield is to be preserved whole?"

Thus he is preserved and the world does him homage.

第二十三章

希言自然。故飘风不终朝,骤雨不终日。孰为此者? 天地。天地尚
不能久,而况于人乎? 故从事于道者同于道,德者同于德,失者同于失。
同于道者,道亦乐得之;同于德者,德亦乐得之;同于失者,失亦乐得之。
信不足焉,有不信焉。

Identification with Tao

Nature says few words:

Hence it is that a squall lasts not a whole morning.

A rainstorm continues not a whole day.

Where do they come from?

From Nature.

Even Nature does not last long (in its utterances),

　How much less should human beings?[1]

Therefore it is that:

---

[1]　The meaning of this paragraph could be better understood in conjunction with
the first two lines of the next chapter: "He who stands on tiptoe does not stand
(firm); he who strains his strides does not walk (well)."

He who follows the Tao is identified with the Tao.

He who follows Character (*Teh*) is identified with Character.

He who abandons (Tao) is identified with abandonment (of Tao).

He who is identified with Tao—

Tao is also glad to welcome him.

He who is identified with Character—

Character is also glad to welcome him.

He who is identified with abandonment—

Abandonment is also glad to welcome him.

He who has not enough faith

Will not be able to command faith from others.

第二十四章

企者不立,跨者不行,自见者不明,自是者不彰,自伐者无功,自矜者不长。其在道也,曰余食赘形,物或恶之,故有道者不处。

The Dregs and Tumors of Virtue

He who stands on tiptoe does not stand (firm);

He who strains his strides does not walk (well);

He who reveals himself is not luminous;

He who justifies himself is not far-famed;

He who boasts of himself is not given credit;

He who prides himself is not chief among men.

These in the eyes of Tao

Are called "the dregs and tumors of virtue,"

Which are things of disgust.

Therefore the man of Tao spurns them.

第二十五章

有物混成,先天地生。寂兮寥兮,独立不改,周行而不殆,可以为天下母。吾不知其名,字之曰道,强为之名曰大。大曰逝,逝曰远,远曰反。故道大,天大,地大,王亦大。域中有四大,而王居其一焉。人法地,地法天,天法道,道法自然。

The Four Eternal Models

Before the Heaven and Earth existed

There was something nebulous:

    Silent, isolated,

    Standing alone, changing not,

    Eternally revolving without fail,

    Worthy to be the Mother of All Things.

I do not know its name

    And address it as Tao.

If forced to give it a name, I shall call it "Great."

Being great implies reaching out in space,

Reaching out in space implies far-reaching,

Far-reaching implies reversion to the original point.

Therefore: Tao is Great,

        The Heaven is great,

        The Earth is great,

        The King is also great.[1]

These are the Great Four in the universe,

And the King is one of them.

Man models himself after the Earth;

---

[1] An ancient text reads "man" in place of "King."

The Earth models itself after Heaven;

The Heaven models itself after Tao;

Tao models itself after Nature. ①

4 力量之源
The Source of Power

第二十六章

重为轻根,静为躁君。是以圣人终日行不离辎重。虽有荣观,燕处超然,奈何万乘之主,而以身轻天下? 轻则失本,躁则失君。

Heaviness and Lightness

The solid② is the root of the light;

The Quiescent is the master of the Hasty.

Therefore the Sage travels all day,

    Yet never leaves his provision-cart. ③

In the midst of honor and glory,

    He lives leisurely, undisturbed.

How can the ruler of a great country

    Make light of his body in the empire?④

In light frivolity, the Center is lost;

In hasty action, self-mastery is lost.

---

① *Tse-jan*, lit. "self-so," "self-formed," "that which is so by itself."

② Literally "heavy," with the Earth as model. In Chinese, "heaviness" or "thickness" of character, meaning "honesty," "generosity," is associated with the idea of stable luck and endurance, whereas "thinness" or "lightness" of character, meaning "frivolity" or "sharpness," is associated with lack of stable luck.

③ A pun on the phrase, containing the word "heavy."

④ By rushing about.

第二十七章

善行无辙迹,善言无瑕谪,善数不用筹策,善闭无关楗而不可开,善结无绳约而不可解。是以圣人常善救人,故无弃人;常善救物,故无弃物。是谓袭明。故善人者,不善人之师;不善人者,善人之资。不贵其师,不爱其资,虽智大迷。是谓要妙。

On Stealing the Light

A good runner leaves no track.

A good speech leaves no flaws for attack.

A good reckoner makes use of no counters.

A well-shut door makes use of no bolts,

    And yet cannot be opened.

A well-tied knot makes use of no rope,

    And yet cannot be untied.

Therefore the Sage is good at helping men;

    For that reason there is no rejected (useless) person.

He is good at saving things;

    For that reason there is nothing rejected. ①

    —This is called stealing② the light.

Therefore the good man is the Teacher of the bad.

And the bad man is the lesson③ of the good.

He who neither values his teacher

    Nor loves the lesson

---

① The Sage uses each according to his talent.

② *Hsi*, to enter or secure by devious means such as invasion, attack at night, penetration, etc. The idea is cunningly to make use of knowledge of Nature's law to obtain the best results.

③ *Tse*, raw-material, resources, help, something to draw upon for profit, such as a lesson.

Is one gone far astray,

Though he be learned.

—Such is the subtle secret.

第二十八章

知其雄,守其雌,为天下溪。为天下溪,常德不离,复归于婴儿。知其白,守其黑,为天下式。为天下式,常德不忒,复归于无极。知其荣,守其辱,为天下谷。为天下谷,常德乃足,复归于朴。朴散则为器,圣人用之则为官长。故大制不割。

Keeping to the Female

He who is aware of the Male

But keeps to the Female

Becomes the ravine① of the world.

Being the ravine of the world,

He has the original character② which is not cut up,

And returns again to the (innocence of the) babe.

He who is conscious of the white (bright)

But keeps to the black (dark)

Becomes the model for the world.

Being the model for the world,

He has the eternal power which never errs,

And returns again to the Primordial Nothingness.

He who is familiar with honor and glory

But keeps to obscurity

───────────────

① See Ch.6. The valley, or ravine, is symbol of the Female Principle, the receptive, the passive.

② *Teh*.

Becomes the valley of the world.

Being the valley of the world,

He has an eternal power which always suffices,

And returns again to the natural integrity of uncarved wood.

Break up this uncarved wood

And it is shaped into vessel,

In the hands of the Sage,

They become the officials and magistrates.

Therefore the great ruler does not cut up.

第二十九章

将欲取天下而为之,吾见其不得已。天下神器,不可为也。为者败之,执者失之。故物或行或随,或歔或吹,或强或羸,或挫或隳。是以圣人去甚,去奢,去泰。

Warning Against Interference

There are those who will conquer the world

And make of it (what they conceive or desire).

I see that they will not succeed.

(For) the world is God's own Vessel

It cannot be made (by human interference).

He who makes it spoils it.

He who holds it loses it.

For: Some things go forward,

Some things follow behind;

Some blow hot,

And some blow cold;[①]

Some are strong,

And some are weak;

Some may break,

And some may fall.

Hence the Sage eschews excess,

eschews extravagance,

eschews pride.

第三十章

以道佐人主者，不以兵强天下。其事好还。师之所处，荆棘生焉。大军之后，必有凶年。善者果而已，不敢以取强。果而勿矜，果而勿伐，果而勿骄，果而不得已，果而勿强。物壮则老，是谓不道，不道早已。

Warning Against the Use of Force

He who by Tao purposes to help the ruler of men

Will oppose all conquest by force of arms. [②]

For such things are wont to rebound.

Where armies are, thorns and brambles grow.

The raising of a great host

Is followed by a year of dearth. [③]

---

① Literally, "blow out," "blow in." I follow Waley's rendering, which conveys the meaning perfectly.

② The Chinese character for "military" is composed of two parts: "stop" and "arms." Chinese pacifists interpret this as meaning disapproval of arms ("stop armament"), whereas it may just as well mean to "stop" the enemy "by force." Etymologically, however, the word for "stop" is a picture of a footprint, so the whole is a picture of a "spear" over "footprints."

③ These six lines are by Waley, for they cannot be improved upon.

Therefore a good general effects his purpose and stops.

He dares not rely upon the strength of arms;

Effects his purpose and does not glory in it;

Effects his purpose and does not boast of it;

Effects his purpose and does not take pride in it;

Effects his purpose as a regrettable necessity;

Effects his purpose but does not love violence.

(For) things age after reaching their prime.

That (violence) would be against the Tao.

And he who is against the Tao perished young.

第三十一章

夫兵者,不祥之器,物或恶之,故有道者不处。君子居则贵左,用兵则贵右。兵者,不祥之器,非君子之器,不得已而用之,恬淡为上。胜而不美,而美之者,是乐杀人。夫乐杀人者,则不可以得志于天下矣。吉事尚左,凶事尚右。偏将军居左,上将军居右,言以丧礼处之。杀人之众,以悲哀泣之,战胜,以丧礼处之。

Weapons of Evil

Of all things, soldiers[1] are instruments of evil,

Hated by men.

Therefore the religious man (possessed of Tao) avoids them.

The gentleman favors the left in civilian life,

But on military occasions favors the right. [2]

---

[1] Another reading, "fine weapons". *Ping* can mean both "soldiers" and "weapons."

[2] These are ceremonial arrangements. The left is a symbol of good omen, the creative; the right is a symbol of bad omen, the destructive.

Soldiers are weapons of evil.

They are not the weapons of the gentleman.

When the use of soldiers cannot be helped,

　The best policy is calm restraint.

Even in victory, there is no beauty,①

And who calls it beautiful

　Is one who delights in slaughter.

He who delights in slaughter

　Will not succeed in his ambition to rule the world.

[The things of good omen favor the left.

The things of ill omen favor the right.

The lieutenant general stands on the left,

The general stands on the right.

That is to say, it is celebrated as Funeral Rite.]

The slaying of multitudes should be mourned with sorrow.

A victory should be celebrated with the Funeral Rite.②

第三十二章

道常无名。朴虽小,天下莫能臣也。侯王若能守之,万物将自宾。天地相合以降甘露,民莫之令而自均。始制有名。名亦既有,夫亦将知止。

---

① Another equally good reading："no boasting,""and who boasts of victory."

② One of the five Cardinal Rites of *Chou-li*. The last five lines but two read like a commentary, interpolated in the text by mistake. The evidence is conclusive：(1) The terms "lieutenant general" and "general" are the only ones in the whole text that are anachronisms, for these terms did not exist till Han times. (2) The commentary by Wang Pi is missing in this chapter, so it must have slipped into the text by a copyist's mistake. See also Ch.69. Cf. Mencius, "The best fighter should receive the supreme punishment"；again, "Only he who does not love slaughter can unify the empire."

知止所以不殆。譬道之在天下,犹川谷之于江海。

Tao Is Like the Sea

Tao is absolute and has no name.

Though the uncarved wood is small,

 It cannot be employed (used as vessel) by anyone.

If kings and barons can keep (this unspoiled nature),

 The whole world shall yield them lordship of their own accord.

The Heaven and Earth join,

 And the sweet rain falls,

Beyond the command of men,

 Yet evenly upon all.

Then human civilization arose and there were names. [1]

Since there were names,

 It were well one knew where to stop.

He who knows where to stop

 May be exempt from danger.

Tao in the world

 May be compared to rivers that run into the sea. [2]

第三十三章

知人者智,自知者明。胜人者有力,自胜者强。知足者富,强行者有志。不失其所者久,死而不亡者寿。

Knowing Oneself

He who knows others is learned;

---

[1] Names imply differentiation of things and loss of original state of Tao.

[2] Really to be compared to the sea, or to the rivers seeking repose in the sea.

He who knows himself is wise.

    He who conquers others has power of muscles;

He who conquers himself is strong.

    He who is contented is rich;

He who is determined has strength of will.

    He who does not lose his center endures;

He who dies yet (his power) remains has long life.

第三十四章

大道泛兮,其可左右。万物恃之以生而不辞,功成不名有,衣养万物而不为主。常无欲,可名于小;万物归焉而不为主,可名为大。以其终不自为大,故能成其大。

The Great Tao Flows Everywhere

The Great Tao flows everywhere,

    (Like a flood) it may go left or right.

The myriad things derive their life from it,

    And it does not deny them.

When its work is accomplished,

    It does not take possession.

It clothes and feeds the myriad things,

    Yet does not claim them as its own.

Often (regarded) without mind or passion,[①]

    It may be considered small.

Being the home[②] of all things, yet claiming not,

    It may be considered great.

----

①   Compare Ch.1.

②   Literally "All things return, or belong to it."

Because to the end it does not claim greatness,

Its greatness is achieved.

第三十五章

执大象，天下往；往而不害，安平太。乐与饵，过客止。道之出口，淡乎其无味，视之不足见，听之不足闻，用之不足既。

The Peace of Tao

Hold the Great Symbol①

And all the world follows.

Follows without meeting harm,

（And lives in）health, peace, commonwealth.

Offer good things to eat

And the wayfarer stays.

But Tao is mild to the taste.

Looked at, it cannot be seen;

Listened to, it cannot be heard;

Applied, its supply never fails.

第三十六章

将欲歙之，必固张之；将欲弱之，必固强之；将欲废之，必固兴之；将欲夺之，必固与之，是谓微明。柔弱胜刚强。鱼不可脱于渊，国之利器不可以示人。

The Rhythm of Life

He who is to be made dwindle（in power）

---

① The symbol of Nature, Heaven or Earth. This chapter consists of rhymed three-word lines.

Must first be caused to expand.

He who is to be weakened

Must first be made strong.

He who is to be laid low

Must first be exalted to power.

He who is to be taken away from

Must first be given.

—This is the Subtle Light.

Gentleness overcomes strength:

Fish should be left in the deep pool,

And sharp weapons of the state should be left

Where none can see them.

第三十七章

道常无为而无不为,侯王若能守之,万物将自化。化而欲作,吾将镇之以无名之朴。镇之以无名之朴,夫将无欲。不欲以静,天下将自定。

World Peace

The Tao never does

Yet through it everything is done.

If princes and dukes can keep the Tao,

The world will of its own accord be reformed.

When reformed and rising to action,

Let it be restrained by the Nameless pristine simplicity.

The Nameless pristine simplicity

Is stripped of desire (for contention).

By stripping of desire quiescence is achieved,

And the world arrives at peace of its own accord.

第三十八章

上德不德,是以有德;下德不失德,是以无德。上德无为而无以为;下德为之而有以为。上仁为之而无以为。上义为之而有以为。上礼为之而莫之应,则攘臂而扔之。故失道而后德,失德而后仁,失仁而后义,失义而后礼。夫礼者,忠信之薄而乱之首。前识者,道之华而愚之始。是以大丈夫处其厚,不居其薄,处其实,不居其华。故去彼取此。

Degeneration

The man of superior character is not (conscious of his) character,

Hence he has character.

The man of inferior character (is intent on) not losing character,

Hence he is devoid of character.

The man of superior character never acts,

Nor ever (does so) with an ulterior motive.

The man of inferior character acts,

And (does so) with an ulterior motive.

The man of superior kindness acts,

But (does so) without an ulterior motive.

The man of superior justice acts,

And (does so) with an ulterior motive.

(But when) the man of superior *li*[①] acts and finds no response,

He rolls up his sleeves to force it on others.

Therefore:

After Tao is lost, then (arises the doctrine of) humanity.

After humanity is lost, then (arises the doctrine of) justice.

After justice is lost, then (arises the doctrine of) *li*.

---

① *Li*, Confucian doctrine of social order and control, characterized by rituals; also courtesy, good manners.

Now *li* is the thinning out of loyalty and honesty of heart,

  And the beginning of chaos.

The prophets are the flowering of Tao

  And the origin of folly.

Therefore the noble man dwells in the heavy (base),

  And not in the thinning (end).

He dwells in the fruit,

  And not in the flowering (expression).

Therefore he rejects the one and accepts the other.

第三十九章

昔之得一者,天得一以清,地得一以宁,神得一以灵,谷得一以盈,万物得一以生,侯王得一以为天下正。其致之一也。天无以清将恐裂,地无以宁将恐发,神无以灵将恐歇,谷无以盈将恐竭,万物无以生将恐灭,侯王无以贵高将恐蹶。故贵以贱为本,高以下为基。是以侯王自谓孤寡不谷。此非以贱为本耶?非乎?故致舆无舆。不欲琭琭如玉,珞珞如石。

Unity through Complements

There were those in ancient times possessed of the One:

  Through possession of the One, the Heaven was clarified,

  Through possession of the One, the Earth was stabilized,

  Through possession of the One, the gods were spiritualized,

  Through possession of the One, the valleys were made full,

  Through possession of the One, all things lived and grew,

  Through possession of the One, the princes and dukes became

    the ennobled of the people.

  —That was how each became so.

Without clarity, the Heavens would shake,

Without stability, the Earth would quake,

Without spiritual power, the gods would crumble,

Without being filled, the valleys would crack,

Without the life-giving power, all things would perish,

Without the ennobling power, the princes and dukes would stumble.

Therefore the nobility depend upon the common man for support,

And the exalted ones depend upon the lowly for their base.

That is why the princes and dukes call themselves "the orphaned,"

   "the lonely one," "the unworthy."

Is it not true then that they depend upon the common man for support?

Truly, take down the parts of a chariot,

   And there is no chariot (left). ①

Rather than jingle like the jade,

   Rumble like the rocks.

第四十章

反者道之动;弱者道之用。天下万物生于有,有生于无。

The Principle of Reversion

Reversion is the action of Tao.

   Gentleness is the function of Tao.

The things of this world come from Being,

   And Being (comes) from Non-being.

---

① Another commonly accepted reading through word-substitution in the text: "Truly, the highest prestige requires no praise." Apart from the forced substitution of words, this reading makes no sense in the context.

5　生活准则
The Conduct of Life

第四十一章

上士闻道,勤而行之;中士闻道,若存若亡;下士闻道,大笑之,不笑不足以为道。故建言有之:明道若昧,进道若退,夷道若纇;上德若谷,大白若辱,广德若不足,建德若偷,质真若渝。大方无隅,大器晚成,大音希声,大象无形。道隐无名,夫唯道,善贷且成。

Qualities of the Taoist

When the highest type of men hear the Tao (truth),

　　They try hard to live in accordance with it;

When the mediocre type hear the Tao,

　　They seem to be aware and yet unaware of it;

When the lowest type hear the Tao,

　　They break into loud laughter—

　　If it were not laughed at, it would not be Tao.

Therefore there is the established saying:

　　"Who understands Tao seems dull of comprehension;

　　Who is advanced in Tao seems to slip backwards;

　　Who moves on the even Tao (Path) seems to go up and down."

Superior character appears like a hollow (valley);

Sheer white appears like tarnished;

Great character appears like insufficient;

Solid character appears like infirm;

Pure worth appears like contaminated.

　　Great space has no corners;

Great talent takes long to mature;

Great music is faintly heard;

Great form has no contour;

And Tao is hidden without a name.

It is this Tao that is adept at lending (its power) and bringing fulfillment.

第四十二章

道生一,一生二,二生三,三生万物。万物负阴而抱阳,冲气以为和。人之所恶,唯孤寡不谷,而王公以为称。故物或损之而益,或益之而损。人之所教,我亦教之。强梁者不得其死,吾将以为教父。

The Violent Man

Out of Tao, One is born;

Out of One, Two;

Out of Two, Three;

Out of Three, the created universe.

The created universe carries the *yin* at its back and the *yang* in front;

Through the union of the pervading principles it reaches harmony.

To be "orphaned," "lonely" and "unworthy" is what men hate most.

Yet the princes and dukes call themselves by such names.

For sometimes things are benefited by being taken away from,

And suffer by being added to.

Others have taught this maxim,

Which I shall teach also:

"The violent man shall die a violent death."

This I shall regard as my spiritual teacher.

第四十三章

天下之至柔,驰骋天下之至坚。无有入无间。吾是以知无为之有益。不言之教,无为之益,天下希及之。

The Softest Substance

The softest substance of the world

    Goes through the hardest.

That-which-is-without-form penetrates that-which-has-no-crevice;

Through this I know the benefit of taking no action.[①]

The teaching without words

And the benefit of taking no action

    Are without compare in the universe.

第四十四章

名与身孰亲? 身与货孰多? 得与亡孰病? 是故甚爱必大费,多藏必厚亡。知足不辱,知止不殆,可以长久。

Be Content

Fame or one's own self, which does one love more?

One's own self or material goods, which has more worth?

Loss (of self) or possession (of goods), which is the greater evil?

Therefore: he who loves most spends most,

    He who hoards much loses much.

The contented man meets no disgrace;

Who knows when to stop runs into no danger—

    He can long endure.

---

① Pervading influence of the spirit reaches everywhere, in contrast with superficial activities which create obstacles of their own.

第四十五章

大成若缺,其用不弊。大盈若冲,其用不穷。大直若屈,大巧若拙,大辩若讷。躁胜寒,静胜热。清静为天下正。

Calm Quietude

The highest perfection is like imperfection,[①]

And its use is never impaired.

The greatest abundance seems meager,

And its use will never fail.

What is most straight appears devious,

The greatest skill appears like clumsiness;

The greatest eloquence seems like stuttering.

Movement overcomes cold,

(But) keeping still overcomes heat.

Who is calm and quiet becomes the guide for the universe.

第四十六章

天下有道,却走马以粪;天下无道,戎马生于郊。祸莫大于不知足,咎莫大于欲得,故知足之足,常足矣。

Racing Horses

When the world lives in accord with Tao,

Racing horses are turned back to haul refuse carts.

When the world lives not in accord with Tao,

Cavalry abounds in the countryside.

There is no greater curse than the lack of contentment.

No greater sin than the desire for possession.

---

①   Because it assumes fluid form according to circumstances.

Therefore he who is contented with contentment shall be always
content.

第四十七章

不出户,知天下;不窥牖,见天道。其出弥远,其知弥少。是以圣人不
行而知,不见而明,不为而成。

Pursuit of Knowledge

Without stepping outside of one's doors,

One can know what is happening in the world;

Without looking out of one's windows,

One can see the Tao of Heaven.

The farther one pursues knowledge,

The less one knows.

Therefore the Sage knows without running about,

Understands without seeing,

Accomplishes without doing.

第四十八章

为学日益,为道日损。损之又损,以至于无为。无为而无不为。取天
下常以无事,及其有事,不足以取天下。

Conquering the World by Inaction

The student of knowledge (aims at) learning day by day;

The student of Tao (aims at) losing day by day.

By continual losing

One reaches doing nothing (*laissez-faire*).

By doing nothing everything is done.

He who conquers the world often does so by doing nothing. ①

When one is compelled to do something, ②

    The world is already beyond his conquering.

第四十九章

圣人无常心,以百姓心为心。善者吾善之;不善者吾亦善之,德善。信者吾信之;不信者吾亦信之,德信。圣人在天下歙歙焉,为天下浑其心。圣人皆孩之③。

The People's Hearts

The Sage has no decided opinions and feelings, ④

But regards the people's opinions and feelings as his own.

The good ones I declare good;

The bad ones I also declare good.

    That is the goodness of virtue.

The honest ones I believe;

The liars I also believe.

    That is the faith of virtue.

The Sage dwells in the world peacefully, harmoniously.

The people of the world are brought into a continuity of heart,

And the Sage regards them all as his own children.

———————————

①   By moral influence.

②   By ordering people about.

③   有的版本此句之前有"百姓皆注其耳目"的文字,林语堂的译文没有对应翻译。——编者注

④   *Hsin*, lit. "heart." Both thinking and feeling are denoted by this word. It is impossible to say a "decided heart."

第五十章

出生入死。生之徒十有三,死之徒十有三。人之生,动之于死地,亦十有三。夫何故? 以其生生之厚。盖闻善摄生者,陆行不遇兕虎,入军不被甲兵。兕无所投其角,虎无所措其爪,兵无所容其刃。夫何故? 以其无死地。

The Preserving of Life

Out of life, death enters.

The companions (organs) of life are thirteen;[1]

The companions (organs) of death are (also) thirteen.

What send man to death in this life are also (these) thirteen.

   How is it so?

Because of the intense activity of multiplying life.

It has been said that he who is a good preserver of life

   Meets no tigers or wild buffaloes on land,

   Is not vulnerable to weapons in the field of battle.

The horns of the wild buffalo are powerless against him;

The paws of the tiger are useless against him;

The weapons of the soldier cannot avail against him.

   How is it so?

Because he is beyond death.[2]

第五十一章

道生之,德畜之,物形之,势成之。是以万物莫不尊道而贵德。道之尊,德之贵,夫莫之命而常自然。故道生之,德畜之,长之育之,亭之毒之,

---

[1] According to Han Fei, the four limbs and nine external cavities. Another orthodox reading is "three-tenths," but this makes less sense.

[2] Lit. "deathless."

养之覆之。生而不有,为而不恃,长而不宰,是谓玄德。

The Mystic Virtue

Tao gives them birth.

Teh (character) fosters them.

The material world gives them form.

The circumstances of the moment complete them.

Therefore all things of the universe worship Tao and exalt Teh.

Tao is worshipped and Teh is exalted

Without anyone's order but is so of its own accord.

Therefore Tao gives them birth,

Teh fosters them,

Makes them grow, develops them,

Gives them a harbor, a place to dwell in peace,

Feeds them and shelters them.

It gives them birth and does not own them,

Acts (helps) and does not appropriate them,

Is superior, and does not control them.

—This is the Mystic Virtue.

第五十二章

天下有始,以为天下母。既得其母,以知其子;既知其子,复守其母,没身不殆。塞其兑,闭其门,终身不勤。开其兑,济其事,终身不救。见小曰明,守柔曰强。用其光,复归其明,无遗身殃,是谓习常①。

---

① 有的版本为"袭常",林语堂的译文"to rest in the Absolute"对应的似乎是"习常",但该章标题的翻译"Stealing the Absolute"对应的则很有可能是"袭常",因为在第二十七章,林语堂还把"袭明"译为"Stealing the Light"。——编者注

Stealing the Absolute

There was a beginning of the universe

    Which may be regarded as the Mother of Universe.

From the Mother, we may know her sons.

    After knowing the sons, keep to the Mother.

    Thus one's whole life may be preserved from harm.

Stop its apertures,

Close its doors,

And one's whole life is without toil.

Open its apertures,

Be busy about its affairs,

And one's whole life is beyond redemption.

He who can see the small is clear-sighted;

He who stays by gentility is strong.

    Use the light,

    And return to clear-sightedness—

Thus cause not yourself later distress

—This is to rest in the Absolute.

第五十三章

使我介然有知,行于大道,唯施是畏。大道甚夷,而民好径。朝甚除,田甚芜,仓甚虚。服文彩,带利剑,厌饮食,财货有余,是谓盗夸。非道也哉!

Brigandage

If I were possessed of Austere Knowledge,

Walking on the Main Path (Tao),

I would avoid the by-paths.

The Main Path is easy to walk on,

Yet people love the small by-paths.

The (official) courts are spic and span,

(While) the fields go untilled.

And the (people's) granaries are very low.

(Yet) clad in embroidered gowns,

And carrying fine swords,

Surfeited with good food and drinks,

(They are) splitting with wealth and possessions.

——This is to lead the world toward brigandage.

Is it not the corruption of Tao?

第五十四章

善建者不拔,善抱者不脱,子孙以祭祀不辍。修之于身,其德乃真;修之于家,其德乃余;修之于乡,其德乃长;修之于国,其德乃丰;修之于天下,其德乃普。故以身观身,以家观家,以乡观乡,以国观国,以天下观天下。吾何以知天下然哉? 以此。

The Individual and the State

Who is firmly established is not easily shaken.

Who has a firm grasp does not easily let go.

From generation to generation his ancestral sacrifices

Shall be continued without fail.

Cultivated in the individual, character will become genuine;

Cultivated in the family, character will become abundant;

Cultivated in the village, character will multiply;

Cultivated in the state, character will prosper;

Cultivated in the world, character will become universal.

Therefore:

　According to (the character of) the individual, judge the
　　individual;

　According to (the character of) the family, judge the family;

　According to (the character of) the village, judge the village;

　According to (the character of) the state, judge the state;

　According to (the character of) the world, judge the world.

　How do I know the world is so?

　By this. ①

第五十五章

含德之厚,比于赤子。毒虫不螫,猛兽不据,攫鸟不搏。骨弱筋柔而握固。未知牝牡之合而朘作,精之至也。终日号而不嗄,和之至也。知和曰常,知常曰明,益生曰祥,心使气曰强。物壮则老,谓之不道,不道早已。

The Character of the Child

Who is rich② in character

Is like a child.

　No poisonous insects sting him,

　No wild beasts attack him,

And no birds of prey pounce upon him.

His bones are soft, his sinews tender, yet his grip is strong.

Not knowing the union of male and female, yet his organs are
　complete,

　Which means his vigor is unspoiled.

---

① From within myself; or the meaning could be very well developed in the following chapter, since the chapter division is arbitrary.

② Lit. "thick," "heavy."

Crying the whole day, yet his voice never runs hoarse,

　　Which means his (natural) harmony is perfect.

To know harmony is to be in accord with the eternal,

(And) to know eternity is called discerning.

(But) to improve upon life is called an ill-omen;

To let go the emotions through impulse[1] is called assertiveness.

(For) things age after reaching their prime;

That (assertiveness) would be against Tao.

And he who is against Tao perishes young. [2]

第五十六章

知者不言,言者不知。塞其兑,闭其门,挫其锐,解其纷,和其光,同其尘,是谓玄同。故不可得而亲,不可得而疏;不可得而利,不可得而害;不可得而贵,不可得而贱,故为天下贵。

Beyond Honor and Disgrace

He who knows does not speak;

He who speaks does not know.

　　Fill up its apertures,

　　Close its doors,

　　Dull its edges,

　　Untie its tangles,

　　Soften its light,

　　Submerge its turmoil,

---

[1]　*Hsin*, lit. "mind," or "heart."

[2]　The last three lines are almost a repetition of the last three lines of Ch. 30, where they more properly belong.

—This is the Mystic Unity. ①

Then love and hatred cannot touch him.

Profit and loss cannot reach him.

Honor and disgrace cannot affect him.

Therefore is he always the honored one of the world.

6 治国之道
The Theory of Government

第五十七章

以正治国,以奇用兵,以无事取天下。吾何以知其然哉? 以此。天下多忌讳,而民弥贫;民多利器,国家滋昏;人多伎巧,奇物滋起;法令滋彰,盗贼多有。故圣人云:我无为而民自化,我好静而民自正,我无事而民自富,我无欲而民自朴。

The Art of Government

Rule a kingdom by the Normal.

Fight a battle by (abnormal) tactics of surprise. ②

Win the world by doing nothing.

How do I know it is so?

Through this—

The more prohibitions there are,

　　the poorer the people become.

The more sharp weapons there are,

　　The greater the chaos in the state.

_____

① All submerged in the One.

② *Cheng*, the normal, the straight, the righteous; *ch'i*, the abnormal, the deceitful, the surprising.

The more skills of technique,

    The more cunning[①] things are produced.

The greater the number of statutes,

    The greater the number of thieves and brigands.

Therefore the Sage says:

I do nothing and the people are reformed[②] of themselves.

I love quietude and the people are righteous by themselves.

I deal in no business and the people grow rich by themselves.

I have no desires and the people are simple and honest by themselves.

第五十八章

其政闷闷,其民淳淳;其政察察,其民缺缺。祸兮福之所倚,福兮祸之所伏。孰知其极? 其无正也。正复为奇,善复为妖。人之迷,其日固久。是以圣人方而不割,廉而不刿,直而不肆,光而不耀。

Lazy Government

When the government is lazy and dull,

    Its people are unspoiled.

When the government is efficient and smart,

    Its people are discontented.

Disaster is the avenue of fortune,

(And) fortune is the concealment of disaster.

    Who would be able to know its ultimate results?

(As it is), there would never be the normal,

---

①   *Ch'i*, same word as that used for "surprise tactics."

②   *Hua*, touched, transformed, "civilized" by moral influence. The best explanation of "doing nothing."

But the normal would (immediately) revert to the deceitful,

And the good revert to the sinister.

Thus long has mankind gone astray!

Therefore the Sage is square (has firm principles),

But not cutting (sharp-cornered),

Has integrity but does not hurt (others),①

Is straight, but not high-handed,

Bright, but not dazzling.

第五十九章

治人事天,莫若嗇。夫唯嗇,是谓早服。早服谓之重积德;重积德则无不克;无不克则莫知其极;莫知其极,可以有国;有国之母,可以长久。是谓深根固柢,长生久视之道。

Be Sparing

In managing human affairs, there is no better rule than to be
sparing.②

To be sparing is to forestall;

To forestall is to be prepared and strengthened;

To be prepared and strengthened is to be ever-victorious;

To be ever-victorious is to have infinite capacity;

He who has infinite capacity is fit to rule a country,

And the Mother (principle) of a ruling country can long endure.

This is to be firmly rooted, to have deep strength,

The road to immorality and enduring vision.

---

① In removing corruption by artificial laws and statutes and punishments.

② Never do too much.

第六十章

治大国若烹小鲜。以道莅天下，其鬼不神。非其鬼不神，其神不伤人；非其神不伤人，圣人亦不伤人。夫两不相伤，故德交归焉。

Ruling a Big Country

Rule a big country as you would fry small fish. ①

Who rules the world in accord with Tao

    Shall find that the spirits lose their power.

It is not that the spirits lose their power,

    But they cease to do people harm.

It is not (only) that they cease to do people harm,

    The Sage (himself) also does no harm to the people.

When both do not do each other harm,

    The original character is restored.

第六十一章

大国者下流，天下之交，天下之牝。牝常以静胜牡，以静为下。故大国以下小国，则取小国；小国以下大国，则取大国。故或下以取，或下而取。大国不过欲兼畜人，小国不过欲入事人。夫两者各得其所欲，大者宜为下。

Big and Small Countries

A big country (should be like) the delta low-regions,

    Being the concourse of the world,

    (And) the Female of the world.

The Female overcomes the Male by quietude,

And achieves the lowly position by quietude.

---

①   Let alone, or the fish will become paste by constant turning about.

Therefore if a big country places itself below a small country,

　　It absorbs[①] the small country.

(And) if a small country places itself below a big country,

　　It absorbs the big country.

Therefore some place themselves low to absorb (others),

Some are (naturally) low and absorb (others).

　　What a big country wants is but to shelter others,

　　And what a small country wants is but to be able to come in and
　　　be sheltered.

Thus (considering) that both may have what they want,

　　A big country ought to place itself low.

第六十二章

道者万物之奥,善人之宝,不善人之所保。美言可以市,尊行可以加人。[②] 人之不善,何弃之有? 故立天子,置三公,虽有拱璧以先驷马,不如坐进此道。古之所以贵此道者何? 不曰:以求得有罪以免邪? 故为天下贵。

The Good Man's Treasure

Tao is the mysterious secret of the universe,

The good man's treasure,

And the bad man's refuge.

　　Beautiful saying can be sold at the Market,

　　Noble conduct can be presented as a gift.

Though there be bad people,

---

① *Ch'ü*, takes, conquers, overcomes, wins over.

② 有的版本为"美言可以市尊,美行可以加人",根据林语堂的对应译文可知此非林所据。——编者注

Why reject them?

Therefore on the crowning of an emperor,

    On the appointment of the Three Ministers,

    Rather than send tributes of jade and teams of four horses,

    Send in the tribute of Tao.

Wherein did the ancients prize this Tao?

Did they not say, "to search for the guilty ones and pardon them?"

Therefore is (Tao) the treasure of the world.

第六十三章

为无为,事无事,味无味。大小多少,报怨以德。图难于其易,为大于其细。天下难事,必作于易;天下大事,必作于细。是以圣人终不为大,故能成其大。夫轻诺必寡信,多易必多难。是以圣人犹难之,故终无难矣。

Difficult and Easy

Accomplish do-nothing.

Attend to no-affairs.

Taste the flavorless.

Whether it is big or small, many or few,

    Requite hatred with virtue.

Deal with the difficult while yet it is easy;

Deal with the big while yet it is small.

The difficult (problems) of the world

    Must be dealt with while they are yet easy;

The great (problems) of the world

    Must be dealt with while they are yet small.

Therefore the Sage by never dealing with great (problems)

    Accomplishes greatness.

He who lightly makes a promise

　　Will find it often hard to keep his faith.

He who makes light of many things

　　Will encounter many difficulties.

Hence even the Sage regards things as difficult,

　　And for that reason never meets with difficulties.

第六十四章

其安易持,其未兆易谋,其脆易泮,其微易散。为之于未有,治之于未乱。合抱之木,生于毫末;九层之台,起于累土;千里之行,始于足下。为者败之,执者失之。是以圣人无为,故无败;无执,故无失。民之从事,常于几成而败之。慎终如始,则无败事。是以圣人欲不欲,不贵难得之货;学不学,复众人之所过。以辅万物之自然,而不敢为。

Beginning and End

That which lies still is easy to hold;

　　That which is not yet manifest is easy to forestall;

That which is brittle (like ice) easily melts;

　　That which is minute easily scatters.

Deal with a thing before it is there;

Check disorder before it is rife.

　　A tree with a full span's girth begins from a tiny sprout;

　　A nine-storied terrace begins with a clod of earth;

　　A journey of a thousand *li* begins at one's feet.

He who acts, spoils;

He who grasps, lets slip.

Because the Sage does not act, he does not spoil;

Because he does not grasp, he does not let slip.

The affairs of men are often spoiled within an ace of completion.

By being careful at the end as at the beginning

Failure is averted.

Therefore the Sage desires to have no desire,

And values not objects difficult to obtain.

Learns that which is unlearned,

And restores what the multitude have lost.

That he may assist in the course of Nature

And not presume to interfere.

第六十五章

古之善为道者,非以明民,将以愚之。民之难治,以其智多。故以智治国,国之贼;不以智治国,国之福。知此两者亦稽式。常知稽式,是谓玄德。玄德深矣,远矣,与物反矣,然后乃至大顺。

The Grand Harmony

The ancients who knew how to follow the Tao

Aimed not to enlighten the people,

But to keep them ignorant.

The reason it is difficult for the people to live in peace

Is because of too much knowledge.

Those who seek to rule a country by knowledge

Are the nation's curse.

Those who seek not to rule a country by knowledge

Are the nation's blessing.

Those who know these two (principles)

Also know the ancient standard,

And to know always the ancient standard

Is called the Mystic Virtue.

When the Mystic Virtue becomes clear, far-reaching,

And things revert back (to their source),

Then and then only emerges the Grand Harmony.

第六十六章

江海所以能为百谷王者,以其善下之,故能为百谷王。是以欲上民,必以言下之;欲先民,必以身后之。是以圣人处上而民不重,处前而民不害。是以天下乐推而不厌。以其不争,故天下莫能与之争。

The Lords of the Ravines

How did the great rivers and seas become the Lords of the
　　Ravines?

By being good at keeping low.

That was how they become the Lords of the Ravines. ①

Therefore in order to be the chief among the people,

　　One must speak like their inferiors.

In order to be foremost among the people,

　　One must walk behind them.

Thus it is that the Sage stays above,

　　And the people do not feel his weight;

Walks in front,

　　And the people do not wish him harm.

Then the people of the world are glad to uphold him forever.

Because he does not contend,

　　No one in the world can contend against him.

———————————

① 　See Ch.6.

第六十七章

天下皆谓我道大,似不肖。夫唯大,故似不肖。若肖,久矣其细也夫。我有三宝,持而保之:一曰慈,二曰俭,三曰不敢为天下先。慈,故能勇;俭,故能广;不敢为天下先,故能成器长。今舍慈且勇,舍俭且广,舍后且先,死矣!夫慈,以战则胜,以守则固。天将救之,以慈卫之。

The Three Treasures

All the world says: my teaching (Tao) greatly resembles folly.

Because it is great; therefore it resembles folly.

If it did not resemble folly,

It would have long ago become petty indeed!

I have Three Treasures;

Guard them and keep them safe:

    The first is Love. ①

    The second is, Never too much. ②

    The third is, Never be the first in the world.

Through Love, one has no fear;

Through not doing too much, one has amplitude (of reserve power);

Through not presuming to be the first in the world,

    One can develop one's talent and let it mature.

If one forsakes love and fearlessness,

    forsakes restraint and reserve power,

    forsakes following behind and rushes in front,

He is doomed!

For love is victorious in attack,

---

① *Ts'e*, tender love (associated with the mother).

② *Chien*, lit. "frugality," "be sparing"; see Ch.59.

And invulnerable in defense.

Heaven arms with love

Those it would not see destroyed.

第六十八章

善为士者不武,善战者不怒,善胜敌者不与,善用人者为之下。是谓不争之德,是谓用人之力,是谓配天古之极。

The Virtue of Not-Contending

The brave soldier is not violent;

The good fighter does not lose his temper;

The great conqueror does not fight (on small issues);

The good user of men places himself below others.

—This is the virtue of not-contending,

　　Is called the capacity to use men,

　　Is reaching to the height of being

　　　Mated to Heaven, to what was of old.

第六十九章

用兵有言:吾不敢为主而为客,不敢进寸而退尺。是谓行无行,攘无臂,扔无敌,执无兵。① 祸莫大于轻敌,轻敌几丧吾宝。故抗兵相加,哀者胜矣。

Camouflage

There is the maxim of military strategists:

———————————

① 该句有的版本为:"是谓行无行,攘无臂,执无兵,乃无敌矣。"——编者注

I dare not be the first to invade, but rather be the invaded. ①

Dare not press forward an inch, but rather retreat a foot.

That is, to march without formations,

To roll not up the sleeves,

To charge not in frontal attacks,

To arm without weapons. ②

There is no greater catastrophe than to underestimate the enemy.

To underestimate the enemy might entail the loss of my treasures. ③

Therefore when two equally matched armies meet,

It is the man of sorrow④ who wins.

第七十章

吾言甚易知,甚易行。天下莫能知,莫能行。言有宗,事有君。夫唯无知,是以不我知。知我者希,则我者贵。是以圣人被褐而怀玉。

They Know Me Not

My teachings are very easy to understand and very easy to practice,

But no one can understand them and no one can practice them.

In my words there is a principle.

---

① *Invader* and *invaded*, lit. "host" and "guest." It is possible to read it differently by supplying the often dropped *when*: "When I dare not to be the invader, then I will be the defender."

② Or to feel like being in this condition, i.e., the subjective condition of humility. This is entirely consistent with Laotse's philosophy of camouflage, the earliest in the world. Cf. "great eloquence is like stuttering," etc., Ch.45.

③ Possibly the "Three Treasures" in Ch.67.

④ Who hated killing. See Ch.31. The corrected text of Yü Yeüh would make this read, "The man who yields wins."

In the affairs of men there is a system.

Because they know not these,

They also know me not.

    Since there are few that know me,

    Therefore I am distinguished.

Therefore the Sage wears a coarse cloth on top

    And carries jade within his bosom.

第七十一章

知不知,尚矣;不知知,病也。夫唯病病,是以不病。圣人不病,以其病病,是以不病。

Sick-Mindedness

Who knows that he does not know is the highest;

Who (pretends to) know what he does not know is sick-minded.

And who recognizes sick-mindedness as sick-mindedness is not sick-
    minded.

    The Sage is not sick-minded.

    Because he recognizes sick-mindedness as sick-mindedness,

    Therefore he is not sick-minded.

第七十二章

民不畏威,则大威至。无狎其所居,无厌其所生。夫唯不厌,是以不厌。是以圣人自知不自见,自爱不自贵。故去彼取此。

On Punishment (1)

When people have no fear of force,[①]

> Then (as is the common practice) great force descends upon them.

Despise not their dwellings,

Dislike not their progeny.

> Because you do not dislike them,
>
> You will not be disliked yourself.

Therefore the Sage knows himself, but does not show himself,

> Loves himself, but does not exalt himself.

Therefore he rejects the one (force) and accepts the other (gentility).

第七十三章

勇于敢则杀,勇于不敢则活。此两者,或利或害。天之所恶,孰知其故? 是以圣人犹难之。天之道,不争而善胜,不言而善应,不召而自来,坦然而善谋。天网恢恢,疏而不失。

On Punishment (2)

Who is brave in daring (you) kill,

Who is brave in not daring (you) let live.

In these two,

> There is some advantage and some disadvantage.

---

① *Wei*, military force or authority; sometimes also used in connection with "God's anger." Another interpretation, "When the people have no fear of God, then God's anger descends upon them." But this does not fit in so well with the context. See the next two chapters on the futility of punishment, especially the first two lines, Ch. 74.

(Even if) Heaven dislikes certain people,

Who would know (who are to be killed and) why?

Therefore even the Sage regards it as a difficult question.

Heaven's Way (Tao) is good at conquest without strife,

Rewarding (vice and virtue) without words,

Making its appearance without call,

Achieving results without obvious design.

The heaven's net is broad and wide.[1]

With big meshes, yet letting nothing slip through.

第七十四章

民不畏死,奈何以死惧之? 若使民常畏死,而为奇者,吾得执而杀之, 孰敢? 常有司杀者杀,夫代司杀者杀,是谓代大匠斫。夫代大匠斫者,希 有不伤其手矣。

On Punishment (3)

The people are not afraid of death;

Why threaten them with death?

Supposing that the people *are* afraid of death,

And we can seize and kill the unruly,

Who would dare to do so?[2]

Often it happens that the executioner is killed.

And to take the place of the executioner

Is like handling the hatchet for the master carpenter.

He who handles the hatchet for the master carpenter

---

[1] This has now become a Chinese proverb for "virtue always rewarded, vice always punished."

[2] Notice the similarity of construction with the first five lines of Ch. 73.

Seldom escapes injury to his hands.

第七十五章

民之饥,以其上食税之多,是以饥。民之难治,以其上之有为,是以难治。民之轻死,以其①求生之厚,是以轻死。夫唯无以生为者,是贤于贵生。

On Punishment (4)

When people are hungry,

It is because their rulers eat too much tax-grain.

    Therefore the unruliness of hungry people

    Is due to the interference of their rulers.

    That is why they are unruly.

The people are not afraid of death,

Because they are anxious to make a living.

That is why they are not afraid of death.

It is those who interfere not with their living

    That are wise in exalting life.

7　箴　言
Aphorisms

第七十六章

人之生也柔弱,其死也坚强。万物草木之生也柔脆,其死也枯槁。故坚强者死之徒,柔弱者生之徒。是以兵强则不胜,木强则折。强大处下,柔弱处上。

---

① 这里的"其"有的版本为"其上",林语堂的译文依据的应该是"其"。——编者注

Hard and Soft

When man is born, he is tender and weak;

At death, he his hard and stiff.

When the things and plants are alive, they are soft and supple;

When they are dead, they are brittle and dry.

Therefore hardness and stiffness are the companions of death,

And softness and gentleness are the companions of life.

Therefore when an army is headstrong,[①] it will lose in battle.

When a tree is hard, it will be cut down.

The big and strong belong underneath.

The gentle and weak belong at the top.[②]

第七十七章

天之道,其犹张弓欤? 高者抑之,下者举之;有余者损之,不足者补之。天之道,损有余而补不足。人之道则不然,损不足以奉有余。孰能有余以奉天下? 唯有道者。是以圣人为而不恃,功成而不处,其不欲见贤。

Bending the Bow

The Tao (way) of Heaven,

Is it not like the bending of a bow?

The top comes down and the bottom-end goes up,

The extra (length) is shortened, the insufficient (width) is

expanded.

It is the Way of Heaven to take away from those that have

too much

---

① *Ch'iang* means "stiff," "strong," and "headstrong."

② As with twigs and trunks.

And give to those that have not enough.

Not so with man's way：

He takes away from those that have not

And gives it as tribute to those that have too much.

Who can have enough and to spare to give to the entire world?

Only the man of Tao.

Therefore the Sage acts, but does not possess,

Accomplishes but lays claim to no credit,

Because he has no wish to seem superior.

第七十八章

天下莫柔弱于水,而攻坚强者莫之能胜,其无以易之。弱之胜强,柔之胜刚,天下莫不知,莫能行。是以圣人云:受国之垢,是谓社稷主;受国不祥,是为天下王。正言若反。

Nothing Weaker than Water

There is nothing weaker than water

But none is superior to it in overcoming the hard,

For which there is no substitute.

That weakness overcomes strength

And gentleness overcomes rigidity,

No one does not know；

No one can put into practice.

Therefore the Sage says：

"Who receives unto himself the calumny of the world

Is the preserver of the state.

Who bears himself the sins of the world

Is the king of the world."

Straight words seem crooked.

第七十九章

和大怨,必有余怨,安可以为善? 是以圣人执左契,而不责于人。有德司契,无德司彻。天道无亲,常与善人。

Peace Settlements

Patching up a great hatred is sure to leave some hatred behind.

How can this be regarded as satisfactory?

Therefore the Sage holds the left tally,①

And does not put the guilt on the other party.

The virtuous man is for patching up;

The vicious is for fixing guilt. ②

But "the way of Heaven is impartial;

It sides only with the good man."③

第八十章

小国寡民,使有什伯之器而不用,使民重死而不远徙。虽有舟舆,无所乘之;虽有甲兵,无所陈之。使民复结绳而用之。甘其食,美其服,安其居,乐其俗。邻国相望,鸡犬之声相闻,民至老死不相往来。

The Small Utopia

(Let there be) a small country with a small population,

Where the supply of goods are tenfold or hundredfold, more

---

① Sign of inferiority in an agreement.

② Wang Pi's commentary: "for pointing out faults." This in modern days is embodied in the "guilt clause," which is always determined by the victor in the battle.

③ An ancient quotation appearing in many ancient texts.

than they can use.

Let the people value their lives① and not migrate far.

Though there be boats and carriages,

None be there to ride them.

Though there be armor and weapons,

No occasion to display them.

Let the people again tie ropes for reckoning,

Let them enjoy their food,

Beautify their clothing,

Be satisfied with their homes,

Delight in their customs.

The neighboring settlements overlook one another

So that they can hear the barking of dogs and crowing of cocks of
their neighbors,

And the people till the end of their days shall never have been
outside their country.

第八十一章

信言不美,美言不信。善者不辩,辩者不善。知者不博,博者不知。
圣人不积,既以为人,已愈有;既以与人,已愈多。天之道,利而不害。圣
人之道,为而不争。

The Way of Heaven

True words are not fine-sounding;

Fine-sounding words are not true.

A good man does not argue;

---

① Lit. "death."

He who argues is not a good man.

The wise one does not know many things;

He who knows many things is not wise.

The Sage does not accumulate (for himself);

He lives for other people,

And grows richer himself;

He gives to other people,

And has greater abundance.

The Tao of Heaven

Blesses, but does not harm.

The Way of the Sage

Accomplishes, but does not contend.

论 语
Aphorisms of Confucius[①]

叶公问孔子于子路,子路不对。子曰:"女奚不曰:其为人也,发愤忘食,乐以忘忧,不知老之将至云尔。"

Duke Yeh (of Ch'u) asked Tselu about Confucius, and Tselu did not make a reply. Confucius said, "Why didn't you tell him that I am a person who forgets to eat when he is enthusiastic about something, forgets all his worries when he is happy, and is not aware that old age is coming on?"

子曰:"吾十有五而志于学,三十而立,四十而不惑,五十而知天命,六十而耳顺,七十而从心所欲,不逾矩。"

Confucius said, "At fifteen I began to be seriously interested in study. At thirty I had formed my character. At forty I had no more perplexities. At fifty I knew the will of heaven. At sixty nothing that I heard disturbed me.[②] At seventy I could let my thought wander

---

① 林语堂在《孔子的智慧》(*The Wisdom of Confucius*)一书中对《论语》进行了重新排列(未全译),并加有分标题,此处仅节选其中的部分内容。　编者注

② Here is an example of the great responsibility and room for conjecture on the part of a translator of ancient text. The original text merely consists of two words "Ears accord."

without trespassing the moral law."

子曰:"饭疏食饮水,曲肱而枕之,乐亦在其中矣。不义而富且贵,于我如浮云。"

Confucius said, "There is pleasure in lying pillowed against a bent arm after a meal of simple vegetables with a drink of water. On the other hand, to enjoy wealth and power without coming by it through the right means is to me like so many floating clouds."

子曰:"君子道者三,我无能焉:仁者不忧,知者不惑,勇者不惧。"子贡曰:"夫子自道也。"

Confucius said, "There are three things about the superior man that I have not been able to attain. The true man has no worries; the wise man has no perplexities; and the brave man has no fear." Tsekung said, "But, Master, you are exactly describing yourself."

子曰:"十室之邑,必有忠信如丘者焉,不如丘之好学也。"

Confucius said, "In every hamlet of ten families, there are always some people as honest and faithful as myself, but none who is so devoted to study."

子曰:"默而识之,学而不厌,诲人不倦,何有于我哉?"

Confucius said, "To silently appreciate a truth, to learn continually and to teach other people unceasingly—that is just natural with me."

子曰:"盖有不知而作之者,我无是也。多闻,择其善者而从之,多见而识之,知之次也。"

Confucius said, "There are some people who do not understand a subject, but go ahead and invent things out of their own head. I am not like those people. One can come to be a wise man by hearing a great deal and following the good, and by seeing a great deal and remembering it."

子曰:"吾尝终日不食,终夜不寝,以思,无益,不如学也。"

Confucius said, "Sometimes I have gone the whole day without food and a whole night without sleep, occupied in thinking and unable to arrive at any results. So I decided to study again."

子曰:"三人行,必有我师焉。择其善者而从之,其不善者而改之。"

Confucius said, "Whenever walking in a company of three, I can always find my teacher among them (or one who has something to teach me). I select a good person and follow his example, or I see a bad person and correct it in myself."

子曰:"不愤不启,不悱不发。举一隅不以三隅反,则不复也。"

Confucius said, "I won't teach a man who is not anxious to learn, and will not explain to one who is not trying to make things clear to himself. And if I explain one-fourth and the man doesn't go back and reflect and think out the implications in the remaining three-fourths for himself, I won't bother to teach him again."

子以四教:文、行、忠、信。

Confucius taught four things: Literature, personal conduct, being one's true self and honesty in social relationships.

子绝四：毋意，毋必，毋固，毋我。

Confucius denounced or tried to avoid completely four things: arbitrariness of opinion, dogmatism, narrow-mindedness and egoism.

颜渊喟然叹曰："仰之弥高，钻之弥坚。瞻之在前，忽焉在后。夫子循循然善诱之，博我以文，约我以礼。欲罢不能，既竭吾才，如有所立卓尔。虽欲从之，末由也已。"

Yen Huei heaved a sigh and said, "You look up to it and it seems so high. You try to drill through it and it seems so hard. You seem to see it in front of you, and all of a sudden it appears behind you. The Master is very good at gently leading a man along and teaching him. He taught me to broaden myself by the reading of literature and then to control myself by the observance of proper conduct. I just felt being carried along, but after I have done my very best, or developed what was in me, there still remains something austerely standing apart, uncatchable. Do what I could to reach his position, I can't find the way."

子曰："兴于诗，立于礼，成于乐。"

Confucius said, "Wake yourself up with poetry, establish your character in *li* and complete your education in music."

子路、曾皙、冉有、公西华侍坐。子曰："以吾一日长乎尔，毋吾以也。居则曰：'不吾知也！'如或知尔，则何以哉？"子路率尔而对曰："千乘之国，摄乎大国之间，加之以师旅，因之以饥馑，由也为之，比及三年，可使有勇，且知方也。"夫子哂之。"求，尔何如？"对曰："方六七十，如五六十，求也为之，比及三年，可使足民。如其礼乐，以俟君子。""赤，尔何如？"对曰："非曰能之，愿学焉。宗庙之事，如会同，端章甫，愿为小相焉。""点，尔何如？"

鼓瑟希，铿尔，舍瑟而作，对曰："异乎三子者之撰。"子曰："何伤乎？亦各言其志也。"曰："暮春者，春服既成，冠者五六人，童子六七人，浴乎沂，风乎舞雩，咏而归。"夫子喟然叹曰："吾与点也！"

Tselu, Tseng Hsi, Jan Ch'iu and Kunghsi Hua were sitting together one day and Confucius said, "Do not think that I am a little bit older than you and therefore am assuming airs. You often say among yourselves that people don't know you. Suppose someone should know you, I should like to know how you would appear to that person." Tselu immediately replied, "I like to rule over a country with a thousand carriages, situated between two powerful neighbors, involved in war and suffering from famine. I like to take charge of such a country and in three years, the nation will become strong and orderly." Confucius smiled at this remark and said, "How about you, Ah Ch'iu?" Jan Ch'iu replied, "Let me have a country sixty or seventy *li* square or perhaps only fifty or sixty *li* square. Put it in my charge, and in three years, the people will have enough to eat, but as for teaching them moral order and music, I shall leave it to the superior man." (Turning to Kunghsi Hua) Confucius said, "How about you, Ah Ch'ih?" Kunghsi Hua replied, "Not that I say I can do it, but I'm willing to learn this. At the ceremonies of religious worship and at the conference of the princes, I should like to wear the ceremonial cap and gown and be a minor official assisting at the ceremony." "How about you, Ah Tien?" The latter (Tseng Hsi) was just playing on the *seh*, and with a bang he left the instrument and arose to speak. "You know my ambition is different from theirs." "It doesn't matter," said Confucius, "we are just trying to find out what each would like to do." Then he replied, "In late spring, when the new spring dress is made, I would like to go with five or six grown-ups and six or seven children to bathe in the

River Ch'i, and after the bath go to enjoy the breeze in the Wuyi woods, and then sing on our way home." Confucius heaved a deep sigh and said, "You are the man after my own heart."

子问公叔文子于公明贾曰:"信乎,夫子不言,不笑,不取乎?"公明贾对曰:"以告者过也,夫子时然后言,人不厌其言;乐然后笑,人不厌其笑;义然后取,人不厌其取。"子曰:"其然? 岂其然乎?"

Confucius asked Kungming Chia about Kungsun Wentse, "Is it true that your Master doesn't talk, doesn't smile and doesn't take goods from the people?" Kungming Chia replied, "That is an exaggerated story. My Master talks only when he should talk and people are not bored with his talk. He smiles only when he is happy, and people are not bored with his smiles. And he takes goods from the people only when it is right to do so, and people do not mind his taking their goods." Confucius said, "Really! Is that so?"

子曰:"予欲无言。"子贡曰:"子如不言,则小子何述焉?"子曰:"天何言哉? 四时行焉,百物生焉。天何言哉?"

Confucius said, "I am going to remain quiet!" Tsekung remarked, "If you remain quiet, how can we ever learn anything to teach to the others?" And Confucius said, "Does Heaven talk? The four seasons go their way in succession and the different things are produced. Does Heaven talk?"

子曰:"吾与回言终日,不违,如愚。退而省其私,亦足以发。回也不愚。"

Confucius said, "I have sometimes talked with Huei for a whole day, and he just sits still there like a fool. But then he goes into his own room and thinks about what I have said and is able to think out some ideas of his own. He is not a fool."

子曰:"知之为知之,不知为不知,是知也。"
Confucius said, "To know that you know and know what you don't know is the characteristic of one who knows."

子曰:"过而不改,是谓过矣。"
Confucius said, "A man who has committed a mistake and doesn't correct it is committing another mistake."

子曰:"君子耻其言而过其行。"
Confucius said, "A man who brags without shame will find great difficulty in living up to his bragging."

子曰:"知之者不如好之者,好之者不如乐之者。"
Confucius said, "The man who loves truth (or learning) is better than the man who knows it, and the man who finds happiness in it is better than the man who loves it."①

子曰:"君子不以言举人,不以人废言。"
Confucius said, "A gentleman does not praise a man (or put him in office) on the basis of what he says, nor does he deny the truth of what one says because he dislikes the person who says it (if it is good)."

———————

① There is no indication in the text as to whether the reference is to loving truth or loving learning. It uses only the word "it."

子曰:"不患人之不己知,患己无能也。"

Confucius said, "Do not worry about people not knowing your ability, but worry that you have not got it."

子曰:"君子求诸己,小人求诸人。"

Confucius said, "A gentleman blames himself, while a common man blames others."

子曰:"人无远虑,必有近忧。"

Confucius said, "A man who does not think and plan long ahead will find trouble right by his door."

子曰:"巧言乱德。小不忍,则乱大谋。"

Confucius said, "Polished speech often confuses our notion of who is good and who is bad. A man who cannot put up with small losses or disadvantages will often spoil a big plan."

子曰:"性相近也,习相远也。"

Confucius said, "Men are born pretty much alike, but through their habits they gradually grow further and further apart from each other."

子曰:"君子不重则不威,学则不固。主忠信,无友不如己者。过则勿惮改。"

Confucius said, "If the superior man is not deliberate in his appearance (or conduct), then he is not dignified. Learning prevents one from being narrow-minded. Try to be loyal and faithful as your main principle. Have no friends who are not as good as yourself. When you have mistakes, don't be afraid to correct them."

子曰:"见贤思齐焉,见不贤而内自省也。"

Confucius said, "When you see a good man, try to emulate his example, and when you see a bad man, search yourself for his faults."

子曰:"三军可夺帅也,匹夫不可夺志也。"

Confucius said, "You can kill the general of an army, but you cannot kill the ambition in a common man."

子曰:"道不远人,远人非道。"

Confucius said, "Truth may not depart from human nature. If what is regarded as truth departs from human nature, it may not be regarded as truth."

子曰:"仁远乎哉? 我欲仁,斯仁至矣。"

Confucius said, "Is the standard of true manhood so far away, after all? When I want true manhood, there it is right by me."

子贡问曰:"有一言而可以终身行之者乎?"子曰:"其'恕'乎? 己所不欲,勿施于人。"

Tsekung asked, "Is there one single word that can serve as a principle of conduct for life?" Confucius replied, "Perhaps the word 'reciprocity' (*shu*) will do. Do not do unto others what you do not want others to do unto you."

子曰:"仁之难成久矣。唯君子能之。是故君子不以其所能者病人,不以人之所不能者愧人。"

Confucius said, "For a long time it has been difficult to see examples of true men. Only the superior man can reach that state. Therefore the superior man does not try to criticize people for what he himself fails in, and he does not put people to shame for what they fail in..." (*Liki*, Ch. XXXII)[①]

子曰:"中庸之为德也,其至矣乎! 民鲜久矣。"

Confucius said, "To find the central clue to our moral being which unites us to the universal order (or to attain central harmony), that indeed is the highest human attainment. For a long time people have seldom been capable of it."

颜渊问仁。子曰:"克己复礼为仁。一日克己复礼,天下归仁焉。为仁由己,而由人乎哉?"

Yen Huei asked about true manhood, and Confucius said, "True manhood consists in realizing your true self and restoring the moral order or discipline (or *li*). If a man can just for one day realize his true self, and restore complete moral discipline, the world will follow him. To be a true man depends on yourself. What has it got to do with others?"

子曰:"唯仁者能好人,能恶人。"

Confucius said, "Only a true man knows how to love people and how to hate people."

---

① 此段选自《礼记·表记》第三十二。林语堂对"君子不以其所能者病人"的理解可能有误。——编者注

子曰："君子去仁,恶乎成名? 君子无终食之间违仁。造次必于是,颠沛必于是。"①

Confucius said, "How can the superior man keep up his reputation when he departs from the level of the true man? The superior man never departs from the level of true manhood for the time of a single meal. In his most casual moments, he lives in it, and in the most compromising circumstances, he stills lives in it."

子曰："君子喻于义,小人喻于利。"

Confucius said, "The superior man understands what is right; the inferior man understands what will sell."

子曰："君子易事而难说也。说之不以道,不说也;及其使人也,器之。小人难事而易说也。说之虽不以道,说也;及其使人也,求备焉。"

Confucius said, "The superior man is easy to serve, but difficult to please, for he can be pleased by what is right, and he uses men according to their individual abilities. The inferior man is difficult to serve, but easy to please, for you can please him (by catering to his weaknesses) without necessarily being right, and when he comes to using men, he demands perfection."

子曰："君子不器。"

Confucius said, "The superior man is not one who is good for only one particular kind of position."

---

① 林语堂的译文是按主题重新安排的,所以有些译文并不是原文的整句或整段翻译。——编者注

子曰:"君子和而不同,小人同而不和。"

Confucius said, "The superior man is broad-minded toward all and not a partisan; the inferior man is a partisan, but not broad-minded toward all."

子曰:"君子坦荡荡,小人长戚戚。"

Confucius said, "The superior man is always candid and at ease (with himself or others); the inferior man is always worried about something."

子曰:"君子泰而不骄,小人骄而不泰。"

Confucius said, "The superior man is dignified, but not proud; the inferior man is proud, but not dignified."

子曰:"君子食无求饱,居无求安,敏于事而慎于言,就有道而正焉,可谓好学也已矣。"

Confucius said, "The superior man doesn't insist on good food and good lodging. He is attentive to his duties and careful in his speech, and he finds a great man and follows him as his guide. Such a person may be called a lover of learning."

孔子曰:"君子有三戒:少之时,血气未定,戒之在色;及其壮也,血气方刚,戒之在斗;及其老也,血气既衰,戒之在得。"

Confucius said, "A gentleman is careful about three things: In his youth, when his blood is strong, he is careful about sex. When he is grown up, and his blood is full, he is careful about getting into a fight (or struggle in general). When he is old and his blood is getting thinner, he is careful about money." (A young man loves women; a middle-aged man loves struggle; and an old man loves money.)[①]

子曰：“质胜文则野，文胜质则史。文质彬彬，然后君子。”

Confucius said, "When a man has more solid worth than polish, he appears uncouth, and when a man has more polish than solid worth, he appears urbane. The proper combination of solid worth and polish alone makes a gentleman."

子曰：“为政以德，譬如北辰，居其所而众星拱之。”

Confucius said, "A sovereign who governs a nation by virtue is like the North Polar Star, which remains in its place and the other stars revolve around it."

子曰：“其身正，不令而行；其身不正，虽令不从。”

Confucius said, "When the ruler himself does what is right, he will have influence over the people without giving commands, and when the ruler himself does not do what is right, all his commands will be of no avail."

有子曰：“礼之用，和为贵。先王之道，斯为美。小大由之。有所不行，知和而和，不以礼节之，亦不可行也。”

Yutse said, "Among the functions of *li*, the most valuable is that it establishes a sense of harmony. This is the most beautiful heritage of the ancient kings. It is a guiding principle for all things, big and small. If things do not go right, and you are bent only on having social harmony (or pcacc) without regulating the society by the pattern of *li*

---

① 括号里的文字是林语堂在译文后的解释说明，在此一并附上。——编者注

(or the principle of social order), ①still things won't go right."

子曰:"知及之,仁不能守之,虽得之,必失之。知及之,仁能守之,不庄以莅之,则民不敬。知及之,仁能守之,庄以莅之,动之不以礼,未善也。"

Confucius said, "If you have the wisdom to perceive a truth, but have not the manhood to keep to it, you will lose it again, though you have discovered it. If you have the wisdom to perceive a truth, and the true manhood to keep to it, and fail to preserve decorum in your public appearance, you will not gain the people's respect for authority. If you have the wisdom to perceive a truth, the manhood to keep to it, and have decorum of appearance, but fail to be imbued with the spirit of *li* (or social discipline) in your actions or conduct, it is also not satisfactory."

子曰:"诗三百,一言以蔽之,曰:思无邪。"

Confucius said, "One phrase will characterize all the three hundred poems (actually three hundred and five), and that is: Keep the heart right."

子曰:"学而不思则罔,思而不学则殆。"

Confucius said, "Reading without thinking gives one a disorderly mind, and thinking without reading makes one flighty (or unbalanced)."

———————

① See Chapters VI, VII, VIII, "Discourses on the Social Order." (章节安排详见林语堂原著——编者注)

子曰:"学而时习之,不亦说乎?"

Confucius said, "Isn't it a great pleasure to learn and relearn again?"

子曰:"温故而知新,可以为师矣。"

Confucius said, "A man who goes over what he has already learned and gains some new understanding from it is worthy to be a teacher."

子曰:"古之学者为己,今之学者为人。"

Confucius said, "The ancient scholars studied for their own sake; today the scholars study for the sake of others (out of obligations to their teachers, their parents, etc.)."

孔子曰:"生而知之者,上也;学而知之者,次也;困而学之,又其次也。困而不学,民斯为下矣。"

Confucius said, "Those who are born wise are the highest type of people; those who become wise through learning come next; those who learn by sheer diligence and industry, but with difficulty, come after that. Those who are slow to learn, but still won't learn, are the lowest type of people."

子曰:"弟子入则孝,出则悌,谨而信,泛爱众,而亲仁。行有余力,则以学文。"

Confucius said, "The young people should be good sons at home, polite and respectful in society; they should be careful in their conduct and faithful, love the people, and associate themselves with the kind people. If after learning all this, they still have energy left, let them read books."

大 学
The Higher Education^①

大学之道,在明明德,在亲民,在止于至善。知止而后有定,定而后能静,静而后能安,安而后能虑,虑而后能得。物有本末,事有终始。知所先后,则近道矣。

The principles of the higher education consist in preserving man's clear character, in giving new life to the people, and in dwelling (or resting) in perfecting, or the ultimate good. Only after knowing the goal of perfection where one should dwell, can one have a definite purpose in life. Only after having a definite purpose in life can one achieve calmness of mind. Only after having achieved calmness of mind, can one have peaceful repose. Only after having peaceful repose can one begin to think. Only after one has learned to think, can one achieve knowledge. There are a foundation and a superstructure in the constitution of things, and a beginning and an end in the course of events. Therefore to know the proper sequence or relative order of things is the beginning of wisdom.

---

① 林语堂在《孔子的智慧》一书中翻译了《大学》全文,此处仅节选部分重要内容,未必是连续的。——编者注

古之欲明明德于天下者,先治其国。欲治其国者,先齐其家者,先修其身。欲修其身者,先正其心。欲正其心者,先诚其意。欲诚其意者,先致其知。致知在格物。物格而后知至,知至而后意诚,意诚而后心正,心正而后身修,身修而后家齐,家齐而后国治,国治而后天下平。自天子以至于庶人,壹是皆以修身为本。其本乱而末治者否矣。其所厚者薄,而其所薄者厚,未之有也。此谓知本。

The ancients who wished to preserve the fresh or clear character of the people of the world, would first set about ordering their national life. Those who wished to order their national life, would first set about regulating their family life. Those who wished to regulate their family life would set about cultivating their personal life. Those who wished to cultivate their personal life would first set about setting their hearts right. Those who wished to set their hearts right would first set about making their wills sincere. Those who wished to make their wills sincere would first set about achieving knowledge. The achieving of true knowledge depended upon the investigation of things. When things investigated, then true knowledge is achieved; when true knowledge is achieved, then the will becomes sincere; when the will is sincere, then the heart is set right (or then the mind sees right); when the heart is set right, then the personal life is cultivated; when the personal life is cultivated, then the family life is regulated; when the family life is regulated, then the national life is orderly; and when the national life is orderly, then there is peace in the world. From the emperor down to the common men, all must regard the cultivation of the personal life as the root or foundation. There is never an orderly upshoot or superstructure when the root or foundation is disorderly. There is never yet a tree whose truck is slim and slender and whose top branches are thick and heavy. This is called "to know the root or foundation of things. "①

    所谓诚其意者,毋自欺也。如恶恶臭,如好好色,此之谓自谦。故君子必慎其独也。小人闲居为不善,无所不至,见君子而后厌然,掩其不善而著其善。人之视己,如见其肺肝然,则何益矣。此谓诚于中,形于外,故君子必慎其独也。曾子曰:"十目所视,十手所指,其严乎!"富润屋,德润身,心广体胖,故君子必诚其意。

    What is meant by "making the will sincere" is that one should not deceive oneself. This sincerity should be like the sincerity with which we hate a bad smell or love what is beautiful. This is called satisfying your own conscience. Therefore, a superior man is watchful over himself when he is alone. The common man does wrong without any kind of self-restraint in his private life, and then when he sees the superior man, he is ashamed of himself, and tries to hide the bad and show off the good in him. But what is the use? For people see into their very hearts when they look at them. That is what is meant when we say, "What is true in a man's heart will be shown in his outward

---

①   The original text (Cheng Hsuan's), before the re-editing of Chu Hsi, ends with two lines: "This is called 'to know the root of things. ' This is called 'achieving true knowledge. '"(即"此谓知之至也"——编者注) The second line then leads off to what are here Sections 4 and 5, which causes an abrupt break in the discussion. Actually, I believe these two lines belong to Section 3, where Confucius said that he was as good a judge as anyone, but that he would make it so that people who had committed crimes would be ashamed to defend themselves, and the people would be in awe of the great wise judge—as an illustration of achieving true knowledge or wisdom. I believe that this paragraph is in uncorrupted text before Cheng merely ended with the line "This is called 'to know the root or foundation of things. '" Chu Hsi, on the other hand, took the two lines at the end of this paragraph in the text he was trying to re-edit and transposed them to a latter part, considering them the last lines of a missing paragraph.

appearance." Therefore the superior man (or the prince) must be watchful over himself when he is alone. Tsengtse said, "What ten eyes are beholding and what ten hands are pointing to—isn't it frightening?" Just as wealth beautifies a house, so character beatifies the body. A big-hearted man also has big proportions. (Probably a proverb, like "A fat man is good-natured.") Therefore a superior man must make his will sincere.

所谓修身在正其心者,身有所忿懥,则不得其正;有所恐惧,则不得其正;有所好乐,则不得其正;有所忧患,则不得其正。心不在焉,视而不见,听而不闻,食而不知其味。此谓修身在正其心。

What is meant by saying that "the cultivation of the personal life depends on setting one's heart right" is this: When one is upset by anger, then the heart is not in its right place; when one is disturbed by fear, then the heart is not in its right place; when one is blinded by love, then the heart is not in its right place; when one is involved in worries and anxieties, then the heart is not in its right place (or the mind has lost its balance). When the mind isn't there, we look but do not see, listen but do not hear and eat but do not know the flavor of the food. This is what is meant by saying that the cultivation of the personal life depends on setting the heart right.

四

中 庸
Central Harmony[①]

天命之谓性,率性之谓道,修道之谓教。道也者,不可须臾离也,可离非道也。是故君子戒慎乎其所不睹,恐惧乎其所不闻。莫见乎隐,莫显乎微,故君子慎其独也。喜怒哀乐之未发,谓之中;发而皆中节,谓之和。中也者,天下之大本也;和也者,天下之达道也。致中和,天地位焉,万物育焉。

What is God-given is what we call human nature. To fulfil the law of our human nature is what we call the moral law. The cultivation of the moral law is what we call culture.

The moral law is a law from whose operation we cannot for one instant in our existence escape. A law from which we may escape is not the moral law. Wherefore it is that the moral man (or the superior man) watches diligently over what his eyes cannot see and is in fear and awe of what his ears cannot hear.

There is nothing more evident than that which cannot be seen by the eyes and nothing more palpable than that which cannot be perceived by the senses. Wherefore the moral man watches diligently

---

① 林语堂在《孔子的智慧》一书中"翻译"了《中庸》全文(其实是借用了辜鸿铭的译文),此处仅节选部分重要内容(未必是连续的),同时也省略了林语堂添加的一些章节小标题。——编者注

over his secret thoughts.

When the passions, such as joy, anger, grief, and pleasure, have not awakened, that is our *central self*, or moral being (*chung*). When these passions awaken and each and all attain due measure and degree, that is *harmony*, or the moral order (*ho*). Our central self or moral being is the great basis of existence, and *harmony* or moral order is the universal law in the world.

When our true central self and harmony are realised, the universe then becomes a cosmos and all things attain their full growth and development.

仲尼曰:"君子中庸,小人反中庸。君子之中庸也,君子而时中;小人之反中庸也①,小人而无忌惮也。"

Confucius remarked: " The life of the moral man is an exemplification of the universal moral order (*chungyung*, usually translated as "the Mean").② The life of the vulgar person, on the other hand, is a contradiction of the universal moral order."

The moral man's life is an exemplification of the universal order, because he is a moral person who unceasingly cultivates his true self or moral being. The vulgar person's life is a contradiction of the universal order, because he is a vulgar person who in his heart has no regard for, or fear of, the moral law.

子曰:"舜其大知也与! 舜好问而好察迩言。隐恶而扬善。执其两端,用其中于民。其斯以为舜乎!"

---

① 此处有的版本为"小人之中庸也"。——编者注
② *Chung* means "central," and *yung* means "constant." The whole idea expresses the conception of a norm.

Confucius remarked: "There was the Emperor Shun. He was perhaps what may be considered a truly great intellect. Shun had a natural curiosity of mind and he loved to inquire into ordinary conversation. He ignored the bad (words?) and broadcast the good. Taking two extreme counsels, he took the mean between them and applied them in dealings with his people. This was the characteristic of Shun's great intellect."

君子之道,费而隐。夫妇之愚,可以与知焉;及其至也,虽圣人亦有所不知焉。夫妇之不肖,可以能行焉;及其至也,虽圣人亦有所不能焉。天地之大也,人犹有所憾。故君子语大,天下莫能载焉;语小,天下莫能破焉。《诗》云:"鸢飞戾天,鱼跃于渊。"言其上下察也。君子之道,造端乎夫妇;及其至也,察乎天地。

The moral law is to be found everywhere, and yet it is a secret.

The simple intelligence of ordinary men and women of the people may understand something of the moral law; but in its utmost reaches there is something which even the wisest and holiest of men cannot understand. The ignoble natures of ordinary men and women of the people may be able to carry out the moral law; but in its utmost reaches even the wisest and holiest of men cannot live up to it.

Great as the Universe is, man is yet not always satisfied with it. For there is nothing so great but the mind of the moral man can conceive of something still greater which nothing in the world can hold. There is nothing so small but the mind of the moral man can conceive of something still smaller which nothing in the world can split.

The *Book of Songs* says: "The hawk soars to the heavens above and fishes dive to the depths below." That is to say, there is no place in the highest heavens above nor in the deepest waters below where the moral law is not to be found. The moral man finds the moral law beginning in the relation between man and woman; but ending in the vast reaches of the universe.

君子素其位而行，不愿乎其外。素富贵，行乎富贵；素贫贱，行乎贫贱；素夷狄，行乎夷狄；素患难，行乎患难。君子无入而不自得焉。在上位，不陵下；在下位，不援上。正己而不求于人，则无怨。上不怨天，下不尤人。故君子居易以俟命，小人行险以侥幸。

子曰："射有似乎君子，失诸正鹄，反求诸其身。"

The moral man conforms himself to his life circumstances; he does not desire anything outside of his position. Finding himself in a position of wealth and honor, he lives as becomes one living in a position of wealth and honor. Finding himself in a position of poverty and humble circumstances, he lives as becomes one living in a position of poverty and humble circumstances. Finding himself in uncivilized countries, he lives as becomes one living in uncivilized countries. Finding himself in circumstances of danger and difficulty, he acts according to what is required of a man under such circumstances. In one word, the moral man can find himself in no situation in life in which he is not master of himself.

In a high position he does not domineer over his subordinates. In a subordinate position he does not court the favors of his superiors. He puts in order his own personal conduct and seeks nothing from others; hence he has no complaint to make. He complains not against God, nor rails against men.

Thus it is that the moral man lives out the even tenor of his life, calmly waiting for the appointment of God, whereas the vulgar person takes to dangerous courses, expecting the uncertain chances of luck.

Confucius remarked: "In the practice of archery we have something resembling the principle in a moral man's life. When the archer misses the center of the target, he turns round and seeks for the cause of his failure within himself."

哀公问政。子曰:"文武之政,布在方策。其人存,则其政举;其人亡,则其政息。人道敏政,地道敏树。夫政也者,蒲卢也。故为政在人,取人以身,修身以道,修道以仁。仁者,人也,亲亲为大;义者,宜也。尊贤为大。亲亲之杀,尊贤之等,礼所生也。在下位不获乎上,民不可得而治矣。故君子不可以不修身;思修身,不可以不事亲;思事亲,不可以不知人;思知人,不可以不知天。天下之达道五,所以行之者三。曰:君臣也,父子也,夫妇也,昆弟也,朋友之交也;五者天下之达道也。知,仁,勇,三者天下之达德也。所以行之者一也。或生而知之,或学而知之,或困而知之,及其知之一也。或安而行之,或利而行之,或勉强而行之,及其成功,一也。"

Duke Ai (ruler of Lu, Confucius' native state) asked what constituted good government.

Confucius replied: "The principles of good government of the Emperors of Wen and Wu are abundantly illustrated in the records preserved. When the men are there, good government will flourish, but when the men are gone, good government decays and becomes extinct. With the right men, the growth of good government is as rapid as the growth of vegetation is in the right soil. Indeed, good government is like a fast-growing plant. The conduct of government, therefore, depends upon the men. The right men are obtained by the ruler's personal character. To cultivate his personal character, the ruler must use the moral law (tao). To cultivate the moral law, the ruler must use the moral sense (*jen* , or principles of true manhood).

"The moral sense is the characteristic attribute of man. To feel natural affection for those nearly related to us is the highest expression of the moral sense. The sense of justice (*yi* or propriety) is the recognition of what is right and proper. To honor those who are worthier than ourselves is the highest expression of the sense of justice. The relative degrees of natural affection we ought to feel for those who are nearly related to us and the relative grades of honor we ought to show to those worthier than ourselves: these give rise to the forms and distinctions in social life (*li* , or principles of social order). For unless social inequalities have a true and moral basis (or unless those being ruled feel their proper place with respect to their rulers), government of the people is impossibility.

"Therefore it is necessary for a man of the governing class to set about regulating his personal conduct and character. In considering how to regulate his personal conduct and character, it is necessary for him to do his duties toward those nearly related to him. In considering how to do his duties toward those nearly related to him, it is necessary for him to understand the nature and organization of human society. In considering the nature and organization of human society, it is necessary for him to understand the laws of God.

"The duties of universal obligation are five, and the moral qualities by which they are carried out are three. The duties are those between ruler and subject, between father and son, between husband and wife, between elder brother and younger, and those in the intercourse between friends. These are the five duties of universal obligation. Wisdom, compassion and courage①—these are the three universally recognized moral qualities of man. It matters not in what way men come to the exercise of these moral qualities, the result is one and the same.

"Some men are born with the knowledge of these moral qualities; some acquire it as the result of education; some acquire it as the result of hard experience. But when the knowledge is acquired, it comes to one and the same thing. Some exercise these moral qualities naturally and easily; some because they find it advantageous to do so; some with effort and difficulty. But when the achievement is made it comes to one and the same thing."

子曰:"好学近乎知,力行近乎仁,知耻近乎勇。知斯三者,则知所以修身;知所以修身,则知所以治人;知所以治人,则知所以治天下国家矣。凡为天下国家有九经,曰:修身也,尊贤也,亲亲也,敬大臣也,体群臣也,子庶民也,来百工也,柔远人也,怀诸侯也。修身,则道立;尊贤,则不惑;亲亲,则诸父昆弟不怨;敬大臣,则不眩;体群臣,则士之报礼重;子庶民,则百姓劝;来百工,则财用足;柔远人,则四方归之;怀诸侯,则天下畏之。齐明盛服,非礼不动,所以修身也;去谗远色,贱货而贵德,所以劝贤也;尊其位,重其禄,同其好恶,所以劝亲亲也;官盛任使,所以劝大臣也;忠信重禄,所以劝士也;时使薄敛,所以劝百姓也;日省月试,既廪称事,所以劝百工也;送往迎来,嘉善而矜不能,所以柔远人也;继绝世,举废国,治乱持危,朝聘以时,厚往而薄来,所以怀诸侯也。凡为天下国家有九经,所以行之者一也。凡事豫则立,不豫则废。言前定,则不跲;事前定,则不困;行前定,则不疚;道前定,则不穷。在下位不获乎上,民不可得而治矣;获乎

---

① Ku translates them as "intelligence, moral character and courage."(Ku 指辜鸿铭——编者注)

上有道,不信乎朋友,不获乎上矣;信乎朋友有道,不顺乎亲,不信乎朋友矣;顺乎亲有道,反诸身不诚,不顺乎亲矣;诚身有道,不明乎善,不诚乎身矣。诚者,天之道也;诚之者,人之道也。诚者,不勉而中,不思而得,从容中道,圣人也。诚之者,择善而固执之者也。博学之,审问之,慎思之,明辨之,笃行之。有弗学,学之弗能,弗措也;有弗问,问之弗知,弗措也;有弗思,思之弗得,弗措也;有弗辨,辨之弗明,弗措也;有弗行,行之弗笃,弗措也。人一能之,己百之;人十能之,己千之。果能此道矣,虽愚必明,虽柔必强。"

Confucius went on to say: "Love of knowledge is akin to wisdom. Strenuous attention to conduct is akin to compassion. Sensitiveness to shame is akin to courage.

"When a man understands the nature and use of these three moral qualities, he will then understand how to put in order his personal conduct and character. When a man understands how to put in order his personal conduct and character, he will understand how to govern men. When a man understands how to govern men, he will then understand how to govern nations and empires.

"For every one called to the government of nations and empires there are nine cardinal directions to be attended to:

1. Cultivating his personal conduct.

2. Honoring worthy men.

3. Cherishing affection for, and doing his duty toward, his kindred.

4. Showing respect to the high ministers of state.

5. Identifying himself with the interests and welfare of the whole body of public officers.

6. Showing himself as a father to the common people.

7. Encouraging the introduction of all useful arts.

8. Showing tenderness to strangers from far countries.

9. Taking interest in the welfare of the princes of the Empire.

"When the ruler pays attention to the cultivation of his personal conduct, there will be respect for the moral law. When the ruler honors worthy men, he will not be deceived (by the crafty officials). When the ruler cherishes affection for his kindred, there will be no disaffection among the members of his family. When the ruler shows respect to the high ministers of state, he will not make mistakes. When the ruler identifies himself with the interests and welfare of the body of public officers, there will be a strong spirit of loyalty among the gentlemen of the country. When the ruler becomes a father to the common people, the mass of the people will exert themselves for the good of the state. When the ruler encourages the introduction of all useful arts, there will be sufficiency of wealth and revenue in the country. When the ruler shows kindness to the strangers from far countries, people from all quarters of the world will flock to the country. When the ruler takes interest in the condition and welfare of the princes of the empire, he will inspire awe and respect for his authority throughout the whole world.

"By attending to the cleanliness and purity of his person and to the propriety and dignity of his dress, and in every word and act permitting nothing which is contrary to good taste and decency; that is how the ruler cultivates his personal conduct. By banishing all flatterers and keeping away from the society of women, holding in low estimation possession of worldly goods, but valuing moral qualities in men—that is how the ruler gives encouragement to worthy men. By raising them to high places of honor and bestowing ample emoluments for their maintenance; sharing and sympathizing with their tastes and opinions—that is how the ruler inspires love for his person among the members of his family. By extending the powers of their functions and allowing them discretion in the employment of their subordinates—that is how the ruler gives encouragement to the high ministers of state. By dealing loyally and punctually with them in all engagements which he makes with them and allowing a liberal scale of pay—that is how the ruler gives encouragement to men in the public service. By strictly limiting the time of their service and making all imposts as light as possible—that is how the ruler gives encouragement to the mass of the people. By ordering daily inspection and monthly examination and rewarding each according to the degree of his workmanship—that is how the ruler encourages the artisan class. By welcoming them when they come and giving them protection when they go, commending what is good in them and making allowance for their ignorance—this is how the ruler shows kindness to strangers from far countries. By restoring lines of broken succession and reviving subjugated states, putting down anarchy and disorder wherever they are found, and giving support to the weak against the strong, fixing stated times for their attendance and the attendance of their envoys at court, loading them with presents when they leave, while exacting little from them in the way of contribution when they come—this is how the ruler takes interest in the welfare of the princes of the empire.

"For every one who is called to government of nations and empire, these are the nine cardinal directions to be attended to; and there is only one way by which they can be carried out.

"In all matters success depends on preparation; without preparation there will always be failure. When what is to be said is previously determined, there will be no difficulty in carrying it out.

When a line of conduct is previously determined, there will be no occasion for vexation. When general principles are previously determined, there will be no perplexity to know what to do."

"If the people in inferior positions do not have confidence in those above them, government of the people is an impossibility. There is only one way to gain confidence for one's authority: if a man is not trusted by his friends, he will not have confidence in those above him. There is only one way to be trusted by his friends: if a man is not affectionate toward his parents, he will not be trusted by his friends. There is only one way to be affectionate toward one's parents: if a man, looking into his own heart, is not true to himself, he will not be affectionate toward his parents. There is only one way for a man to be true to himself. If he does not know what is good, a man cannot be true to himself.

"Being true to oneself is the law of God. To try to be true to oneself is the law of man. ①

"He who is naturally true to himself is one who, without effort, hits upon what is right, and without thinking understands what he wants to know, whose life is easily and naturally in harmony with the moral law. Such a one is what we call a saint or a man of divine nature. He who learns to be his true self is one who finds out what is good and holds fast to it.

"In order to learn to be one's true self, it is necessary to obtain a wide and extensive knowledge of what has been said and done in the world; critically to inquire into it; carefully to ponder over it; clearly

---

① This part from the beginning of the section is found in the *Book of Mencius*, Book IV, Part 1. The complete interview is found also in *Confucius' Family Records* (*K'ungtse Chiayu*) without the section that follows immediately.

to sift it; and earnestly to carry it out.

"It matters not what you learn; but when you once learn a thing, you must never give it up until you have mastered it. It matters not what you inquire into, but when you inquire into a thing, you must never give it up until you have thoroughly understood it. It matters not what you try to think out, but when you once try to think out a thing, you must never give it up until you have got what you want. It matters not what you try to sift out, but when you once try to sift out a thing, you must never give it up until you have sifted it out clearly and distinctly. It matters not what you try to carry out, but when you once try to carry out a thing, you must never give it up until you have done it thoroughly and well. If another man succeed by one effort, you will use a hundred efforts. If another man succeed by ten efforts, you will use a thousand efforts.

"Let a man really proceed in this manner, and, though dull, he will surely become intelligent; though weak, he will surely become strong."

自诚明,谓之性;自明诚,谓之教。诚则明矣,明则诚矣。

To arrive at understanding from being one's true self is called nature, and to arrive at being one's true self from understanding is called culture. He who is his true self has thereby understanding, and he who has understanding finds thereby his true self. [1]

唯天下至诚,为能尽其性;能尽其性,则能尽人之性;能尽人之性,则

---

[1] This paragraph constitutes a "chapter" by itself in the Chinese text. The translation of this paragraph and the following two paragraphs is entirely mine, differing from Ku's.

能尽物之性；能尽物之性，则可以赞天地之化育；可以赞天地之化育，则可以与天地参矣。

Only those who are their absolute true selves in the world can fulfil their own nature; only those who fulfil their own nature can fulfil the nature of others; only those who fulfil the nature of others can fulfil the nature of things; those who fulfil the nature of things are worthy to help Mother Nature in growing and sustaining life; and those who are worthy to help Mother Nature in growing and sustaining life are the equals of heaven and earth.

其次致曲，曲能有诚。诚则形，形则著，著则明，明则动，动则变，变则化。唯天下至诚为能化。

The next in order are those who are able to attain to the apprehension of a particular branch of study. By such studies, they are also able to apprehend the truth. Realization of the true self compels expression; expression becomes evidence; evidence becomes clarity or luminosity of knowledge; clarity or luminosity of knowledge activates; active knowledge becomes power and power becomes a pervading influence. Only those who are absolutely their true selves in this world can have pervading influence.

至诚之道，可以前知。国家将兴，必有祯祥；国家将亡，必有妖孽。见乎蓍龟，动乎四体。祸福将至，善，必先知之；不善，必先知之。故至诚如神。

It is an attribute of the possession of the absolute true self to be able to foreknow. When a nation or a family is about to flourish, there are sure to be lucky omens. When a nation or family is about to perish, there are sure to be signs and prodigies. These things manifest themselves in the instruments of divination and in the agitation of the human body. When happiness or calamity is about to come, it can be known beforehand. When it is good, it can be known beforehand. When it is evil, it can also be known beforehand. Therefore he who has realized his true self is like a celestial spirit.

诚者,自成也;而道,自道也。诚者,物之终始,不诚无物。是故君子诚之为贵。诚者,非自成己而已也,所以成物也。成己,仁也;成物,知也。性之德也,合外内之道也,故时措之宜也。

Truth means the fulfilment of our self; and moral law means following the law of our being. Truth is the beginning and end (the substance) of material existence. Without truth there is no material existence. It is for this reason that the moral man values truth.

Truth is not only the fulfilment of our own being; it is that by which things outside of us have an existence. The fulfilment of our being is moral sense. The fulfilment of the nature of things outside of us is intellect. These, moral sense and intellect, are the powers or faculties of our being. They combine the inner or subjective and outer or objective use of the power of the mind. Therefore, with truth, everything done is right.

故至诚无息。不息则久,久则征,征则悠远,悠远则博厚,博厚则高明。博厚,所以载物也;高明,所以覆物也;悠久,所以成物也。博厚配地,高明配天,悠久无疆。如此者,不见而章,不动而变,无为而成。天地之道,可一言而尽也:其为物不贰,则其生物不测。天地之道,博也,厚也,高也,明也,悠也,久也。今夫天,斯昭昭之多,及其无穷也,日月星辰系焉,万物覆焉。今夫地,一撮土之多,及其广厚,载华岳而不重,振河海而不泄,万物载焉。今夫山,一卷石之多,及其广大,草木生之,禽兽居之,宝藏兴焉。今夫水,一勺之多,及其不测,鼋鼍蛟龙鱼鳖生焉,货财殖焉。《诗》曰:"惟天之命,于穆不已。"盖曰天之所以为天也。"于乎不显,文王之德之纯。"盖曰文王之所以为文也,纯亦不已。

Thus absolute truth is indestructible. Being indestructible, it is eternal. Being eternal, it is self-existent. Being self-existent, it is infinite. Being infinite, it is vast and deep. Being vast and deep, it is transcendental and intelligent. It is because it is vast and deep that it contains all existence. It is because it is transcendental and intelligent that it embraces all existence. It is because it is infinite and eternal that it fulfills or perfects all existence. In vastness and depth it is like the Earth. In transcendental intelligence it is like Heaven. Infinite and eternal, it is the Infinite itself.

Such being the nature of absolute truth, it manifests itself without being seen; it produces effects without motion; it accomplishes its ends without action.

The principle in the course and operation of nature may be summed up in one word: because it obeys only its own immutable law, the way in which it produces the variety of things is unfathomable.

Nature is vast, deep, high, intelligent, infinite and eternal. The heaven appearing before us is only this bright, shining mass; but in its immeasurable extent, the sun, the moon, stars and constellations are suspended in it, and all things are embraced under it. The earth, appearing before us, is but a handful of soil; but in all its breadth and depth, it sustains mighty mountains without feeling their weight; rivers and seas dash against it without causing it to leak. The mountain appearing before us is only a mass of rock; but in all the vastness of its size, grass and vegetation grow upon it, birds and beasts dwell on it, and treasures of precious minerals are found in it. The water appearing before us is but a ladleful of liquid; but in all its unfathomable depths, the largest crustaceans, dragons, fishes, and turtles are produced in them, and all useful products abound in them.

In the *Book of Songs* it is said:

> "The ordinance of God,
>
> How inscrutable it is and goes on for ever."

That is to say, this is the essence of God. It is again said:

> "How excellent it is,
>
> The moral perfection of King Wen."

That is to say, this is the essence of the noble character of the Emperor Wen. Moral perfection also never dies.

唯天下至诚,为能经纶天下之大经,立天下之大本,知天地之化育。夫焉有所倚? 肫肫其仁! 渊渊其渊! 浩浩其天! 苟不固聪明圣知达天德者,其孰能知之?

It is only he in this world who has realized his absolute self that can order and adjust the great relations of human society, fix the fundamental principles of morality, and understand the laws of growth and reproduction of the Universe.

Now, where does such a man derive his power and knowledge, except from himself? How simple and self-contained his true manhood![1] How unfathomable the depth of his mind! How infinitely grand and vast the moral height of his nature! Who can understand such a nature except he who is gifted with the most perfect intelligence and endowed with the highest divine qualities of character, and who has reached in his moral development the level of the gods?

---

[1] Ch'en Li regards this phrase as the best description of *jen*, or "true manhood."

五

礼 记
Liki[①]

大道之行也,天下为公。选贤与能,讲信修睦,故人不独亲其亲,不独子其子,使老有所终,壮有所用,幼有所长,鳏寡孤独废疾者,皆有所养。男有分,女有归。货恶其弃于地也,不必藏于己;力恶其不出于身也,不必为己。是故谋闭而不兴,盗窃乱贼而不作,故外户而不闭。是谓大同。

When the great Tao prevailed (i. e., in the Golden Age), the world was a common state (not belonging to any particular ruling family), rulers were elected according to their wisdom and ability and mutual confidence and peace prevailed. Therefore people not only regarded their own parents as parents and their own children as children. The old people were able to enjoy their old age, the young men were able to employ their talents, the juniors had the elders to look up to, and the helpless widows, orphans and cripples and deformed were well taken care of. The men had their respective occupations and the women had their homes. If the people didn't want to see goods lying about on the ground, they did not have to keep them for themselves, and if people had too much energy for work, they did

---

① 林语堂在《孔子的智慧》一书中翻译了《礼记》的《礼运》《学记》《乐记》三篇的部分内容,此处仅节选部分重要内容,未必是连续的。——编者注

not have to labor for their own benefit. Therefore there was no cunning or intrigue and there were no bandits or burglars, and as a result, there was no need to shut one's outer gate (at night). This was the period of *tat'ung*, or the Great Commonwealth. ①

今大道既隐,天下为家。各亲其亲,各子其子,货力为己。大人世及以为礼,城郭沟池以为固,礼义以为纪,以正君臣,以笃父子,以睦兄弟,以和夫妇,以设制度,以立田里,以贤勇知,以功为己。故谋用是作,而兵由此起。禹汤文武成王周公,由此其选也。此六君子者,未有不谨于礼者也。以著其义,以考其信,著有过,刑仁讲让,示民有常。如有不由此者,在执者去,众以为殃。是谓小康。

But now the great Tao no longer prevails, and the world is divided up into private families (or becomes the possession of private families), and people regard only their own parents as parents and only their own children as children. They acquire goods and labor each for his own benefits. A hereditary aristocracy is established and different states build cities, outer cities and moats each for its own defence. The principles of *li* (or forms of social intercourse) and righteousness serve as the principles of social discipline. By means of these principles, people try to maintain the official status of rulers and subjects, to teach the parents and children and elder brothers and younger brothers and husbands and wives to live in harmony, to establish social institutions and to live in groups of hamlets. The physically strong and the mentally clever are raised to prominence and each one tries to carve his own career. Hence there is deceit and cunning and from these wars arise. (The great founders of dynasties like) Emperors Yu, T'ang,

---

① *Ta* means "great" and *t'ung* means "common."

Wen, Wu, and Ch'eng and Duke Chou were the best men of his age. Without a single exception, these six gentlemen were deeply concerned over the principle of *li*, through which justice was maintained, general confidence was tested, errors or malpractices were exposed. An ideal of true manhood, *jen*, was set up and good manners or courtesy was cultivated, as solid principles for the common people to follow. A ruler who violates these principles would then be denounced as a public enemy and driven off from his office. This is called the Period of *Hsiaok'ang* or "The Period of Minor Peace."

虽有嘉肴,弗食,不知其旨也;虽有至道,弗学,不知其善也。

Just as one cannot know the taste of food without eating it, however excellent it may be, so without education one cannot come to know the excellence of a great body of knowledge, although it may be there.

是故学然后知不足,教然后知困。知不足,然后能自反也;知困,然后能自强也。故曰:教学相长也。《兑命》曰:"学学半。"其此之谓乎?

Therefore only through education does one come to be dissatisfied with his own knowledge, and only through teaching others does one come to realize the uncomfortable inadequacy of his knowledge. Being dissatisfied with his own knowledge, one then realizes that the trouble lies with himself, and realizing the uncomfortable inadequacy of his knowledge, one then feels stimulated to improve himself. Therefore it is said, "The processes of teaching and learning stimulate one another." That is the meaning of the passage in the *Advice to Fu Yueh* which says, "Teaching is the half of learning."

大学之法：禁于未发之谓豫，当其可之谓时，不陵节而施之谓孙，相观而善之谓摩。此四者，教之所由兴也。

The principles of college education are as follows: First, prevention, or preventing bad habits before they arise. Secondly, timeliness, or giving the students things when they are ready for them. Thirdly, order, or teaching the different subjects in proper sequence. Fourthly, mutual stimulation（literally "friction"）, or letting the students admire the excellence of other students. These four things ensure the success of education.

学者有四失，教者必知之。人之学也，或失则多，或失则寡，或失则易，或失则止。此四者，心之莫同也。知其心，然后能救其失也。教也者，长善而救其失者也。

There are four common errors in education which the teacher must beware of. Some students try to learn too much or too many subjects, some learn too little or too few subjects, some learn things too easily and some are too easily discouraged. These four things show that individuals differ in their mental endowments, and only through a knowledge of the different mental endowments can the teacher correct their mistakes. A teacher is but a man who tries to bring out the good and remedy the weaknesses of his students.

善学者，师逸而功倍，又从而庸之。不善学者，师勤而功半，又从而怨之。善问者，如攻坚木，先其易者，后其节目，及其久也，相说以解。不善问者反此。善待问者如撞钟，叩之以小者则小鸣，叩之以大者则大鸣，待其从容，然后尽其声。不善答问者反此。此皆进学之道也。

With a good student, the teacher doesn't have much to do and the results are double, besides getting the students' respect. With a bad student, the teacher has to work hard and the results are only half of what is to be expected, besides getting hated by the student. A good questioner proceeds like a man chopping wood—he begins at the easier end, attacking the knots last, and after a time the teacher and student come to understand the point with a sense of pleasure. A bad questioner does just exactly the opposite. One who knows how to answer questions is like a group of bells. When you strike the big bell, the big one rings, and when you strike the small bell, the small one rings. It is important, however, to allow time for its tone gradually to die out. One who does not know how to answer questions is exactly the reverse of this. These are all suggestions for the process of teaching and learning.

凡音之起,由人心生也。人心之动,物使之然也。感于物而动,故形于声。声相应,故生变,变成方,谓之音。比音而乐之,及干戚、羽旄,谓之乐。

Music rises from the human heart when the human heart is touched by the external world. When touched by the external world, the heart is moved, and therefore finds its expression in sounds. These sounds echo, or combine with, one another and produce a rich variety, and when the various sounds become regular, then we have rhythm. The arrangements of tones for our enjoyment in combination with the military dance, with shields and hatchets, and the civil dance, with long feathers and pennants of ox-tails, is called music.

凡音者,生人心者也。情动于中,故形于声;声成文,谓之音。是故治世之音安以乐,其政和;乱世之音怨以怒,其政乖;亡国之音哀以思,其民困。声音之道,与政通矣。

Music rises from the human heart. When the emotions are touched, they are expressed in sounds, and when the sounds take definite forms, we have music. Therefore the music of a peaceful and prosperous country is quiet and joyous, and the government is orderly; the music of a country in turmoil shows dissatisfaction and anger, and the government is chaotic; and the music of a destroyed country shows sorrow and remembrance, and the people are distressed. Thus we see music and government are directly connected with one another.

乐者为同,礼者为异。同则相亲,异则相敬。乐胜则流,礼胜则离。合情饰貌者,礼乐之事也。礼义立,则贵贱等矣。乐文同,则上下和矣。

Music unites while rituals differentiate. Through union the people come to be friendly toward one another, and through differentiation the people come to learn respect for one another. If music predominates, the social structure becomes too amorphous, and if rituals predominate, social life becomes too cold. To bring the people's inner feelings and their external conduct into balance is the work of rituals and music. The establishment of rituals gives a well-defined sense of order and discipline, while the general spread of music and song establishes the general atmosphere of peace in the people.

乐者,天地之和也;礼者,天地之序也。和,故百物皆化;序,故群物皆别。乐由天作,礼以地制。过制则乱,过作则暴。明于天地,然后能兴礼乐也。

Music expresses the harmony of the universe, while rituals express the order of the universe. Through harmony all things are influenced, and through order all things have a proper place. Music arises from heaven, while rituals are patterned on the earth. To go beyond these patterns would result in violence and disorder. In order to have the proper rituals and music, we must understand the principles of Heaven and Earth...

德者,性之端也;乐者,德之华也;金石丝竹,乐之器也。诗,言其志也;歌,咏其声也;舞,动其容也。三者本于心,然后乐器从之。是故情深而文明,气盛而化神,和顺积中而英华发外,唯乐不可以为伪。

Character is the backbone of our human nature, and music is the flowering of character. The metal, stone, string and bamboo instruments are the instruments of music. The poem gives expression to our heart, the song gives expression to our voice, and the dance gives expression to our movements. These three arts take their rise from the human soul, and then are given further expression by means of musical instruments. Therefore, from the depth of sentiment comes the clarity of form, and from the strength of the mood comes the spirituality of its atmosphere. This harmony of spirit springs forth from the soul and finds expression or blossoms forth in the form of music. Therefore music is the one thing in which there is no use trying to deceive others or make false pretenses...

六

孟　子
Mencius[①]

孟子曰:"乃若其情,则可以为善矣,乃所谓善也。若夫为不善,非才之罪也。恻隐之心,人皆有之;羞恶之心,人皆有之;恭敬之心,人皆有之;是非之心,人皆有之。恻隐之心,仁也;羞恶之心,义也;恭敬之心,礼也;是非之心,智也。仁义礼智,非由外铄我也,我固有之也,弗思耳矣。故曰,'求则得之,舍则失之。'或相倍蓰而无算者,不能尽其才者也。《诗》曰:'天生蒸民,有物有则。民之秉彝,好是懿德。'孔子曰:'为此诗者,其知道乎! 故有物必有则,民之秉彝也,故好是懿德。'"

"If you let them follow their original nature," replied Mencius, "then they are all good. That is why I say human nature is good. If men become evil, that is not the fault of their original endowment. The sense of mercy is found in all men; the sense of shame is found in all men; the sense of respect is found in all men; the sense of right and wrong is found in all men. The sense of mercy is what we call benevolence or charity. The sense of shame is what we call righteousness. The sense of respect is what we call propriety. The sense of right and wrong is what we call wisdom, or moral consciousness.

① 林语堂在《孔子的智慧》一书中翻译了《孟子·告子》上篇,此处仅节选部分重要内容,未必是连续的。——编者注

Charity, righteousness, propriety and moral consciousness are not something that is drilled into us; we have got them originally with us, only we often forget about them (or neglect or ignore them). Therefore it is said, 'Seek and you will find it, neglect and you will lose it.' This moral consciousness is developed in different persons to different degrees, some five times, some ten times and some infinitely more than others, because people have not developed to the full extent what is in them. The *Book of Songs* says, 'Heaven created the common people with laws governing their affairs. When the people keep to the central (or common) principles, they will love a beautiful character.' Confucius commented upon this poem, saying, 'The writer of this poem understood the moral law, and therefore he recognized that there were laws governing human affairs. Because the people keep to the central principles, therefore they have come to love beautiful character.'"

"故曰,口之于味也,有同耆焉;耳之于声也,有同听焉;目之于色也,有同美焉。至于心,独无所同然乎?心之所同然者何也?谓理也,义也。圣人先得我心之所同然耳。故理义之悦我心,犹刍豢之悦我口。"

"Therefore I say there is a common love for flavors in our mouths, a common sense for sounds in our ears, and a common sense for beauty in our eyes. Why then do we refuse to admit that there is something common in our souls also? What is that thing that we have in common in our souls? It is reason and a sense of right. The Sage is the man who has first discovered what is common to men's souls. Therefore, reason and the sense of right please our minds as beef and mutton and pork please our palates."

　　孟子曰："鱼,我所欲也;熊掌,亦我所欲也。二者不可得兼,舍鱼而取熊掌者也。生,亦我所欲也;义,亦我所欲也。二者不可得兼,舍生而取义者也。生亦我所欲,所欲有甚于生者,故不为苟得也。死亦我所恶,所恶有甚于死者,故患有所不辟也。如使人之所欲莫甚于生,则凡可以得生者,何不用也? 使人之所恶莫甚于死者,则凡可以辟患者,何不为也? 由是则生而有不用也,由是则可以辟患而有不为也。是故所欲有甚于生者,所恶有甚于死者。非独贤者有是心也,人皆有之,贤者能勿丧耳。"

Mencius said, "I like fish, but I also like bear's paw, but if I can't have both at the same time, I will forgo the fish and eat the bear's paw. I love life, but I also love righteousness, and if I can't have both at the same time, I will sacrifice life to have righteousness. I love life, but there is something that I love more than life, and therefore I would not have life at any price. I also hate death, but there is something that I hate more than death, and therefore I would not avoid danger at any price. If there is nothing that man loves more than life, then does he not permit himself to do anything in order to save it? And if there is nothing that man hates more than death, then why does he not always avoid dangers that could be avoided? And so there are times when a man would forsake his life, and there are times when a man would not avoid danger. It is not only the good men who have this feeling that there are times when they would forsake life and there are times when they would not avoid danger.

All men have this feeling, only the good men have been able to preserve it. "①

---

① In the Chinese text, Mencius used the word "heart," which I have translated here as "feelings" (elsewhere also as the "soul"), because of the limitations of this word "heart" in the English usage. The whole Mencian philosophy centers around "keeping the heart" and not "losing" it. At other places I have found it necessary to render the same word by "mind" or "intelligence." Of course the English word "heart" comes closest to what Mencius calls *hsin*, since it is primarily a matter of feeling and not of thinking. But the same word is used in Chinese to express the "mind" also, and it should be strongly emphasized that the Chinese language does not admit of a clear distinction of, or separation between, the head and the heart. That is not only grammatically, but also historically a true fact. Mencius, however, uses three important words, "the heart" (including the mind or intelligence), "sentiment" (which is interpreted as the heart in action), and "talent" (or innate capacity, which is more or less fully developed in individuals according to the circumstances).

七

列　子
Book of Liehtse[①]

两小儿辩日

孔子东游,见两小儿辩斗,问其故。

一儿曰:"我以日始出时去人近,而日中时远也。"一儿以日初出远,而日中时近也。

一儿曰:"日初出大如车盖,及日中则如盘盂,此不为远者小而近者大乎?"

一儿曰:"日初出沧沧凉凉,及其日中如探汤,此不为近者热而远者凉乎?"

孔子不能决也。两小儿笑曰:"孰为汝多知乎?"

Confucius and the Children

Confucius was travelling east and met two children arguing with one another. He asked them what they were arguing about, and one child said, "I say the sun is nearer to us in the morning and farther away from us at noon, and he says the sun is farther away from us in the morning and nearer to us at noon." One child said, "When the sun begins to come up, it is big like a carriage cover, and at noon it is like a dinner plate. So it must be farther away when it looks smaller, and

---

① 此处仅收录两则著名的寓言故事。——编者注

nearer us when it looks bigger." The other child said, "When the sun comes up, the air is very cool, and at noon it burns like hot soup. So it must be nearer when it is hot and father away when it is cool." Confucius could not decide who was right, and the children laughed at him and said, "Whoever said that you were a wise guy?"

愚公移山

太行、王屋二山,方七百里,高万仞,本在冀州之南,河阳之北。

北山愚公者,年且九十,面山而居。惩山北之塞,出入之迂也。聚室而谋曰:"吾与汝毕力平险,指通豫南,达于汉阴,可乎?"杂然相许。其妻献疑曰:"以君之力,曾不能损魁父之丘,如太行、王屋何? 且焉置土石?"杂曰:"投诸渤海之尾,隐土之北。"遂率子孙荷担者三夫,叩石垦壤,箕畚运于渤海之尾。邻人京城氏之孀妻有遗男,始龀,跳往助之。寒暑易节,始一反焉。

河曲智叟笑而止之曰:"甚矣,汝之不惠! 以残年余力,曾不能毁山之一毛,其如土石何?"北山愚公长息曰:"汝心之固,固不可彻,曾不若孀妻弱子。虽我之死,有子存焉;子又生孙,孙又生子;子又有子,子又有孙;子子孙孙无穷匮也,而山不加增,何苦而不平?"河曲智叟亡以应。

操蛇之神闻之,惧其不已也,告之于帝。帝感其诚,命夸娥氏二子负二山,一厝朔东,一厝雍南。自此,冀之南,汉之阴,无陇断焉。

The Old Man Who Would Move Mountains

The two mountains Taihang (in Shansi) and Wangwu cover a territory of seven hundred square *li*, and are ten thousand cubits high. They were formerly situated in the south of Chichow and north of Hoyang. Old Man Fool of the North Mountain was about ninety years old and he lived in a house facing the mountain. He did not like to go up and down the mountain when he left home, and asked his family to come together and said to them, "You and I shall set to work with all our strength and level this mountain so that we may have a level path leading straight to Yunan (Honan), and reaching clear to the northern bank of the Han River (in Hupeh). What do you say?" The family agreed, but his wife said, "With your strength, you can't even do anything with the K'ueifu Hill. How can you do anything with the Taihang and Wangwu? Besides, where are you going to put away all the rocks and soil?" The various people said, "We can throw them into the end of the Puhai (Gulf of Peichili, south of Manchuria) and north of Yintu (Siberia)."

He then led three of his children and grandchildren who could carry loads, and began to chip the rocks and shovel the soil, and carried them in baskets to the end of Puhai. An orphan boy of the neighbor's widow by the name of Chingch'eng, who had just shed his milk teeth, jumped along and came to help them, and returned home only once a season.

The wise man of Hoch'ü laughed at the old man and tried to stop him, saying, "What a fool you are! With all the strength and years left to you, you can't even scratch the surface of this mountain. What can you do about the rocks and soil?" Old Man Fool of North Mountain drew a deep sigh and said, "It's only your mind that is not made up; when it is made up, nothing can stop it. You are of less use than the widow's son. When I die, there will be my children (to carry on the work), and the children will have grandchildren, and the grandchildren will again have children, and the children will again have children, and the children will again have grandchildren. So my children and grandchildren are endless, while the mountain cannot grow bigger in size. Why shouldn't it be leveled some day?" The wise man could not make any reply.

Now the Snake Spirit heard about it and was worried about his own safety, and he went to speak to God. God had pity on the old man's sincerity of heart and ordered the two sons of K'uafu to carry the two mountains and placed one in Sutung and one in Yungnan. From then on, the south of Chichow and north of Han River became level ground.

八

庄　子
Book of Chuangtse[①]

鱼游濠上

庄子与惠子游于濠梁之上。庄子曰："鲦鱼出游从容，是鱼之乐也。"

惠子曰："子非鱼，安知鱼之乐？"

庄子曰："子非我，安知我不知鱼之乐？"

惠子曰："我非子，固不知子矣；子固非鱼矣，子之不知鱼之乐，全矣。"

庄子曰："请循其本。子曰'汝安知鱼乐'云者，既已知吾知之而问我，我知之濠上也。"

How Do You Know?

Chuangtse and Hueitse had strolled onto the bridge over the Hao when the former observed, "See how the small fish are darting about! That is the happiness of the fish."

"You are not a fish yourself," said Hueitse; "how can you know the happiness of the fish?"

"And you not being I," retorted Chuangtse, "how can you know that I do not know?"

"If I, not being you, cannot know what you know," urged

---

① 此处仅节选部分片段。——编者注

Hueitse, "it follows that you, not being a fish, cannot know the happiness of the fish."

"Let us go back to your original question," said Chuangtse. "You asked me how I knew the happiness of the fish. Your very question shows that you knew that I knew. I knew it [from my own feelings] on this bridge."

庄周梦蝶

昔者庄周梦为蝴蝶，栩栩然蝴蝶也，自喻适志与！不知周也。俄然觉，则蘧蘧然周也。不知周之梦为蝴蝶与，蝴蝶之梦为周与？周与蝴蝶则必有分矣。此之谓物化。

The Butterfly's Dream

Once upon a time, I, Chuang Chou, dreamt that I was a butterfly, fluttering hither and thither, to all intents and purposes a butterfly. I was conscious only of my happiness as a butterfly, unaware that I was Chou. Soon I awoke, and there I was, veritably myself again. Now I do not know whether I was then a man dreaming that I was a butterfly, or whether I am now a butterfly, dreaming that I am a man. Between a man and a butterfly, there is necessarily a distinction. The transition is called "the transformation of material things."

古之真人

泉涸，鱼相与处于陆，相呴以湿，相濡以沫，不如相忘于江湖。与其誉尧而非桀也，不如两忘而化其道。

夫大块载我以形，劳我以生，佚我以老，息我以死。故善吾生者，乃所以善吾死也。

To Lose Oneself in Tao

When the pond dries up and the fishes are left upon the dry ground, rather than leave them to moisten each other with their damp and spittle, it would be far better to let them forget themselves in their native rivers and lakes. And it would be better than praising Yao and blaming Chieh to forget both [the good and bad] and lose oneself in Tao.

The Great [universe] gives me this form, this toil in manhood, this repose in old age, this rest in death. And surely that which is such a kind arbiter of my life is the best arbiter of my death.

天道与人道

夫有土者,有大物也。有大物者,不可以物;物而不物,故能物物。明乎物物者之非物也,岂独治天下百姓而已哉! 出入六合,游乎九州,独往独来,是谓独有。独有之人,是谓至贵。

何谓道? 有天道,有人道。无为而尊者,天道也;有为而累者,人道也。主者,天道也;臣者,人道也。天道之与人道也,相去远矣,不可不察也。

The Tao of God and the Tao of Man

For to have a territory is to have something great. He who has something great must not regard the material things as material things. Only by not regarding material things as material things can one be the lord of things. The principle of looking at material things as not real things is not confined to mere government of the empire. Such a one may wander at will between the six limits of space or travel over the Nine Continents, unhampered and free. This is to be the Unique One. The Unique One is the highest among man...

What then is Tao? There is the Tao of God, and there is the Tao of man. Honor through inaction comes from the Tao of God; entanglement through action comes from the Tao of man. The Tao of God is fundamental; the Tao of man is accidental. The distance which separates them is great. Let us all take heed thereto!

逍遥游

北冥有鱼,其名为鲲。鲲之大,不知其几千里也。化而为鸟,其名而鹏,鹏之背,不知其几千里也;怒而飞,其翼若垂天之云。是鸟也,海运则将徙于南冥;南冥者,天池也。《齐谐》者,志怪者也。《谐》之言曰:"鹏之徙于南冥也,水击三千里,抟扶摇而上者九万里,去以六月息者也。"野马也,尘埃也,生物之以息相吹也。天之苍苍,其正色邪? 其远而无所至极邪? 其视下也,亦若是则已矣。

且夫水之积也不厚,则其负大舟也无力;覆杯水于坳堂之上,则芥为之舟,置杯焉则胶,水浅而舟大也。风之积也不厚,则其负大翼也无力;故九万里,则风斯在下矣,而后乃今培风;背负青天,而莫之夭阏者,而后乃今将图南。蜩与学鸠笑之曰:"我决起而飞,抢榆枋而止,时则不至,而控于地而已矣。奚以之九万里而南为?"适莽苍者,三餐而反,腹犹果然;适百里者,宿舂粮;适千里者,三月聚粮;之二虫,又何知?

小知不及大知,小年不及大年。奚以知其然也? 朝菌不知晦朔,蟪蛄不知春秋,此小年也。楚之南有冥灵者,以五百岁为春,五百岁为秋;上古有大椿者,以八千岁为春,八千岁为秋。此大年也。而彭祖乃今以久特闻,众人匹之,不亦悲乎?

汤之问棘也是已:"穷发之北,有冥海者,天池也。有鱼焉,其广数千里,未有知其修者,其名为鲲。有鸟焉,其名为鹏,背若泰山,翼若垂天之云,抟扶摇羊角而上者九万里,绝云气,负青天,然后图南,且适南冥也。斥鷃笑之曰:'彼且奚适也? 我腾跃而上,不过数仞而下,翱翔蓬蒿之间,此亦飞之至也。而彼且奚适也?'"此小大之辩也。

故夫知效一官,行比一乡,德合一君,而征一国者,其自视也,亦若此矣。而宋荣子犹然笑之。且举世誉之而不加劝,举世非之而不加沮,定乎内外之分,辩乎荣辱之境,斯已矣。彼其于世,未数数然也;虽然,犹有未树也。

夫列子御风而行,泠然善也,旬有五日而后反,彼于致福者,未数数然也;此虽免乎行,犹有所待者也。若夫乘天地之正,而御六气之辩,以游无穷者,彼且恶乎待哉?

故曰:"至人无己,神人无功,圣人无名。"

A Happy Excursion

In the northern ocean there is a fish, called the *k'un*, I do not know how many thousand *li* in size. This *k'un* changes into a bird, called the *p'eng*. Its back is I do not know how many thousand *li* in breadth. When it is moved, it flies, its wings obscuring the sky like clouds.

When on a voyage, this bird prepares to start for the Southern Ocean, the Celestial Lake. And in the *Records of Marvels* we read that when the *p'eng* flies southwards, the water is smitten for a space of three thousand *li* around, while the bird itself mounts upon a great wind to a height of ninety thousand *li*, for a flight of six months' duration.

There mounting aloft, the bird saw the moving white mists of spring, the dust-clouds, and the living things blowing their breaths among them. It wondered whether the blue of the sky was its real color, or only the result of distance without end, and saw that the things on earth appeared the same to it.

If there is not sufficient depth, water will not float large ships. Upset a cupful into a hole in the yard, and a mustard-seed will be your boat. Try to float the cup, and it will be grounded, due to the disproportion between water and vessel.

So with air. If there is not sufficient a depth, it cannot support large wings. And for this bird, a depth of ninety thousand *li* is necessary to bear it up. Then, gliding upon the wind, with nothing save the clear sky above, and no obstacles in the way, it starts upon its journey to the south.

A cicada and a young dove laughed, saying, "Now, when I fly with all my might, 'tis as much as I can do to get from tree to tree. And sometimes I do not reach, but fall to the ground midway. What then can be the use of going up ninety thousand *li* to start for the south?"

He who goes to the countryside taking three meals with him comes back with his stomach as full as when he started. But he who travels a hundred *li* must take ground rice enough for an overnight stay. And he who travels a thousand *li* must supply himself with provisions for three months. Those two little creatures, what should they know?

Small knowledge has not the compass of great knowledge any more than a short year has the length of a long year. How can we tell that this is so? The fungus plant of a morning knows not the alternation of day and night. The cicada knows not the alternation of spring and autumn. Theirs are short years. But in the south of Ch'u there is a *mingling* (tree) whose spring and autumn are each of five hundred years' duration. And in former days there was a large tree which had a spring and autumn each of eight thousand years. Yet, P'eng Tsu[①] is known for reaching a great age and is still, alas! An object of envy to all!

---

① He is reputed to have lived 800 years.

It was on this very subject that the Emperor Tang[①] spoke to Chi, as follows:—"At the north of Ch'iungfa, there is a Dark Sea, the Celestial Lake. In it there is a fish several thousand *li* in breadth, and I know not how many in length. It is called the *k'un*. There is also a bird, called the *p'eng*, with a back like Mount T'ai, and wings like clouds across the sky. It soars up upon a whirlwind to a height of ninety thousand *li*, far above the region of the clouds, with only the clear sky above it. And then it directs its flight towards the Southern Ocean.

"And a lake sparrow laughed, and said: Pray, what may that creature be going to do? I rise but a few yards in the air and settle down again, after flying around among the reeds. That is as much as any one would want to fly. Now, where ever can this creature be going to?" Such, indeed, is the difference between small and great.

Take, for instance, a man who creditably fills some small office, or whose influence spreads over a village, or whose character pleases a certain prince. His opinion of himself will be much the same as that lake sparrow's. The philosopher Yung of Sung would laugh at such a one. If the whole world flattered him, he would not be affected thereby, nor if the whole world blamed him would he be dissuaded from what he was doing. For Yung can distinguish between essence and superficialities, and understand what is true honor and shame. Such men are rare in their generation. But even he has not established himself.

Now Liehtse[②] could ride upon the wind. Sailing happily in the

---

① B. C. 1783.

② Philosopher about whose life nothing is known. The book *Liehtse* is considered a later compilation.

cool breeze, he would go on for fifteen days before his return. Among mortals who attain happiness, such a man is rare. Yet although Liehtse could dispense with walking, he would still have to depend upon something.①As for one who is charioted upon the eternal fitness of Heaven and Earth, driving before him the changing elements as his team to roam through the realms of the Infinite, upon what, then, would such a one have need to depend?

Thus it is said, "The perfect man ignores self; the divine man ignores achievement; the true Sage ignores reputation."

① The wind.

九

墨 子
Book of Motse[①]

非 攻

今有一人，入人园圃，窃其桃李。众闻则非之，上为政者得则罚之。此何也？以亏人自利也。至攘人犬豕鸡豚者，其不义又甚入人园圃窃桃李。是何故也？以亏人愈多，其不仁兹甚，罪益厚。至入人栏厩，取人马牛者，其不仁义又甚攘人犬豕鸡豚。此何故也？以其亏人愈多，苟亏人愈多，其不仁兹甚，罪益厚。至杀不辜人也，扡其衣裘，取戈剑者，其不义又甚入人栏厩取人马牛。此何故也？以其亏人愈多，苟亏人愈多，其不仁兹甚矣，罪益厚。当此，天下之君子皆知而非之，谓之不义。今至大为攻国，则弗知非，从而誉之，谓之义。此可谓知义与不义之别乎？

杀一人谓之不义，必有一死罪矣。若以此说往，杀十人十重不义，必有十死罪矣；杀百人百重不义，必有百死罪矣。当此，天下之君子皆知而非之，谓之不义。今至大为不义攻国，则弗知非，从而誉之，谓之义，情不知其不义也，故书其言以遗后世。若知其不义也，夫奚说书其不义以遗后世哉？今有人于此，少见黑曰黑，多见黑曰白，则以此人不知白黑之辩矣；少尝苦曰苦，多尝苦曰甘，则必以此人为不知甘苦之辩矣。今小为非，则知而非之；大为非攻国，则不知非，从而誉之，谓之义。此可谓知义与不义之辩乎？是以知天下之君子也，辩义与不义之乱也。

---

① 此处仅收录《非攻》一文。——编者注

Against Wars of Aggression

If a man breaks into a private garden and steals peaches and plums, and it is found out, the people will condemn it as wrong. If he is caught by the authorities, he is punished. Why? Because he injures others.

If a man robs his neighbor of chicken and pigs and dogs, it is considered a more serious offense. Why? Because the injury done to others is greater. If the injury committed is greater, the man is considered to be worse and the punishment is greater.

If a man now goes into someone's stables and steals his horses or cattle, he is considered to be still worse than the stealer of chicken and pigs and dogs. Why? Because the injury done is greater, he does more harm to others, and his crime is still greater.

To go further, if a man kills an innocent man, takes away his clothing and his spear and sword, the offense is still greater than that of stealing horses and cattle. Why? Because the more harm he does to others, the worse he is considered to be and the greater the crime.

All educated men condemn such actions and call them wrong. But the same persons do not realize that a war of aggression against another country is wrong, but instead praise it and give it their support. They consider that it is right to do so. Can these people be said to know the difference between right and wrong?

It is considered wrong to kill one person, and the crime is punished for one murder. Following this reasoning, the crime of committing ten murders is ten times worse than that of killing one man, and the murderer's crime is ten times greater. To kill one hundred persons would be a hundred times worse and the crime is multiplied a hundredfold.

All educated men condemn such murders and call them wrong. But the same persons do not realize that a war of aggression against another country is wrong, but instead praise it and give it their support. They consider that it is right to do so. They are really not conscious that it is wrong, for they write about such wars of aggression in their history books. If they knew that it was wrong, they would not have done so.

If a man calls something which is a little black "black," but calls deep black "white," then it may be said of him that he does not know the difference between black and white. If a man tastes something slightly bitter and calls it "bitter," but calls what is very bitter "sweet," he, too, may be said not to know the difference between sweetness and bitterness.

Now if a man condemns a small wrong as "wrong," but does not consider the great wrong of aggression against a neighbor, but gives it praise and support, how can such a man be said to know the difference between right and wrong?

It is therefore seen that the educated men of this world do not know the difference between right and wrong.

韩非子
Book of Hanfeitse^①

说　难

凡说之难：非吾知之有以说之之难也，又非吾辩之能明吾意之难也，又非吾敢横失而能尽之难也。凡说之难：在知所说之心，可以吾说当之。所说出于为名高者也，而说之以厚利，则见下节而遇卑贱，必弃远矣。所说出于厚利者也，而说之以名高，则见无心而远事情，必不收矣。所说阴为厚利而显为名高者也，而说之以名高，则阳收其身而实疏之；说之以厚利，则阴用其言显弃其身矣。此不可不察也。

The Person Spoken to

The difficulty in speaking to a person is not that of knowing what to say, nor that of method of argument to make one's meaning clear. Nor does it consist in the difficulty of having the courage to speak one's mind fully and frankly. The difficulty lies in knowing the mind of the person spoken to and fitting one's proper approach to it. If the person spoken to likes to have a name for altruism and idealism and you speak to him about utilitarian profits, he will think you vulgar-minded and

---

① 此处仅收录《说难》一文的部分内容。——编者注

keep away from you. On the other hand, if the person spoken to has a good mind for commercial profits and you speak to him about idealism, he will think you an impractical sort of person with whom he will have nothing to do. If the person spoken to likes to appear as a man of principles and is at heart after the profits and you speak to him about principles, he will make a pretense of being close to you but will not take you into his confidence. If you speak to the same person about big profits, he will secretly take your advice but outwardly keep you at a distance. These things one must know.

第二编

古文小品

塞翁失马
The Old Man at the Fort

刘 安（Liu An）

近塞上之人有善术者。马无故亡而入胡，人皆吊之。其父曰："此何遽不为福乎！"居数月，其马将胡骏马而归，人皆贺之。其父曰："此何遽不能为祸乎！"家富良马，其子好骑，堕而折其髀，人皆吊之。其父曰："此何遽不为福乎！"居一年，胡人大入塞，丁壮者引弦而战。近塞之人，死者十九，此独以跛之故，父子相保。故福之为祸，祸之为福，化不可极，深不可测也。

There was an old man at a frontier fort in the north who understood Taoism. One day he lost his horse, which wandered into the land of the Hu tribesmen. His neighbors came to condole with him, and the man said, "How do you know that this is bad luck?"

After a few months, the horse returned with some fine horses of the Hu breed, and the people congratulated him. The old man said, "How do you know that this is good luck?"

He then became very prosperous with so many horses. The son one day broke his legs riding, and all the people came to condole with him again. The old man said, "How do you know that this is bad luck?"

One day the Hu tribesmen invaded the frontier fort. All the young men fought with arrows to defend it, and nine tenths of them were killed. Because the son was a cripple, both father and son escaped unharmed.

Therefore, good luck changes into bad, and bad luck changes into good. The workings of events are beyond comprehension.

舌存齿亡
How the Tongue Survived the Teeth

刘　向（Liu Shiang）

　　常枞有疾，老子往问焉，曰："先生疾甚矣，无遗教可以语诸弟子者乎？"常枞曰："子虽不问，吾将语子。"常枞曰："过故乡而下车，子知之乎？"老子曰："过故乡而下车，非谓其不忘故耶？"常枞曰："嘻！是已。"常枞曰："过乔木而趋，子知之乎？"老子曰："过乔木而趋，非谓敬老耶？"常枞曰："嘻！是已。"张其口而示老子曰："吾舌存乎？"老子曰："然！""吾齿存乎？"老子曰："亡！"常枞曰："子知之乎？"老子曰："夫舌之存也，岂非以其柔耶？齿之亡也，岂非以其刚耶？"常枞曰："嘻！是已。天下之事已尽矣，无以复语子哉①！"

　　Ch'ang Ch'uang was sick and Laotse went to see him. The latter said to Ch'ang Ch'uang, "You are very ill. Have you not something to say to your disciple?" "Even if you did not ask me, I was going to tell you," replied Ch'ang Ch'uang. "Do you know why one has to get down from one's carriage when coming to one's old village?" And Laotse replied, "Doesn't this custom mean that one should not forget one's origins?" "Ah, yes," said Ch'ang Ch'uang.

　　Then the sick man asked again, "Do you know why one should run

---

① 有的版本为"何以复语子哉"。——编者注

when passing under a tall tree?" "Doesn't this custom mean we should respect what is old?" "Ah, yes," said Ch'ang Ch'uang.

Then Ch'ang Ch'uang opened his mouth wide and asked Laotse to look into it, and said, "Is my tongue still there?" "It is," replied Laotse. "Are my teeth still there?" asked the old man. "No," replied Laotse. "And do you know why?" asked Ch'ang Ch'uang. "Does not the tongue last longer because it is soft? And is it not because the teeth are hard that they fall off earlier?" replied Laotse. "Ah, yes", said Ch'ang Ch'uang. "There you have learned all the principles concerning the world, I have nothing else to teach you."

邹忌讽齐王纳谏
Against Yes Men

刘　向（Liu Shiang）

邹忌修八尺有余，而形貌昳丽。朝服衣冠，窥镜，谓其妻曰："我孰与城北徐公美？"其妻曰："君美甚，徐公何能及君也！"城北徐公，齐国之美丽者也。忌不自信，而复问其妾曰："吾孰与徐公美？"妾曰："徐公何能及君也！"且日，客从外来，与坐谈，问之客曰："吾与徐公孰美？"客曰："徐公不若君之美也。"明日，徐公来，孰视之，自以为不如，窥镜而自视，又弗如远甚。暮寝而思之，曰："吾妻之美我者，私我也；妾之美我者，畏我也；客之美我者，欲有求于我也。"

于是入朝见威王，曰："臣诚知不如徐公美，臣之妻私臣，臣之妾畏臣，臣之客欲有求于臣，皆以美于徐公。今齐地方千里，百二十城，宫妇左右莫不私王，朝廷之臣莫不畏王，四境之内莫不有求于王。由此观之，王之蔽甚矣。"

王曰："善。"乃下令："群臣吏民能面刺寡人之过者，受上赏；上书谏寡人者，受中赏；能谤讥于市朝①，闻寡人之耳者，受下赏。"

令初下，群臣进谏，门庭若市；数月之后，时时而间进；期年之后，虽欲言，无可进者。

燕、赵、韩、魏闻之，皆朝于齐。此所谓战胜于朝廷。

---

① 有的版本为"能谤议于市朝"。——编者注

King Wei of Tsi was completely surrounded by courtiers who flattered his vanity and followed his whims. One day, Tsou Chi said to the king:

"Sire, I am not exactly bad-looking. [He was 'eight feet' tall.] But in the north city, there is a Mr. Shu, noted for his handsomeness. One day I stood before the mirror and asked my wife, 'Who do you think is handsomer, Mr. Shu or me?' 'Of course you are,' replied my wife. I dared not take her word for it and asked my concubine the same question. 'How can Mr. Shu compare with you?' was her answer. Next morning a guest came and after a while, I asked him the same question, and he replied, 'Mr. Shu cannot compare with you.' The following day, Mr. Shu himself came to see me. I studied him carefully and thought he was much handsomer than myself. I examined myself in the mirror and was quite convinced that I could not compare with him. So I lay in my bed and thought, my wife praises me because she is partial to me. My concubine praises me because she is afraid of me. My friend praises me because he has something to ask of me.

"Now Tsi is a kingdom of a thousand square *li* with one hundred twenty cities. All the palace ladies and attendants are partial to you. All the courtiers are afraid of your power. And all the people have something to ask of you. So it seems to me that it is hard for you to hear the truth."

"Well said," replied the king. He then issued an order: "All ministers, officials, and common people who can point out my mistakes shall receive the highest class of rewards. Those who write letters to advise me shall receive the second-class reward. And those who can criticize me and my government at the market place so that it reaches my ears shall receive the third-class reward."

When the order was issued, the king was deluged with a torrent of advice, and the court was crowded with people. This went on for several months. After a year, there was no mistake of the government which had not already been thought of and pointed out by somebody.

The neighboring countries Yen, Chao, Han, and Wei heard of what the king had done and came to acknowledge the state of Tsi as their leader. This is called winning the war at home.

四

与山巨源绝交书
Letter Severing Friendship
Letter to Shan Chuyuan①

嵇　康(Chi Kang)

　　前年从河东还,显宗、阿都说足下议以吾自代,事虽不行,知足下故不知之。足下傍通,多可而少怪;吾直性狭中,多所不堪,偶与足下相知耳。间闻足下迁,惕然不喜……

　　……少加孤露,母兄见骄,不涉经学。性复疏懒,筋驽肉缓,头面常一月十五日不洗,不大闷痒,不能沐也。每常小便而忍不起,令胞中略转乃起耳。又纵逸来久,情意傲散,简与礼相背,懒与慢相成,而为侪类见宽,不攻其过。又读《庄》、《老》,重增其放。故使荣进之心日颓,任实之情转笃。此犹禽鹿,少见驯育,则服从教制;长而见羁,则狂顾顿缨,赴蹈汤火;虽饰以金镳,飨以嘉肴,愈思长林而志在丰草也。

　　……又人伦有礼,朝廷有法,自惟至熟,有必不堪者七,甚不可者二。卧喜晚起,而当关呼之不置,一不堪也。抱琴行吟,弋钓草野,而吏卒守之,不得妄动,二不堪也。危坐一时,痹不得摇,性复多虱,把搔无已,而当裹以章服,揖拜上官,三不堪也。素不便书,又不喜作书,而人间多事,堆案盈机,不相酬答,则犯教伤义,欲自勉强,则不能久,四不堪也。不喜吊丧,而人道以此为重,已为未见恕者所怨,至欲见中伤者;虽瞿然

---

① 原文根据林语堂的译文节录,有删节。——编者注

自责,然性不可化,欲降心顺俗,则诡故不情,亦终不能获无咎无誉如此,五不堪也。不喜俗人,而当与之共事,或宾客盈坐,鸣声聒耳,嚣尘臭处,千变百伎,在人目前,六不堪也。心不耐烦,而官事鞅掌,机务缠其心,世故繁其虑,七不堪也。又每非汤、武而薄周、孔,在人间不止,此事会显,世教所不容,此甚不可一也。刚肠疾恶,轻肆直言,遇事便发,此甚不可二也。以促中小心之性,统此九患,不有外难,当有内病,宁可久处人间邪?

又闻道士遗言,饵术、黄精,令人久寿,意甚信之;游山泽,观鱼鸟,心甚乐之;一行作吏,此事便废,安能舍其所乐而从其所惧哉! 夫人之相知,贵识其天性,因而济之。……吾顷学养生之术,方外荣华,去滋味,游心于寂寞,以无为为贵。纵无九患,尚不顾足下所好者。……自卜已审,若道尽途穷则已耳。足下无事冤之,令转于沟壑也。

……足下若嬲之不置,不过欲为官得人,以益时用耳。……自惟亦皆不如今日之贤能也。若以俗人皆喜荣华,独能离之,以此为快;……若吾多病困,欲离事自全,以保余年,此真所乏耳,岂可见黄门而称贞哉! 若趣欲共登王途,期于相致,时为欢益,一旦迫之,必发狂疾。自非重怨,不至于此也。……其意如此,既以解足下,并以为别。嵇康白。

Dear Chuyuan:

I hear that you proposed to recommend me to take your place. You do not really know me. You stand for a lot of things which I cannot stand. When I heard that you were promoted, I was sorry for you...

I lived very much to myself as a child, and used to offend my mother's brother. I did not study the [Confucian] classics and am by nature lazy to the bones. I often go without washing my face for fifteen days, and unless I itch a great deal, I just do not wash. Even when I am pressed to go to the toilet, I would rather delay it by not getting up and letting it turn inside a little. Besides, I have been used to living my life in my own way and cannot stand the forms of social intercourse. My friends are used to it and ignore it. And then the reading of Laotse and Chuangtse makes me yearn for freedom, caring less and less for power and position and more and more for true simplicity. We see that animals are best trained when young; when they are broken after they are grown-up, they chafe at the reins and prance and buck and heave. They may be dressed with a golden harness and fed the finest of foods, yet continue to dream of the tall grass and the deep forests.

I consider that there are seven things in a life in the government which I cannot stand and two things which I am bound to do which will be considered improper. Among the unbearable things comes the first: to be asked to get up for office when my nature is to lie in bed late. Secondly, I love to walk about and sing in the countryside, or go fishing, and I cannot do this with government servants watching me. I shan't dare to make an incorrect move. Thirdly, I love to sit while swinging my legs and scratch myself when bitten by lice on my body. How am I going to do this, wearing the official cap and gown and paying respects to my superiors? Fourthly, I hate correspondence. I cannot in conscience leave it unanswered; yet at best I shall make only interrupted efforts. Fifthly, I never care for attending funerals, which nevertheless are regarded by society as very important. I may offend people by not attending, and some may feel inclined toward revenge for a supposed insult. But I cannot help myself. If I try and pretend and go through the ceremonial weeping, eventually I cannot do a good job of it and shall be blamed for it. Sixthly, I hate to mix up with the common, uncultivated people. I shall have to associate with these and go through the noise and confusion and babble of a public dinner.

Seventhly, I am impatient of business duties, and all the worries and responsibilities that go with an office. Besides all these, I am usually free with my criticism of Confucius and Mencius and their ideal kings. There are other things in this life to attend to. Clearly this will not be permitted by so-called "high" society. Then it is my habit to say what I think, and this again will bring me into trouble.

For these nine grave reasons, I consider myself unfit to go into government. Besides, I strongly believe in the methods of prolonging life recommended by the Taoists, such as eating spiked millet and deer bamboo (*Polygonatum falcatum*). And I love to live in the country and look at the fish and listen to the birds. These things I certainly cannot do when I am burdened with an office. Friends should try to understand one another's individual nature. Human nature is something which cannot be forced... I have been recently interested in the art of prolonging life, and trying to get rid of the ambitions of fame and power and the desires of the senses, in order to let my mind roam about in nothingness. I place the highest value on inaction. Even without the aforementioned nine considerations, I simply do not covet what you regard as worth while... I figure that at the worst, I shall die poor. Don't you try to get me involved, with the risk of being punished for violating some government regulations...

[He goes into his family details.] You are bothering me only because you think you want to enlist some good men for the service of the government... There are others much more able than myself. My only distinction is that I do not care for these things. What I really crave is to be left alone and live my remaining years in peace. I am not trying to be singular. But if you persist and want to drag me into the government, and perhaps even force me to do it, I shall go insane, I am sure. I cannot believe that you have such a bad grudge against me as to wish this on me.

I have explained myself. And this is to say good-bye.

五

兰亭集序

The Past and Future
At the Orchid Pavilion

王羲之（Wang Shichih）

　　永和九年，岁在癸丑。暮春之初，会于会稽山阴之兰亭，修禊事也。群贤毕至，少长咸集。此地有崇山峻岭，茂林修竹，又有清流激湍，映带左右，引以为流觞曲水，列坐其次。虽无丝竹管弦之盛，一觞一咏，亦足以畅叙幽情。是日也，天朗气清，惠风和畅。仰观宇宙之大，俯察品类之盛。所以游目骋怀，足以极视听之娱，信可乐也。

　　夫人之相与，俯仰一世，或取诸怀抱，晤言一室之内；或因寄所托，放浪形骸之外。虽趣舍万殊，静躁不同，当其欣于所遇，暂得于己，快然自足，曾不知老之将至。及其所之既倦，情随事迁，感慨系之矣。向之所欣，俯仰之间，已为陈迹，犹不能不以之兴怀。况修短随化，终期于尽。古人云："死生亦大矣。"岂不痛哉！

　　每览昔人兴感之由，若合一契，未尝不临文嗟悼，不能喻之于怀。固知一死生为虚诞，齐彭殇为妄作。后之视今，亦犹今之视昔。悲夫！故列叙时人，录其所述，虽世殊事异，所以兴怀，其致一也。后之览者，亦将有感于斯文。

That is the ninth year of Yungho (353 A. D.), *kueichou* in the cycle. We met in late spring at the Orchid Pavilion in Shanyin to celebrate the Water Festival.

All the scholar friends are gathered, and there is a goodly mixture of old and young. In the background lie high peaks and deep forests, while a clear, gurgling brook catches the light to the right and to the left. We then arrange ourselves, sitting on its bank, drinking in succession from the goblets as it floats down the stream. No music is provided, but with drinking and with song, our hearts are gay and at ease. It is a clear spring day with a mild, caressing breeze. The vast universe, throbbing with life, lies spread before us, entertaining the eye and pleasing the spirit and all the senses. It is perfect.

Now when men come together, they let their thoughts travel to the past and the present. Some enjoy a quiet conversation indoors and others play about outdoors, occupied with what they love. The forms of amusement differ according to temperaments, but when each has found what he wants he is happy and never feels old. Then as time passes on and one is tired of his pursuits, it seems that what fascinated him not so long ago has become a mere memory. What a thought! Besides, whether individually we live a long life or not, we all return to nothingness. The ancients regarded death as the great question. Is it not sad to think of it?

I often thought that the people of the past lived and felt exactly as we of today. Whenever I read their writings I felt this way and was seized with its pathos. It is cool comfort to say that life and death are different phases of the same thing and that a long span of life or a short one does not matter. Alas! The people of the future will look upon us as we look upon those who have gone before us. Hence I have recorded here those present and what they said. Ages may pass and times may change, but the human sentiments will be the same. I know that future readers who set their eyes upon these words will be affected in the same way.

六

桃花源记
The Peach Colony

陶渊明（Tao Yuanming）

晋太元中，武陵人捕鱼为业，缘溪行，忘路之远近。忽逢桃花林，夹岸数百步，中无杂树，芳草鲜美，落英缤纷，渔人甚异之，复前行，欲穷其林。

林尽水源，便得一山，山有小口，仿佛若有光。便舍船，从口入。初极狭，才通人。复行数十步，豁然开朗。土地平旷，屋舍俨然，有良田、美池，桑竹之属，阡陌交通，鸡犬相闻。其中往来种作，男女衣着，悉如外人。黄发垂髫，并怡然自乐。

见渔人，乃大惊，问所从来，具答之。便要还家，设酒杀鸡作食。村中闻有此人，咸来问讯。自云先世避秦时乱，率妻子邑人来此绝境，不复出焉，遂与外人间隔。问今是何世，乃不知有汉，无论魏晋。此人一一为具言所闻，皆叹惋。余人各复延至其家，皆出酒食。停数日，辞去。此中人语云："不足为外人道也。"

既出，得其船，便扶向路，处处志之。及郡下，诣太守，说如此。太守即遣人随其往，寻向所志，遂迷不复得路。

南阳刘子骥，高尚士也，闻之，欣然规往。未果，寻病终。后遂无问津者。

During the reign of Taiyuan① of Chin, there was a fisherman of Wuling. One day he was walking along a bank. After having gone a certain distance, he suddenly came upon a peach grove which extended along the bank for about a hundred yards. He noticed with surprise that the grove had a magic effect, so singularly free from the usual mingling of brushwood, while the ground was covered with its rose petals. He went further to explore, and when he came to the end of the grove, he saw a spring which came from a cave in the hill. Having noticed that there seemed to be a weak light in the cave, he tied up his boat and decided to go in and explore.

At first the opening was very narrow, barely wide enough for one person to go in. After a dozen steps, it opened into a flood of light. He saw before his eyes a wide, level valley, with houses and fields and farms. There were bamboos and mulberries; farmers were working and dogs and chickens were running about. The dresses of the men and women were like those of the outside world, and the old men and children appeared very happy and contented. They were greatly astonished to see the fisherman and asked him where he had come from. The fisherman told them and was invited to their homes, where wine was served and chicken was killed for dinner to entertain him. The villagers hearing of his coming all came to see him and to talk. They said that their ancestors had come here as refugees to escape from the tyranny of Tsin Shih-huang [builder of Great Wall] some six hundred years ago, and they had never left it. They were thus completely cut off from the world, and asked what was the ruling dynasty now. They had not even heard of the Han Dynasty (two

① 376—396, in the author's own lifetime.

centuries before to two centuries after Christ), not to speak of the Wei (third century) and the Chin (third and fourth centuries). The fisherman told them, which they heard with great amazement. Many of the other villagers then began to invite him to their homes by turn and feed him dinner and wine.

After a few days, he took leave of them and left. The villagers begged him not to tell the people outside about their colony. The man found his boat and came back, marking a mental note of the direction of the route he had followed. He went to the magistrate's office and told the magistrate about it. The latter sent someone to go with him and find the place, but they got lost and could never find it again. Liu Tsechi of Nanyang was a great idealist. He heard of this story, and planned to go and find it, but was taken ill and died before he could fulfill his wish. Since then, no one has gone in search of this place.

归去来辞
Ah, Homeward Bound I Go! ①

陶渊明(Tao Yuanming)

　　归去来兮,田园将芜,胡不归? 既自以心为形役,奚惆怅而独悲? 悟已往之不谏,知来者之可追。实迷途其未远,觉今是而昨非。舟遥遥以轻飏,风飘飘而吹衣。问征夫以前路,恨晨光之熹微。乃瞻衡宇,载欣载奔。僮仆欢迎,稚子候门。三径就荒,松菊犹存。携幼入室,有酒盈樽。引壶觞以自酌,眄庭柯以怡颜。倚南窗以寄傲,审容膝之易安。园日涉以成趣,门虽设而常关。策扶老以流憩,时矫首而遐观。云无心以出岫,鸟倦飞而知还。景翳翳以将入,抚孤松而盘桓。

　　归去来兮,请息交以绝游。世与我而相违,复驾言兮焉求? 悦亲戚之情话,乐琴书以消忧。农人告余以春及,将有事于西畴。或命巾车,或棹孤舟。既窈窕以寻壑,亦崎岖而经丘。木欣欣以向荣,泉涓涓而始流。善万物之得时,感吾生之行休。

　　已矣乎! 寓形宇内复几时,曷不委心任去留? 胡为乎遑遑欲何之? 富贵非吾愿,帝乡不可期。怀良辰以孤往,或植杖而耘耔。登东皋以舒啸,临清流而赋诗。聊乘化以归尽,乐夫天命复奚疑!

---

① This poem is in the form of a *fu*, progressing in parallel constructions, like the *Psalms*, and sometimes rhymed.

Ah, homeward bound I go! Why not go home, seeing that my field and gardens with weeds are overgrown? Myself have made my soul serf to my body: why have vain regrets and mourn alone?

Fret not over bygones and the forward journey take. Only a short distance have I gone astray, and I know today I am right, if yesterday was a complete mistake.

Lightly floats and drifts the boat, and gently flows and flaps my gown. I inquire the road of a wayfarer, and sulk at the dimness of the dawn.

Then when I catch sight of my old roofs, joy will my steps quicken. Servants will be there to bid me welcome, and waiting at the door are the greeting children.

Gone to seed, perhaps, are my garden paths, but there will still be the chrysanthemums and the pine! I shall lead the youngest boy in by the hand, and on the table there stands a cup full of wine!

Holding the pot and cup, I give myself a drink, happy to see in the courtyard the hanging bough. I lean upon the southern window with an immense satisfaction, and note that the little place is cosy enough to walk around.

The garden grows more familiar and interesting with the daily walks. What if no one knocks at the always closed door! Carrying a cane I wander at peace, and now and then look aloft to gaze at the blue above.

There the clouds idle away from their mountain recesses without any intent or purpose, and birds, when tired of their wandering flights, will think of home. Darkly then fall the shadows and, ready to come home, I yet fondle the lonely pines and loiter around.

Ah, homeward bound I go! Let me from now on learn to live

alone! The world and I are not made for one another, and why drive round like one looking for what he has not found?

Content shall I be with conversations with my own kin, and there will be music and books to while away the hours. The farmers will come and tell me that spring is here and there will be work to do at the western farm.

Some order covered wagons; some row in small boats. Sometimes we explore quiet, unknown ponds, and sometimes we climb over steep, rugged mounds.

There the trees, happy of heart, grow marvelously green, and spring water gushes forth with a gurgling sound. I admire how things grow and prosper according to their seasons, and feel that thus, too, shall my life go its round.

Enough! How long yet shall I this mortal shape keep? Why not take life as it comes, and why hustle and bustle like one on an errand bound?

Wealth and power are not my ambitions, and unattainable is the abode of the gods! I would go forth alone on a bright morning, or perhaps, planting my cane, begin to pluck the weeds and till the ground.

Or I would compose a poem beside a clear stream, or perhaps go up to Tungkao and make a long-drawn call on top of the hill. So would I be content to live and die, and without questionings of the heart, gladly accept Heaven's will.

八

春夜宴桃李园序
The Universe a Lodging House
From "A Night Feast"[①]

李　白（Li Po）

夫天地者，万物之逆旅；光阴者，百代之过客。而浮生若梦，为欢几何？古人秉烛夜游，良有以也。

The universe is a lodging house for the myriad things, and time itself is a traveling guest of the centuries. This floating life is like a dream. How can one enjoy oneself? It is for this reason that the ancient people held candles to celebrate the night.

---

① 此处仅节选部分内容。——编者注

愚溪诗序
The River of Folly
Preface to "Folly River Poems"

柳宗元（Liu Tsungyuan）

灌水之阳有溪焉，东流入于潇水。或曰：冉氏尝居也，故姓是溪为冉溪。或曰：可以染也，名之以其能，故谓之染溪。予以愚触罪，谪潇水上。爱是溪，入二三里，得其尤绝者家焉。古有愚公谷，今予家是溪，而名莫能定，士之居者，犹龂龂然，不可以不更也，故更之为愚溪。

愚溪之上，买小丘，为愚丘。自愚丘东北行六十步，得泉焉，又买居之，为愚泉。愚泉凡六穴，皆出山下平地，盖上出也。合流屈曲而南，为愚沟。遂负土累石，塞其隘，为愚池。愚池之东为愚堂。其南为愚亭。池之中为愚岛。嘉木异石错置，皆山水之奇者，以予故，咸以愚辱焉。

夫水，智者乐也。今是溪独见辱于愚，何哉？盖其流甚下，不可以溉灌；又峻急多坻石，大舟不可入也。幽邃浅狭，蛟龙不屑，不能兴云雨，无以利世，而适类于予，然则虽辱而愚之，可也。

宁武子"邦无道则愚"，智而为愚者也；颜子"终日不违如愚"，睿而为愚者也。皆不得为真愚。今予遭有道而违于理，悖于事，故凡为愚者，莫我若也。夫然，则天下莫能争是溪，予得专而名焉。

溪虽莫利于世，而善鉴万类，清莹秀澈，锵鸣金石，能使愚者喜笑眷慕，乐而不能去也。予虽不合于俗，亦颇以文墨自慰，漱涤万物，牢笼百态，而无所避之。以愚辞歌愚溪，则茫然而不违，昏然而同归，超鸿蒙，混希夷，寂寥而莫我知也！于是作《八愚诗》，纪于溪石上。

There is a river which runs north of the Kuan and flows into the Siao. This is locally called the "Ran River," because, according to some, a Ran clan used to live here and, according to others, because there is a dyeing industry [ran] along the river. I was remanded to this district in the Kuan River district because of my folly, and have come to love this place. It is especially beautiful a few miles up, and I have chosen my home here. Since the written name of the river is yet undecided and the local people are in favor of changing it, I have changed its name to "River of Folly," following the precedent of the Folly Hill in ancient times, which took its name from the "Man of Folly." I bought a small hill above it and named it the "Folly Mount." Sixty paces northeast of the Folly Mount are springs, which I bought and christened "Folly Springs." The Folly Springs consist of six, all coming from the high grounds in different rivulets, which are called the "Folly Rivulets." I then had these springs dammed and surrounded with rocks and made into a pond, which is named the "Folly Pond." East of the Folly Pond stands the Folly Hall, and on the south stands the Folly Pavilion. In the center of the pond, I had a little isle made, called the "Folly Isle." The place is studded with choice, rare plants and special, selected rocks, and all have received the humiliating name of "Folly" because of me.

Water has been proverbially associated with wisdom. Why then is it humiliated here with the name of "Folly"? First, the river current is very low and is useless for irrigation purposes, and secondly, it is too fast and full of rocks in mid-current for navigation by big boats. Thirdly, it is narrow and shallow, unworthy to be a hiding place for dragons who control the rains and the clouds. It is therefore of no benefit to the world, just like myself. I find therefore some excuse for calling it the "River of Folly." Now the *Analects* tells us that Ningwutse "acted like a stupid person in times of chaos" [to save his life]. There we see a man who was clever and chose to appear stupid. Yen Huei [Confucius' favorite disciple] is said to "appear stupid, sitting and thinking all day." There is the case of a man who was a deep thinker and appeared stupid. They were not really stupid. In my case, however,① I live under a wise government, but have been stubborn and self-opinionated. Therefore there is no one more stupid than myself. If so, then, I have the indisputable right to father the name of this river.

Despite its defects, this river has many good points. It is beautiful, and it sounds like music as it rushes down the hills, so that it makes a stupid person like myself find it enchanting, unwilling to tear myself away from it. And like the river, I cannot fit in with the times, but I can console myself with writing which mirrors and reflects all creation and its myriad changes and washes away all impurities, even as the river does. Thus fitting words of folly to celebrate the River of Folly, I lose myself in the universe, becoming a part of the vast creation, go back to the age of the nebulae, and mingle with the Inaudible and the Impalpable, hidden in a primeval stillness, unknown to the world. I haven written eight poems on the River of Folly and have them inscribed on the rocks.

---

① Liu was careful here to say the right thing. For if he "grumbled" or did not admit his fault, the writing might be brought up against him as evidence of his insubordination.

书李贺小传后
Communion with Nature
Postscript to "Li Ho's Life"

陆龟蒙(Lu Kueimeng)

玉溪生传李贺云:长吉常时旦日出游,从小奚奴,骑距驴,背一古破锦囊,遇有所得,即书投囊中。暮归,足成其文。余为儿时,在溧阳闻白头书佐言:孟东野,贞元中以前秀才,家贫,受溧阳尉。溧阳昔为平陵,县南五里有投金濑,濑南八里许道东有故平陵,城周千余步,基址陂陀,裁高三四尺。而草木势甚盛,率多大栎,合数十抱,藂条蒙翳,如坞如洞。地洼下,积水沮洳,深处可活鱼鳖辈。大抵幽邃岑寂,气候古澹可喜,除里民樵罩外无入者。东野得之忘归,或比日,或间日,乘驴领小吏经蓦投金渚一往。至,得荫大栎,隐岩蓧,坐于积水之旁,吟到日西还,尔后裒裒去,曹务多弛废。今秃躁卞急,不佳东野之为,立白王府,请以假尉代东野,分其俸以给之。东野竟以穷去。吾闻淫畋渔者,谓之暴天物。天物既不可暴,又可抉摘刻削,露其情状乎? 使自萌卵至于槁死,不能隐伏,天能不致罚耶? 长吉夭,东野穷,玉溪生官不挂朝籍而死,正坐是哉! 正坐是哉!

Yuchisheng's[①] biographical sketch of Li Ho says that the poet used to go out every day on a donkey, followed by a boy servant. The donkey carried an old bag. Whenever he had a good couple of lines, he

---

① "Yuchisheng" means "Jade River Student."

would write them down and throw the piece of paper into the bag. At night, upon his return, he would take these slips out and compose them into poems. ①

When I was a boy living at Liyang, I was told by a white-haired old clerk of the government this story about the poet Meng Tungyeh. In the reign of Tsengyuan (785—804), he was a poor scholar and was made an assistant magistrate of Liyang, formerly called the Pingling county. About two miles south, there is a rapids called Touchin [Throw Gold] Rapids, extending about two and a half miles in length. On the east of the road, there are the old ruins of the old Pingling city, with a wall enclosure of over one thousand paces. The tumble-down ruins of the walls stand three or four feet high, heavily covered with underbrush. Many old chestnut-leaved oaks, a dozen spans in circumference, cast their shadows over the place, and the ground is covered with wild underbrush and herbs, and is full of caves and depressions. As it lies on a low level, little ponds are formed where fish and turtles make their homes. In general, it is a dark, somber, and deserted place, suggesting the ages past. No one goes there except woodcutters and fishermen. Tungyeh fell in love with it. Every day or every other day, he would go out there on a donkey, accompanied by a young employee of the office, and head for the Touchin islets. Arriving there, he would sit in the shade of an old oak tree, by the side of some pool, and sing his lines until sundown. This habit continued, to the great detriment of his office duties. The magistrate was exasperated and requested permission from the prince to have someone

---

① His mother seeing him so occupied with those slips of paper, said to him, "You are going to kill yourself with those papers."

else do Tungyeh's work and share his salary. Tungyeh's financial condition became difficult and he left.

I have heard it said that those who indulge in hunting and fishing slaughter life which is given by nature. If life may not be destroyed, how is it permissible for a poet to watch and observe and pry into and expose the secret of every little moment of such [plant and animal] life, so that from morning till eve these living things have nowhere to hide? How is it possible that God should not punish such transgressors? Changchi [Li Ho] died young, Tungyeh was poor, and Yuchisheng died before he could secure an office at the capital. It must be so! It must be so, indeed!

丐　论
The Beggar's Philosophy

元　结（Yuan Chieh）

　　天宝戊子中,元子游长安,与丐者为友。或曰:"君友丐者,不太下乎?"对曰:"古人乡无君子,则与云山为友;里无君子,则与松柏为友;坐无君子,则与琴酒为友。出游于国,见君子则友之。丐者,今之君子,吾恐不得与之友也。丐者丐论,子能听乎? 吾既与丐者相友,喻求罢,丐友相喻曰:'子羞吾为丐邪? 有可羞者,亦曾知未也? 呜呼! 于今之世有丐者,丐宗属于人,丐嫁娶于人,丐名位于人,丐颜色于人。甚者则丐权家奴齿,以售邪佞;丐权家婢颜,以容媚惑。有自富丐贫,自贵丐贱;于刑丐命,命不可得,就死丐时,就时丐息,至死丐全形,而终有不可丐者。更有甚者,丐家族于仆围,丐性命于臣妾,丐宗庙而不敢,丐妻子而无辞。有如此者,不可为羞哉! 吾所以丐人之弃衣,丐人之弃食,提罂荷杖,在于路傍,且欲与天下之人为同类耳。不然则无颜容行于人间。夫丐衣食,贫也,以贫乞丐,心不惭,迹与人同,示无异也,此君子之道。吾君子不欲全道邪? 幸不在山林,亦宜具罂杖随我作丐者之状貌,学丐者之言辞,与丐者之相逢,使丐者之无耻,庶几时世始能相容,吾子无矫然取不容也。'"於戏! 丐者言语如斯,可编为《丐论》,以补时规。①

------

① 译文中林语堂做了一定的改写,并且没有翻译从"於戏"开始的最后两句,其他译文也有类似现象,由于删减较少,此处原文未做对应删减。——编者注

In 748, I was living at the capital and had a beggar for a friend. Someone was embarrassed by my conduct and asked me why I did so. I said:

"In ancient times, when there were no gentlemen friends in the village, a scholar befriended the clouds and mountains. When there were no gentlemen friends in the neighborhood, he made friends with the pines and bamboos. When there were no gentlemen friends in the house to talk with, he amused himself with wine and music. But when he went to a strange city, he sought the gentlemen's company. This beggar, I have discovered, is quite a cultivated gentleman. In fact, I am honored by his friendship."

My friend was amazed and asked me to explain.

I told him the beggar's words, as follows:

You ask me why I carry a cane and a pot to beg for people's leftovers and discarded clothing? The explanation is quite simple. I want to merge with the city crowd and be regarded as a man like all of them. People don't like you if you pretend that you are queer or different. I beg because I am poor. There is no shame in it. Some people think it is a shame, but of course this is pure prejudice. We all beg. People all around me beg every day, and beg more shamelessly. Some beg for official posts, some for marriage to a family of some social standing. Have you ever seen their faces when they beg? Some beg the servants of the influential families to help them; some beg the doorkeeper or the maids in order to get in, with sweat on their brows. The poor beg the rich and the rich beg the poor; the powerful beg the common men and the common men beg the powerful for assistance and favors. Prisoners beg to have their sentences commuted and sick men beg to be permitted to live a little longer. And many, mind you, can't even get what they beg and pray for. How many men beg their wives at home? How many beg at the temple? How many beg their own servants at a certain crisis to do them a little favor?

One must go along with the crowd and do what the others do. You should really copy my example and learn a little of the beggar's language and the beggar's shamelessness. That is the way to be tolerated and liked in this world. Don't you try to be different from the world and be persecuted for it.

十二

山中与裴秀才迪书
An Invitation from a Mountain Resident
Letter to Pei Ti, B. A.

王　维(Wang Wei)

近腊月下,景气和畅,故山殊可过。足下方温经,猥不敢相烦,辄便往山中,憩感配寺,与山僧饭讫而去。北涉玄灞,清月映郭。夜登华子冈,辋水沦涟,与月上下。寒山远火,明灭林外。深巷寒犬,吠声如豹。村墟夜春,复与疏钟相间。此时独坐,僮仆静默,多思曩昔,携手赋诗,步仄径,临清流也。当待春中,草木蔓发,春山可望,轻鯈出水,白鸥矫翼,露湿青皋,麦陇朝雊,斯之不远,倘能从我游乎? 非子天机清妙者,岂能以此不急之务相邀。然是中有深趣矣! 无忽。因驮黄檗人往,不一,山中人王维白。

Dear Pei:

In this month of December, the weather has been very mild, and the old mountain is worth a visit. I knew you were immersed in your studies, and did not want to bother you. I may tell you what you missed: I often went into the mountains and stopped at Kanpei Temple where after a meal with the monk, I started off. I crossed the Pa [river] and saw the outer city wall sleep under the moonlight. At night, I went up the Huatsekang [hill]. The golden ripples of the Wang chased and floated with the moon, and on the distant mountainsides, some lights flickered beyond the forests. The sounds of dogs barking from some alley and of farmers pounding rice were punctuated with notes from the temple bells. By that time, the servants accompanying me had fallen asleep and I sat alone, thinking of the days when we wandered together on the mountain paths or sat on the bank of a clear stream and wrote verse. Now I will wait till spring is here, when the green things will have returned and blue hills lie in the distance, minnows chase in the shallow waters and herons flap their wings. You will find pheasants flying in the morning among the wheat fields and dew on the green banks. This will be not so far away. Are you coming? I would not write of these things and invite you to come unless I knew you would appreciate them. But there is a deep, resuscitating joy in it. Don't forget. I am sending this note by a woodcutter.

From a resident in the mountains,

Wang Wei

十三

与友人论文书选
Tungpo on the Art of Writing^①

苏东坡(Su Tungpo)

与谢民师推官书

所示书教及诗赋杂文,观之熟矣。大略如行云流水,初无定质,但常行于所当行,常止于所不可不止,文理自然,姿态横生。孔子曰:"言之不文,行而不远。"又曰:"辞达而已矣。"夫言止于达意,即疑若不文,是大不然。求物之妙,如系风捕影,能使是物了然于心者,盖千万人而不一遇也。而况能使了然于口与手者乎?是之谓辞达。辞至于能达,则文不可胜用矣。扬雄好为艰深之辞,以文浅易之说,若正言之,则人人知之矣……雄之陋,如此比者甚众,可与知者道,难与俗人言也,因论文偶及之耳。欧阳文忠公言,文章如精金美玉,市有定价,非人所能以口舌定贵贱也。

The Style of Sailing Clouds and Flowing Water

I have looked over your poems and prose. In general, writing should be like sailing clouds and flowing water. It has no definite [required] form. It goes where it has to go and stops where it cannot

---

① 此处仅节选部分内容。——编者注

but stop. One has thus a natural style, with all its wayward charms. Confucius said, "If a statement is not beautiful, it will not be read far and wide." Again he said, "In writing, all one asks is successful expression of an idea." One may think that if a statement merely aims at expressing one's thoughts, it will not be beautiful. That is not true. It is not easy to express exactly a fugitive idea or a passing thought. First of all, it is difficult to see and appreciate it in one's mind and heart—not one in a million can do it—and even harder to express it by writing or by word of mouth. When this is done, that thought or idea is given proper expression, and when one can do this, one can do anything with writing. Yang Shiung (53 B. C.—A. D. 18) loved to dress up his superficial ideas in archaic, abstruse language. For if he said clearly what he thought, it would be shown to be something everybody knew already... These are examples of his superficiality. This is something about writing which can be spoken about only to those who really understand. I mention this merely in passing. Ouyang Shiu (1007—1072) said that writing is like gold or jade, with a definite market price for a certain quality. Literary reputation is not something which can be made or minimized by someone's expressed opinion.

— *Letter to Shieh Minshih*

南行前集叙

夫昔之为文者,非能为之为工,乃不能不为之为工也。山川之有云,草木之有华实,充满勃郁,而见于外,夫虽欲无有,其可得耶! 自少闻家君之论文,以为古之圣人有所不能自已而作者。故轼与弟辙为文至多,而未尝敢有作文之意。

The Compulsion to Write

Writers in ancient times wrote, not because they decided they wanted to write, but because they could not help writing. It is like clouds and flowers of vegetation which take form naturally as a result of accumulation of certain forces. They have to seek expression of what is in them. I have heard my father say that the ancient sages said things because they had something which must be said. My brother Cheh and myself have written a great deal, but we have never presumed to think that we are so engaged in writing.

—Preface to "Poems on the Southward Voyage"

答张文潜县丞书

文字之衰,未有如今日者也。其源实出于王氏。王氏之文未必不善也,而患在于好使人同己。自孔子不能使人同,颜渊之仁,子路之勇,不能以相移。而王氏欲以其学同天下。地之美者,同于生物,不同于所生。惟荒瘠斥卤之地,弥望皆黄茅白苇,此则王氏之同也。

The Need of Individuality

Never has the plight of literature been worse than today. The cause for this is to be sought in Mr. Wang (Anshih, 1021—1086).[1] He is a good writer, but he wants everybody to agree with himself. Even Confucius could not make two individuals alike; he could not change the character of his disciples, Yen Huei or Tselu. But Wang wants the entire world to accept his ideas. Two pieces of good land can both produce certain crops, but they do not produce the same kind of crops. Bad land, on the other hand, can produce one kind—a deadening

---

[1] Wang Anshih was a great social reformer, but curiously also a good poet. The emperor had complete confidence in him and gave him power to enforce his socialistic schemes. This he did by driving away from the court every single man who did not agree with him, Su Tungpo among them.

uniformity of reeds and rushes which extend for miles and miles. This is the uniformity of thought which Wang wants.

—Letter to Chang Wenchien (a disciple)

答毛泽民

比日酷暑,不审起居何如?顷承示长笺及诗文一轴,日欲裁谢,因循至今,悚息。今时为文者至多,可喜者亦众,然求如足下闲暇自得,清美可口者,实少也。敬佩厚赐,不敢独飨,当出之知者。世间唯名实不可欺。文章如金玉,各有定价,先后进相汲引,因其言以信于世,则有之矣。至其品目高下,盖付之众口,决非一夫所能抑扬。轼于黄鲁直、张文潜辈数子,特先识之耳。始诵其文,盖疑信者相半,久乃自定,翕然称之,轼岂能为之轻重哉!非独轼如此,虽向之前辈,亦不过如此也,而况外物之进退。此在造物者,非轼事。辱见贶之重,不敢不尽。承不久出都,尚得一见否?

The Universal Values of Writing

It is very hot these last few days, and I do not know how you feel. I have received your long letter and a scroll of prose and poems. I am sorry to have delayed answering until now. There are many people who write today, and many who write agreeably well. But there are few who show that ease and self-mastery and simple freshness as you do. I am glad to have read them, and shall not be selfish but will let the world know about it. There is one thing in life that there is no mistake about: no lasting reputation can be palmed off on the public. Literature is like gold or jade; there is a regular market value for certain qualities. It is true that the elder generation can help the younger writers by their comments. But in the end the quality of a writer will be determined by the reading public, and is not based on any one person's opinion. In the case of a few, like Huang Tingchien, Chang Wenchien [Su's accepted disciples], I was merely a discoverer of their talents. People heard what I said, and held their reservations, and only after a certain time elapsed was there a consensus of opinion, and they got their dues. I did not have the power to create reputations. And not only I, but also the generations preceding me. As to academic honors, these are in the lap of the gods. I have nothing to do with it. I am telling you all I think in this letter. Shall be going away from the capital soon. Can I see you?

—*Letter to Mao Pang*

答黄鲁直

晁君骚辞,细看甚奇丽,信其家多异材耶? 然有少意,欲鲁直以己意微箴之。凡人文字,当务使平和,至足之余,溢为怪奇,盖出于不得已也。晁文奇丽似差早,然不可直云耳。非谓避讳也,恐伤其迈往之气,当为朋友讲磨之语乃宜。不知以为然否?

On the Simple, Natural Style

Mr. Chao (Wuchiu, later one of Su's disciples) sent me his long sentimental poem [*sao*]. On careful reading, I found it had a rich beauty of phraseology. His family seems indeed to have many talents. But I have a little idea to suggest, and I want you to put it to him gently. A man should aim first of all to write naturally and simply, and let that extra richness of thought and expression come naturally when it comes—overflows as it were as a natural, effortless consequence. I think Chao is a little too young. But break it to him gently, not because we want to spare him, but because it may affect that great young drive in him. Put it casually in the course of a friendly conversation. What do you think?

—Letter to Huang Tingchien

答李廌书

惠示古赋近诗,词气卓越,意趣不凡,甚可喜也。但微伤冗,后当稍收敛之,今未可也。足下之文,正如川之方增,当极其所至,霜降水落,自见涯涘,然不可不知也。录示孙之翰《唐论》。仆不识之翰,……议论英发,暗与人意合者甚多。又读欧阳文忠公《志》文、司马君实跋尾,益复慨然。然足下欲仆别书此文入石,以为之翰不朽之托,何也?之翰所立于世者,虽无欧阳公之文可也,而况欲托字画之工以求信于后世,不亦陋乎?足下相待甚厚,而见誉过当,非所以为厚也。近日士大夫皆有偺侈无涯之心,动辄欲人以周、孔誉己,自孟轲以下者,皆怃然不满也。此风殆不可长。又仆细思所以得患祸者,皆由名过其实,造物者所不能堪,与无功而受千钟者,其罪均也。深不愿人造作言语,务相粉饰,以益其疾。

On Cutting Down

I have received your poems in ancient *fu* and modern *shih* forms. I am pleased with the swing of rhythm and the many fresh ideas. But they are a little overwritten. Later you must try to cut down a little. Don't do it now. Your composition gives the impression of a swelling spring river. Let it rise to its highest limits. When the frost comes and the water level goes down, you will find the regular banks. But you should know it now.

You have kindly shown me the essays on Tang history by Sun Chih-han, whom I do not know... He has many ideas there with which I agree. I have also read Ouyang Shiu's biography, with Ssuma Kuang's postscript, which are indeed very expressive. But why do you want me to write this piece by Ouyang in my handwriting for stone inscription so as to "immortalize" Chih-han? He can well enough stand on his own, even without Ouyang's piece.

Why should he have the vulgar idea to want to achieve immortality by means of a good calligraphy? You have always been most kind to me, but don't do it by overcomplimenting me more than I deserve. The scholars of today are overambitious. They want people to compare them to Confucius or the duke of Chou; any comparison from Mencius down would not satisfy them. This is a trend that should be stopped. I have come to realize that I ran into so many troubles because I was actually a lesser man than my reputation made me out to be. God will not stand for this. It is as bad as to receive a high post without having done anything for the country. I really wish people would stop rumors about me that add to my conceit. They will make matters worse for me…

—*Letter to Li Chih* (almost a disciple)

十四

石钟山记
The Stone Bell Mountain

苏东坡（Su Tungpo）

《水经》云："彭蠡之口，有石钟山焉。"郦元以为下临深潭，微风鼓浪，水石相搏，声如洪钟。是说也，人常疑之。今以钟磬置水中，虽大风浪不能鸣也，而况石乎！至唐李渤始访其遗踪，得双石于潭上，扣而聆之，南声函胡，北音清越，枹止响腾，余韵徐歇，自以为得之矣。然是说也，余尤疑之。石之铿然有声者，所在皆是也，而此独以钟名，何哉？

元丰七年六月丁丑，余自齐安舟行适临汝，而长子迈将赴饶之德兴尉，送之至湖口，因得观所谓石钟者。寺僧使小童持斧，于乱石间择其一二扣之，硿硿焉。余固笑而不信也。

至莫夜月明，独与迈乘小舟，至绝壁下。大石侧立千尺，如猛兽奇鬼，森然欲搏人；而山上栖鹘，闻人声亦惊起，磔磔云霄间；又有若老人欬且笑于山谷中者，或曰此鹳鹤也。余方心动欲还，而大声发于水上，噌吰如钟鼓不绝，舟人大恐。徐而察之，则山下皆石穴罅，不知其浅深，微波入焉，涵澹澎湃而为此也。舟回至两山间，将入港口，有大石当中流，可坐百人，空中而多窍，与风水相吞吐，有窾坎镗鞳之声，与向之噌吰者相应，如乐作焉。

因笑谓迈曰："汝识之乎？噌吰者，周景王之无射也；窾坎镗鞳者，魏庄子之歌钟也。古之人不余欺也！"事不目见耳闻而臆断其有无，可乎？郦元之所见闻，殆与余同，而言之不详；士大夫终不肯以小舟夜泊绝壁之

下,故莫能知;而渔工水师,虽知而不能言,此世所以不传也。而陋者乃以
斧斤考击而求之,自以为得其实。余是以记之,盖叹郦元之简,而笑李渤
之陋也。

The *Classic of Waters* says, "At the mouth of Kuli[①] stands the
Stone Bell Mountain." Its commentator Li Taoyuan (died A.D.527)
states that "there is a deep water at its foot, where the winds and waves
striking the rocks make a sound like that of great bells." People often
discredit this statement, for bells and musical stones submerged in
waves do not make such a sound, not to speak of rocks. Not until the
Tang Period did Li Po [not the poet] visit the place, where he found
two rocks from the water. When struck with a wooden handle, they
made a clanging sound, dying away gradually like bells, one in a
clearer and the other in a muffled tone. He thought he had thus
verified the origin of the name. But I had my doubts, for there are
certainly rocks which make a ringing sound when struck, but these
were said to make sounds like bells. In June 1084, I was making a
voyage from Tsi-an to Linju, and my eldest son, Mai, was going to
Tehshing in Kiangse. I sent him off to Hukou,[②] and thus we had an
opportunity to visit it and see the stone bells. A monk sent a boy to
show us. The boy took an ax and struck at some of the rocks near by at
random, but there was nothing unusual about the dull thuds. I gave it
up for hearsay and laughed.

That night, however, there was a bright moon, and I took a boat
with Mai to the foot of the mountain. The river here was flanked by a

---

① 个别原文版本把"彭蠡"误写为"鼓蠡",可能林语堂参考了这样的版本,也可能是
他把"彭"误看成了"鼓"。——编者注
② Where the Poyang Lake empties into the Yangtse River. At this place, there are
now two hills by this name.

high cliff almost a thousand feet high.① As seen in the moonlight, the rocks looked very much like some weird monsters or dark spirits in frightening postures. The hawks nesting above flew up with raucous cries upon hearing our approach. There was another noise like an old man coughing and chortling somewhere in the air. We were told that this came from a species of cranes [daws?]. I was quite moved and was thinking of turning back when a great noise came over the waters, booming and whining like drums and bells, which quite frightened the boatman. Upon close examination, I found that at the foot of the cliff were a number of stone caves of unknown depth. When the waves hit the caves, it made the roaring, surging noise. On turning back past Hanshan, at the point where the lake waters joined the big river, there was a huge rock in the middle of the stream, big enough to hold a hundred people. This huge boulder was full of holes and hollows, and the winds and waters sucking through them swish-swashed and made a booming noise, which joined with the clanging from the water caves to make a symphony.

I said to my son, "Mai, you see. That clanging from the caves will help you to understand the mention in history books of the sound of the bells of the Emperor Ching of Chou Dynasty, and the boom will help you to appreciate the description of the orchestra bells of Wei Shientse.② Evidently, what the ancient books tell us is true. One is often inclined to doubt ancient records until one personally sees these things. Li Taoyuan must have seen what we have seen, but he was not very explicit. The scholars usually would not take the trouble to take a

① Actually about 500—600 feet.
② Su Tungpo could repeat phrases and whole passages from history books.

boat to the foot of the cliff, so they could not have known. The boatmen know about it, of course, but they do not record it in books. Li Po verified it only superficially by knocking at a couple of rocks on land, and he never really found out where the sounds came from."

I write this down, to show that Li Taoyuan did not say enough and Li Po did not know enough.

十五

凌虚台记

Record on the Terrace for Stepping on the Void

苏东坡（Su Tungpo）

国于南山之下，宜若起居饮食与山接也。四方之山，莫高于终南；而都邑之丽山者，莫近于扶风。以至近求最高，其势必得。而太守之居，未尝知有山焉。虽非事之所以损益，而物理有不当然者，此凌虚之所为筑也。

方其未筑也，太守陈公杖履逍遥于其下，见山之出于林木之上者，累累如人之旅行于墙外而见其髻也。曰："是必有异。"使工凿其前为方池，以其土筑台，高出于屋之檐而止。然后人之至于其上者，恍然不知台之高，而以为山之踊跃奋迅而出也。公曰："是宜名凌虚。"以告其从事苏轼，而求文以为记。

轼复于公曰："物之废兴成毁，不可得而知也。昔者荒草野田，霜露之所蒙翳，狐虺之所窜伏，方是时，岂知有凌虚台耶？废兴成毁相寻于无穷，则台之复为荒草野田，皆不可知也。尝试与公登台而望，其东则秦穆之祈年、橐泉也，其南则汉武之长杨，五柞，而其北则隋之仁寿，唐之九成也。计其一时之盛，宏杰诡丽，坚固而不可动者，岂特百倍于台而已哉！然而数世之后，欲求其仿佛，而破瓦颓垣无复存者，既已化为禾黍荆棘丘墟陇亩矣，而况于此台欤？夫台犹不足恃以长久，而况于人事之得丧，忽往而忽来者欤？而或者欲以夸世而自足，则过矣。盖世有足恃者，而不在乎台之存亡也。"既已言于公，退而为之记。

Since the terrace is situated at the foot of the southern hills, it would seem that every day one would eat and sleep and live in close association with the hills, but His Honor the Chief Magistrate was unaware of their existence. When His Honor Sire Chen was walking around in the garden one day, he saw hilltops showing above the trees like the knotted hair of passengers walking outside the walk, and he declared, "This is strange indeed!" His Honor ordered a square pond to be dug in the front part of the garden, and with the dug-up earth he built a terrace to be the level of the house roof, so that future visitors of this terrace would not be aware that they were standing on a high place but the hills would seem to meet their eyes on the level. "Let this terrace be called the Terrace for Stepping on the Void," said His Honor. He told this to his junior colleague, Su Shih [Su Tungpo], and asked the latter to write an inscription for the terrace.

Su Shih replied to His Honor and said: "Who can tell how and when the things of this life rise and decay? When this place was a stretch of wild country, exposed to the dew and frost, and foxes and snakes made their homes therein, who would suspect that one day the Terrace for Stepping on the Void would be erected at this place? Since the laws of rise and decay go on in a continual cycle, who can tell but one day this terrace may once more become a stretch of wasteland and barren fields? Once I went up to the terrace with His Honor and looked around. On the east we saw the prayer temple and springs of Emperor Mu of Chin, on the south we saw the halls and terraces of Emperor Wu of Han, and looking to the north we saw the Jenshou Palace of Sui and the Chiuchen Palace of Tang. I thought of the days of their glory, their magnificence and everlasting solidity, greater a hundred times than this terrace. Yet, after a few centuries, travelers over these ruins found only broken tiles and rubble, and mounds covered with brambles and fields of corn. How much more must this be true of the present terrace? And, if even the solid structure of a terrace cannot last long, how much more deceptive are the successes and failures and the ever changing fortunes of human affairs? It would indeed be a mistake for some people to pride themselves on their present good fortune. For we know that there are things in this life which last forever, but this terrace is not one of them."

论画理
Painting the Inner Law of Things

苏东坡（Su Tungpo）

　　余尝论画，以为人禽、宫室、器用皆有常形。至于山石、竹木、水波、烟云，虽无常形，而有常理。常形之失，人皆知之。常理之不当，虽晓画者有不知。故凡可以欺世而取名者，必托于无常形者也。虽然，常形之失，止于所失，而不能病其全；若常理之不当，则举废之矣。以其形之无常，是以其理不可不谨也。世之工人，或能曲尽其形，而至于其理，非高人逸士不能辨。与可之于竹石枯木，真可谓得其理者矣。如是而生，如是而死，如是而挛拳瘠蹙，如是而条达遂茂，根茎节叶，牙角脉缕，千变万化，未始相袭，而各当其处，合于天造，厌于人意。盖达士之所寓也欤……必有明于理而深观之者，然后知余言之不妄。

It has been my opinion concerning painting that men and animals and buildings and structures have a constant material form. On the other hand, mountains and rocks, bamboos and trees, ripples of water, smoke and clouds do not have a constant form [*shing*] but do have a constant inner spirit [*li*]. Anybody can detect inaccuracy in the constant forms, but even specialists often fail to note mistakes in painting the constant inner spirit of things. Some artists find it much easier to deceive the public and make a name for themselves by painting objects without constant forms. When one makes a mistake in the form or contour of an object, however, the mistake is confined to that particular part and does not spoil the whole, whereas if one misses the inner spirit, the whole painting falls flat. Because such objects do not have a constant form, one must pay special attention to their inner laws. There are plenty of craftsmen who can copy the minute details of objects, but the inner law of things can be comprehended only by the highest human spirits. Yuko's [Wen Tung, c. 1019—1079, a cousin of Su Tungpo] paintings of bamboos, rocks, and dried-up trees may be said to have truly seized the inner spirit of the objects. He understands how these things grow and decay, how they twist and turn and are sometimes blocked and compressed, and how they prosper and thrive in freedom. The roots, stalks, joints, and leaves go through infinite variations, following different rhythms independent of one another. And yet they are all true to nature and completely satisfying to the human spirit. These are records of the inspirations of a great soul… Those who understand the inner spirit of things and examine these paintings carefully will see that I am right.

十七

日 喻

Truth Is Harder to See than the Sun①

苏东坡(Su Tungpo)

生而眇者不识日,问之有目者。或告之曰:"日之状如铜槃。"扣槃而得其声,他日闻钟,以为日也。或告之曰:"日之光如烛。"扪烛而得其形,他日揣籥,以为日也。日之与钟籥亦远矣,而眇者不知其异,以其未尝见而求之人也。道之难见也甚于日,而人之未达也,无以异于眇。达者告之,虽有巧譬善导,亦无以过于槃与烛也。自槃而之钟,自烛而之籥,转而相之,岂有既乎? 故世之言道者,或即其所见而名之,或莫之见意之,皆求道之过也。

There was a man born blind. He had never seen the sun and asked about it of people who could see. Someone told him, "The sun's shape is like a brass tray." The blind man struck the brass tray and heard its sound. Later when he heard the sound of a bell, he thought it was the sun. Again someone told him, "The sunlight is like that of a candle," and the blind man felt the candle, and thought that was the sun's shape. Later he felt a [big] key and thought it was the sun. The sun is quite different from a bell or a key, but the blind man cannot tell their difference because he has never seen the sun. The truth [Tao] is

---

① 此处仅节选部分内容。——编者注

harder to see than the sun, and when people do not know it, they are exactly like the blind man. Even if you do your best to explain by analogies and examples, it still appears like the analogy of the brass tray and the candle. From what is said of the brass tray, one imagines a bell, and from what is said about a candle, one imagines a key. In this way, one gets even further and further away from the truth. Those who speak about *Tao* sometimes give it a name according to what they happen to see, or imagine what it is like without seeing it. These are mistakes in the effort to understand *Tao*.

十八

叙陈正甫会心集
On Zest in Life
Preface to *Hwheishin Collection of Poems of Chen Chengfu*[①]

袁中郎(Yuan Chunglang)

　　世人所难得者唯趣。趣如山上之色、水中之味、花中之光、女中之态，虽善说者不能下一语，唯会心者知之。今之人，慕趣之名，求趣之似，于是有辨说书画、涉猎古董以为清；寄意玄虚、脱迹尘纷以为远。又其下则有如苏州之烧香煮茶者。此等皆趣之皮毛，何关神情！夫趣得之自然者深，得之学问者浅。当其为童子也，不知有趣，然无往而非趣也。面无端容，目无定睛，口喃喃而欲语，足跳跃而不定，人生之至乐，真无逾于此时者。孟子所谓不失赤子，老子所谓能婴儿，盖指此也，趣之正等正觉最上乘也。山林之人，无拘无缚，得自在度日，故虽不求趣而趣近之。愚不肖之近趣也，以无品也。品愈卑，故所求愈下。或为酒肉，或然声伎，率心而行，无所忌惮，自以为绝望于世，故举世非笑之不顾也，此又一趣也。迨夫年渐长，官渐高，品渐大，有身如梏，有心如棘，毛孔骨节俱为闻见知识所缚，入理愈深，然其去趣愈远矣。

---

① 此处仅节选部分内容。——编者注

I find that zest is a rare gift in life. Zest is like hues on the mountains, taste in water, brilliance in flowers, and charm in women. It is appreciated only by those who have understanding, and is difficult to explain in words. True enough, it is common nowadays to find people who affect a taste in certain diversions. Some cultivate a love for painting, calligraphy, and antiques, and others are fascinated by the mystics and recluses and the life of a hermit. Still others are like the people of Soochow who make a hobby of tea and incense, turning it almost into a cult. These are superficial, and have nothing to do with real zest and understanding of the flavor in living.

This zest for living is more born in us than cultivated. Children have most of it. They have probably never heard of the word "zest," but they show it everywhere. They find it hard to look solemn; they wink, they grimace, they mumble to themselves, they jump and skip and hop and romp. That is why childhood is the happiest period of a man's life, and why Mencius spoke of "recovering the heart of a child" and Laotse referred to it as a model of man's original nature. The peasants who live near the mountains and forests do not make a cult of these things; in their life of freedom and absence of social conventions, they enjoy the beauties of nature all as a part of their living. The more degenerate men become, the harder they find it to enjoy life. Some are fascinated by merely sensual enjoyments and call it "fun," and find their pleasure in meats and wines and sex and riotous living and defiance of social customs, saying they are thus liberating themselves. Often as one progresses in life, his official rank becomes higher and his social status grows bigger; his body and mind are fettered with a thousand cares and sober duties. Then knowledge, learning, and life experience stop up even his pores and seep down to his hardened joints. The more he knows, the more befuddled he becomes, and the more removed he is from understanding this zest in living.

十九

祭震女文
In Memory of a Child
Sacrificial Prayer to Ah Chen

沈君烈（Shen Chunlieh）

万历己未年冬下浣之三日,沈承之长女阿震以痘不发而殇,藁葬北邙之次。其母薄氏,日称念梵书,资其冥福,复促作一疏词,笔不忍下也。于其三七,当荐熟食,乃为文哭之,焚于其所生前跳弄之场曰:

呜呼痛哉,汝名阿震,生于丙辰,以丙辰字,故取震名。汝生之初,我实不喜,三十许人,不男而女。迨汝未期,汝即可怜,以额招汝,汝笑哑然。当此之时,周妪褓汝,衣不解带,一夜十起,饱就妪眠,饥就母乳。妪因汝故,亦几委曲,移湿就干,补疮剜肉,烦则母瞋,省则汝哭。

昨岁戊午,我命不济,频出就试,割汝而去。周妪既死,试又不利,归来牵袖,索物而戏,有汝在侧,愁亦快意。汝齿日添,汝慧日多,呼爹呼姆,音不少讹。常手弹门,自问谁何。我侄来时,汝呼曰哥,戏攫汝物,汝窜而波。我舅来时,汝以衣拖,呼声曰母,旋笑呵呵。汝伯来时,作宾主陪,擎杯曰请,笑者如雷。汝祖入乡,汝又往苏,经年不直,问汝识无,应声曰识,白帽白须。汝有外翁,一面未曾,问客何方,即日北京。汝之外姑,视如身生,凡三五次,挈汝苏行,三更索玩,五更索果。父母留汝,汝反不可,顾谓我曰,阿婆思我。

今年六月,汝有疖灾,我特往苏,挈汝归来,摩挲患处,其色甚哀,然不敢哭,恐哭不该。每持果饵,必窥意旨,不色授之,不遽入齿。每所玩弄,误有损伤,小目怒之,敛手退藏。汝母过严,时加梏束,惧汝长大,习惯成熟,我意亦然,但私相嘱,婴孩何知,且随其欲。汝昔在苏,父母归娄,问汝何依,欲去欲留,言虽不决,意在两头。顷汝归斯,喜不自持,诱汝怖汝,假面作痴,小筐提枣,矮座啜糜,口诵大学,手拜阿弥,握枚赌胜,绕屋争驰,哈哈拍掌,自喜为奇。

不勾半月,即汝死期,天乎命乎,神仙莫知。汝未死顷,召医诊视,或云风邪,或云癍子,风不可必,癍似有理,至今思之,不测所以。汝善话言,此际不语,声嘶气断,张目而已,环汝而泣,汝泪亦泚。

呜呼,痛可忍言哉。论世俗情,女死何哭,论我生年,壮大穷独,汝又颇慧,虽女亦足,谁知鬼神,虐我太酷。先汝十日,汝妹阿巽,少汝二岁,与汝同病,同三日亡,汝所狎认,今汝无伴,当与妹并。汝稍能行,妹立未定,往来携手,相好无竞。若逢汝妪,可更一问,父有室顾,父有妣闵,但往依之,必汝提引,所以权厝,亦近顾侧。妹小汝携,汝小顾掖,他年卜地,葬汝同宅。

我今思汝,不能去怀,汝若有知,常入梦来,缘或未尽,可再投胎。所诵金刚,并诸经咒,设羹燔钱,付汝领受。汝见冥王,操手哀叩,侬实不寿,侬实无咎,侬生贫家,侬甘粗陋,穄粒必拾,以畏雷吼,襦履必惜,以爬微垢,神有诛求,侬年实幼,鬼有陵轹,望神为佑。但可如是,莫啼莫哗,地府之中,不比在家。我今作文,汝不识字,但呼阿震,汝父在此,哭汝一声,呼汝一次。

On the twenty-third of December of the year 1619, Shen Chunlieh's eldest daughter, Ah Chen, died of smallpox which failed to appear, and was buried on the northern mounds. Her mother, Madame Po, recited Buddhist sutras daily in her favor, and urged the writing of a sacrificial prayer for her, but he did not have the heart to take up a pen and do it. On the twenty-first day of her death, he prepared for her a sacrifice of cooked food, and composed a piece to weep over her, which was burned on the scene of her childhood games, and is as follows:

Alas! Great is my sorrow! Your name is Ah Chen, written with the components Ping and Chen, because you were born in the year Pingchen (1616). When you were born, I was not truly pleased, for I was a man over thirty, and you came not a boy but a girl. But before you were one year old, you were already adorable. When one nodded to you, you opened your mouth and laughed. During this period, Chouma [amah] was taking care of you, and she woke up ten times a night, and never took off her girdle while going to bed. When you were hungry, you sought for milk from your mama, and when you were well filled, you went to bed with Chouma. And Chouma suffered many misunderstandings on your account. She moved you from a wet place to a dry place, and went to great troubles to lighten a small suffering. If she paid you too much attention, your mother would reprimand her, and if she paid too little attention, you would cry.

Last year, I was unlucky. On account of the examinations, I had to tear myself away from you. I failed in the examinations and Chouma died. When I came back, you pulled at my sleeves and asked for toys. With you by my side, my sorrow was relieved. You grew more teeth and you daily grew in wisdom. You called "Dada" and "Mama" and your pronunciation was perfect. You often knocked at the door and asked "Who is it?" When my nephew came, you called him "Koko" [elder brother]. He took away your toys in play and you ran away and protested. When your maternal uncle came, you pulled at his gown. You called out "Mama" and you laughed in a silvery voice. When your paternal uncle came, you played the host. Lifting the cup, you said, "Ching!" and we roared with laughter. Your grandpa went to the country, and you yourself went to Soochow. For a year you had not seen him, and we asked you if you knew grandpa, and you said, "Yes. White cap and white beard." You have never seen your maternal grandpa, and when we asked you, "Whence comes this guest?" you said "Peking!" Your maternal grandma was very fond of you and regarded you like her own. Several times she took you to Soochow with her. You asked for toys at midnight and asked for fruit at day's dawn. Your own parents asked you to come home, but you refused, saying "Grandma would think of me."

This year in June, you had boils, and I went to Soochow specially to take you home. I touched your affected spots, and your face showed pain. But you did not cry, thinking it was not right. Every time you took a fruit or sweetmeat, you looked at people's faces, and if we did not approve, you would not put it in your mouth. Sometimes you touched things and accidentally spoiled them, and one just looked at you, and your hand would shrink back. Your mama was too strict with you, and she often admonished you, for fear that when you grew up, you would form such habits. I did not agree, and told her in private, "Let the baby alone. What does she know at this young age?" When you were at Soochow, and mama and I were coming home, we asked you if you would come or stay. And your heart lay both ways, and you hesitated to reply. Then you came home, and we were so glad, and we coaxed you and we pulled faces to get your laugh. You carried a toy basket of dates and sat on a low stool to eat porridge. You repeated the *Great Learning*, and you bowed to Buddha. You played at guessing games, and you romped about the house. You clapped your hands and thought yourself very clever.

But within a fortnight, the day of your death came. Was it Heaven's will or was it your fate? Even the fairies do not know. Before you died, we sent for a doctor. Some said it was a cold, and some said it was smallpox. It could not be a cold, and it might be smallpox, and we still wonder what you died of. You were clever at speech, but you were silent then. You only panted and stared at us. We wept around you and you wept, too.

Alas! Great is my sorrow! According to conventions, why should one weep at a daughter's death. According to my age, I am in my prime and poor and alone. You were very intelligent, and I was satisfied with you, although a girl. But who knew that the gods would be so cruel to me? Ten days before you, your younger sister, Ah Shun, died of the same disease in three days. You know her well, and now that you have no company there, you must stick together with your sister. You can already walk about, but your sister can hardly stand steadily. You should take her by the hand and go about together and must be good to each other and never quarrel. If you meet your amah [Chouma], you could ask her, saying, "Pa had a wife by the name of Ku and a mammy by the name of Min." Ask her to take you to them, and they will surely take care of you. You can stay there for the present, and you should be near Ku. Sister is small and you should lead her, and you are small and Ku should protect you. Sometime later, I will find a propitious ground and bury you three in the same grave.

I am thinking of you now, and it is hard to forget you. If you should hear my prayer, come to see me in my dreams. If fate decrees that you must yet live an earthly life, then come again into your mama's womb. I am offering Buddhist sacrifices and prayers, and I have soup here for you, and I am burning paper money for your use. When you see the Judge of the Lower World, hold your hands together and plead to him, "I am young, and I am innocent. I was born in a poor family and I was contented with scanty meals. I never wasted a single grain of rice, and I was never willfully careless of my clothing and my shoes. Whatever thou commandest, I am only a young child. If evil spirits ever bully me, may thou protect me!" You should just put it that way, and you should not cry or make too much noise. For remember you are in a strange underworld, and it is not like it is at home with our own people. Now I am composing this, but you do not yet know how to read. I will only cry, "Ah Chen, your father is here." I can but cry for you and call your name.

二十

西湖七月半
Harvest Moon on West Lake

张　岱(Chang Tai)

西湖七月半,一无可看,止可看看七月半之人。看七月半之人,以五类看之。其一,楼船箫鼓,峨冠盛筵,灯火优傒,声光相乱,名为看月而实不见月者,看之;其一,亦船亦楼,名娃闺秀,携及童娈,笑啼杂之,环坐露台,左右盼望,身在月下而实不看月者,看之;其一,亦船亦声歌,名妓闲僧,浅斟低唱,弱管轻丝,竹肉相发,亦在月下,亦看月而欲人看其看月者,看之;其一,不舟不车,不衫不帻,酒醉饭饱,呼群三五,跻入人丛,昭庆、断桥,嚣呼嘈杂,装假醉,唱无腔曲,月亦看,看月者亦看,不看月者亦看,而实无一看者,看之;其一,小船轻幌,净几煖炉,茶铛旋煮,素瓷静递,好友佳人,邀月同坐,或匿影树下,或逃嚣里湖,看月而人不见其看月之态,亦不作意看月者,看之。

杭人游湖,巳出酉归,避月如仇。是夕好名,逐队争出,多犒门军酒钱,轿夫擎燎,列俟岸上。一入舟,速舟子急放断桥,赶入胜会。以故二鼓以前,人声鼓吹,如沸如撼,如魇如呓,如聋如哑。大船小船一齐凑岸,一无所见,止见篙击篙,舟触舟,肩摩肩,面看面而已。少刻兴尽,官府席散,皂隶喝道去,轿夫叫船上人,怖以关门,灯笼火把如列星,一一簇拥而去。岸上人亦逐队赶门,渐稀渐薄,顷刻散尽矣。吾辈始舣舟近岸,断桥石磴始凉,席其上,呼客纵饮。此时月如镜新磨,山复整妆,湖复颒面,向之浅斟低唱者出,匿影树下者亦出。吾辈往通声气,拉与同坐。韵友来,名妓至,杯箸安,竹肉发。月色苍凉,东方将白,客方散去。吾辈纵舟,酣睡于十里荷花之中,香气拍人,清梦甚惬。

There is nothing to see during the harvest moon on West Lake [Hangchow]. All you can see are people who come out to see the moon. Briefly, there are five categories of these holidaymakers. First, there are those who come out in the name of looking at the harvest moon, but never even take a look at it: the people who, expensively dressed, sit down at gorgeous dinners with music in brightly illuminated boats or villas, in a confusion of light and noise. Secondly, those who do sit in the moonlight, but never look at it: ladies, daughters of high families, in boats and towers, also handsome boys [homosexuals] who sit in open spaces and giggle and chatter and look at other people. Thirdly, boat parties of famous courtesans and monks with time on their hands who enjoy a little sip and indulge in song and flute and string instruments. They are in the moonlight, too, and indeed look at the moon, but want people to see them looking at the moon. Fourthly, there are the young men, who neither ride, nor go into boats, but after a drink and a good dinner, rush about in their rowdy dress and seek the crowd at Chaoching and Tuanchiao where it is thickest, shouting, singing songs of no known melody, and pretending to be drunk. They look at the moon, look at the people looking at the moon, and also look at those not looking at the moon, but actually see nothing. Lastly, there are those who hire a small boat, provided with a clay stove and a clean table and choice porcelain cups and pots, and who get into the boat with a few friends and their sweethearts; they hide under a tree or row out into the Inner Lake in order to escape from the crowd, and look at the moon without letting people see that they are looking at the moon and even without consciously looking at it.

The local Hangchow people come out on the lake, if they do at all, between eleven in the morning and eight in the evening, as if they had morbid fear of the moon. But on this night, they all come out in groups, in the hope of getting good tips. The sedan chair carriers line up on the bank. The moment they get into a boat, they tell the boatman to hurry and row across to the Tuanchiao area, and get lost in the crowd. Therefore in that area before the second watch [ten o'clock], the place is filled with noise and music bands in a weird, boiling confusion, like a roaring sea or a landslide, or a nightmare, or like Bedlam let loose, with all the people in it rendered deaf for the moment. Large and small boats are tied up along the bank, and one can see nothing except boats creaking against boats, punting poles knocking punting poles, shoulders rubbing shoulders, and faces looking at faces. Soon the feasting is over, the officials leave, the *yamen* runners shout to clear the way, the sedan chair carriers scream for fare, the boatmen give warning that the city gates will soon be closed. A grand procession of torches and lanterns, with swarms of retainers, passes on. Those on land also hurry to get into the city before the closing of the gate, and very soon almost the entire crowd is gone.

Only then do we move the boat to Tuanchiao. The rocks have become cool by this time, and we spread a mat on the ground and invite ourselves to a great drink. At this time, the moon looks like a newly polished mirror, the hills appear draped in a new dress, and the face of lake is like a lady after a fresh make-up. Those who have been hiding themselves under a tree and enjoying a quiet sip come out now also. We exchange names and invite them to join us. There we have charming friends and famous courtesans; cups and chopsticks are in place, and songs and music begin, in the chilly dream world of moonlight. The party breaks up at dawn, and we get into the boat again and move it into the miles of lotus-covered surface, where we catch a nap in an air filled with its fragrance, and have a perfect sleep.

二十一

小窗幽记
Sketches by the Little Window[1]

陈继儒(Chen Chiju)

赏花须结豪友,观妓须结淡友,登山须结逸友,泛舟须结旷友,对月须结冷友,待雪须结艳友,捉酒须结韵友。

For enjoying flowers, one must secure big-hearted friends. For going to sing-song houses to have a look at sing-song girls, one must secure temperate friends. For going up a high mountain, one must secure romantic friends. For boating, one must secure friends with an expansive nature. For facing the moon, one must secure friends with a cool philosophy. For anticipating snow, one must secure beautiful friends. For a wine party, one must secure friends with flavor and charm.

法饮宜舒,放饮宜雅;病饮宜小,愁饮宜醉;春饮宜庭,夏饮宜郊,秋饮宜舟,冬饮宜室,夜饮宜月。

Formal drinking should be slow and leisurely, unrestrained drinking should be elegant and romantic; a sick person should drink a small quantity, and a sad person should drink to get drunk. Drinking in

---

① 此处仅节选部分内容。——编者注

the spring should take place in a courtyard, in summer in the outskirts of a city, in autumn on a boat and in winter in the house, and at night it should be enjoyed in the presence of the moon.

凡醉各有所宜。醉花宜昼,袭其光也;醉雪宜夜,清其思也;醉得意宜唱,宜其和也;醉将离宜击钵,壮其神也;醉文人宜谨节奏,畏其侮也;醉俊人宜益觥盂加旗帜,助其怒也;醉楼宜暑,资其清也;醉水宜秋,泛其爽也。此皆审其宜,考其景,反此则失饮矣。

There is a proper time and place for getting drunk. One should get drunk before flowers in the daytime, in order to assimilate their light and color; and one should get drunk in snow in the night-time, in order to clear his thoughts. A man getting drunk when happy at success should sing, in order to harmonize his spirit; and a man getting drunk at a farewell party should strike a musical note, in order to strengthen his spirit. A drunk scholar should be careful in his conduct, in order to avoid humiliations; and a drunk military man should order gallons and put up more flags, in order to increase his military splendor. Drinking in a tower should take place in summer, in order to profit from the cool atmosphere; and drinking on the water should take place in autumn, in order to increase the sense of elated freedom. These are proper ways of drinking in respect of mood and scenery, and to violate these rules is to miss the pleasure of drinking.

吾斋之中,不尚虚礼。凡入此斋,均为知己;随分款留,忘形笑语;不言是非,不侈荣利;闲谈古今,静玩山水;清茶好酒,以适幽趣。臭味之交,如斯而已。

In my studio, all formalities will be abolished, and only the most intimate friends will be admitted. They will be treated with rich or poor fare such as I eat, and we will chat and laugh and forget our own existence. We will not discuss the right and wrong of other people and will be totally indifferent to worldly glory and wealth. In our leisure we will discuss the ancients and the moderns, and in our quiet, we will play with the mountains and rivers. Then we will have thin, clear tea and good wine to fit into the atmosphere of delightful seclusion. That is my conception of the pleasure of friendship.

月夜焚香,古桐三弄,便觉万虑都忘,妄想尽绝。试看香是何味,烟是何色,穿窗之白是何影,指下之余是何音,恬然乐之而悠然忘之者是何趣,不可思量处是何境?

We burn incense on a moonlight night and play three stanzas of music from an ancient instrument, and immediately the myriad worries of our breast are banished and all our foolish ambitions or desires are forgotten. We will then inquire, what is the fragrance of this incense, what is the color of the smoke, what is that shadow that comes through the white papered windows, what is this sound that arises from below my fingertips, what is this enjoyment which makes us so quietly happy and so forgetful of everything else, and what is the condition of the infinite universe?

凡静室,须前栽碧梧,后种翠竹,前檐放步,北用暗窗,春冬闭之,以避风雨,夏秋可开,以通凉爽。然碧梧之趣,春冬落叶,以舒负暄融和之乐,夏秋交荫,以蔽炎烁蒸烈之气,四时得宜,莫此为胜。

For such a quiet studio, one should have *wut'ung* trees in front and and some green bamboos behind. On the south of the house, the eaves will stretch boldly forward, while on the north side, there will be small windows, which can be closed in spring and winter to shelter one from rain and wind, and opened in summer and autumn for ventilation. The beauty of the *wut'ung* tree is that all its leaves fall off in spring and winter, thus admitting us to the full enjoyment of the sun's warmth, while in summer and autumn its shade protects us from the scorching heat.

筑室数楹,编槿为篱,结茅为亭。以三亩荫竹树栽花果,二亩种蔬菜,四壁清旷,空诸所有,蓄山童灌园剃草,置二三胡床着亭下,挟书剑以伴孤寂,携琴弈以迟良友,此亦可以娱老。

Build a house of several beams, grow a hedge of *chin* trees and cover a pavilion with a hay-thatch. Three *mow* of land will be devoted to planting bamboos and flowers and fruit trees, while two *mow* will be devoted to planting vegetables. The four walls of a room are bare and the room is empty, with the exception of two or three rough beds placed in the pavilion. A peasant boy will be kept to water the vegetables and clear the weeds. So then one may arm one's self with books and a sword against solitude, and provide a *ch'in* (a stringed instrument) and chess to anticipate the coming of good friends. This is one of the ways that can make one's old age more lovely.

门内有径,径欲曲;径转有屏,屏欲小;屏进有阶,阶欲平;阶畔有花,花欲鲜;花外有墙,墙欲低;墙内有松,松欲古;松底有石,石欲怪;石面有亭,亭欲朴;亭后有竹,竹欲疏;竹尽有室,室欲幽;室旁有路,路欲分;路合有桥,桥欲危;桥边有树,树欲高;树阴有草,草欲青;草上有渠,渠欲细;渠引有泉,泉欲瀑;泉去有山,山欲深;山下有屋,屋欲方;屋角有圃,圃欲宽;圃中有鹤,鹤欲舞;鹤报有客,客不俗;客至有酒,酒欲不却;酒行有醉,醉欲不归。

Inside the gate there is a footpath and the footpath must be winding. At the turn of the footpath there is an outdoor screen and the screen must be small. Behind the screen there is a terrace and the terrace must be level. On the banks of the terrace there are flowers and the flowers must be bright-colored. Beyond the flowers there is a wall and the wall must be low. By the side of the wall there is a pine tree and the pine must be old. At the foot of the pine tree there are rocks and the rocks must be quaint. Over the rocks there is a pavilion and the pavilion must be simple. Behind the pavilion there are bamboos and the bamboos must be sparse. At the end of the bamboos there is a house and the house must be secluded. By the side of the house there is a road and the road must branch off. At the point where several roads come together, there is a bridge and the bridge must be tantalizing to cross. At the end of the bridge there are trees and the trees must be tall. In the shade of the trees there is grass and the grass must be green. Above the grass plot there is a ditch and the ditch must be slender. At the top of the ditch there is a spring and the spring must gurgle. Above the spring there is a hill and the hill must be undulating. Below the hill there is a hall and the hall must be square. At the corner of the hall there is a vegetable garden and the garden must be big. In the garden there is a stork and the stork must dance. The stork announces there is a guest and the guest must not be vulgar. When the guest arrives he is offered wine and the wine must not be declined. At the drink the guest must get drunk and the drunken guest must not want to go home.

二十二

幽梦影
Quiet Dream Shadows[①]

张　潮(Chang Chao)

1　人　生
Human Life

情之一字,所以维持世界;才之一字,所以粉饰乾坤。

Passion holds up the bottom of the universe, and the poet gives it a new dress.

情必近于痴而始真,才必兼乎趣而始化。

Love is not true love without a form of madness. A literary artist must have zest in life to enter into nature's spirit.

美味以大嚼尽之,奇境以粗游了之,深情以浅语传之,良辰以酒食度之,富贵以骄奢处之,俱失造化本怀。[②]

---

①　此处仅节选部分内容。此外,《幽梦影》原文还有很多张潮亲友的评论(论述),颇有意思,林语堂也翻译了部分译文,并且还时不时地穿插有自己的论述,为节省篇幅,本书中仅收录张潮的文字及其译文。——编者注

②　此句出自朱锡绶的《幽梦影续》,林语堂在自己的评述中也有说明。——编者注

It is against the will of God to eat delicate food hastily, to pass gorgeous scenery hurriedly, to express deep sentiments superficially, to pass a beautiful day steeped in food and drinks, and to enjoy your wealth sunk in luxuries.

律己宜带秋气,处世宜带春气。

One should discipline oneself in the spirit of autumn and live with others in the spirit of spring.

能闲世人之所忙者,方能忙世人之所闲。

Only those who take leisurely what the people of the world are busy about can be busy about what the people of the world take leisurely.

人莫乐于闲,非无所事事之谓也。闲则能读书,闲则能游名胜,闲则能交益友,闲则能饮酒,闲则能著书。天下之乐,孰大于是?

Of all things one enjoys leisure most, not because one does nothing. Leisure confers upon one the freedom to read, to travel, to make friends, to drink, and to write. Where is there a greater pleasure than this?

妾美不如妻贤,钱多不如境顺。

I think it is better to have an understanding wife than a pretty concubine, and better to have peace of mind than wealth.

值太平世,生湖山郡,官长廉静,家道优裕,娶妻贤淑,生子聪慧,人生如此,可云全福。

The perfect life: to live in a world of peace in a lake district where the magistrate is good and honest, and to have an understanding wife and bright children.

有功夫读书,谓之福;有力量济人,谓之福;有学问著述,谓之福;无是非到耳,谓之福;有多闻直谅之友,谓之福。

Blessed are those who have time for reading, money to help others, the learning and ability to write, who are not bothered with gossip and disputes, and who have learned friends frank with advice.

不治生产,其后必致累人;专务交游,其后必致累己。

Those who despise money end up by sponging on their friends; those who mix up freely with all sorts of people will eventually hurt themselves.

胸中小不平,可以酒消之;世间大不平,非剑不能消也。

A small injustice can be drowned by a cup of wine; a great injustice can be drowned only by the sword.

多情者必好色,而好色者未必尽属多情;红颜者必薄命,而薄命者未必尽属红颜;能诗者必好酒,而好酒者未必尽属能诗。

A great lover loves women, but one who loves women is not necessarily a great lover. A beautiful woman often has a tragic life, but not all those who have tragic lives are beautiful. A good poet can always drink, but being a great drinker does not make one a poet.

有青山方有绿水,水惟借色于山;有美酒便有佳诗,诗亦乞灵于酒。

Green hills come with blue waters which borrow their blueness from the hills; good wine produces beautiful poems, which draw sustenance from the spirits.

酒可好不可骂座,色可好不可伤生,财可好不可昧心,气可好不可越理。

Drink by all means, but do not make drunken scenes; have women by all means, but do not destroy your health; work for money by all means, but do not let it blot out your conscience; get mad about something, but do not go beyond reason.

天下无书则已,有则必当读;无酒则已,有则必当饮;无名山则已,有则必当游;无花月则已,有则必当赏玩;无才子佳人则已,有则必当爱慕怜惜。

If there were no books, then nothing need be said about it, but since there are books, they must be read; if there were no wine, then nothing need be said, but since there is, it must be drunk; since there are famous mountains, they must be visited; since there are flowers and the moon, they must be enjoyed; and since there are poets and beauties they must be loved and protected.

不得已而谀之者,宁以口,毋以笔;不可耐而骂之者,亦宁以口,毋以笔。

If one has to praise someone, rather do it by word of mouth than by pen; if there are persons that must be castigated, also do it by word of mouth rather than in writing.

万事可忘,难忘者名心一段;千般易淡,未淡者美酒三杯。

One can forget everything except the thought of fame, and learn to be cool toward everything except three cups of wine.

物之能感人者,在天莫如月,在乐莫如琴,在动物莫如鹃,在植物莫如柳。

Of all things in the universe, those that move men most deeply are the moon in heaven, the *chin* in music, the cuckoo among birds, and the willow among plants.

阅《水浒传》,至鲁达打镇关西,武松打虎,因思人生必有一桩极快意事,方不枉在生一场。即不能有其事,亦须著得一种得意之书,庶几无憾耳。

When you read the *Shuihu* and come to the passage where Luta smashes into the ranks of Chenkuanshi or where Wusung kills the tiger with his bare hands, you feel good. By that I mean something like what Li Po felt when he made the queen hold the inkstone for him when he was commanded to write a poem. A man must have such moments of supreme satisfaction in his life. Then he will not have lived in vain. If he cannot, he can hope to make up for it by writing a fine book.

胸藏丘壑,城市不异山林;兴寄烟霞,阁浮有如蓬岛。梧桐为植物中清品,而形家独忌之甚,且谓梧桐大如斗,主人往外走……俗言之不足据,类如此夫。

In possession of a lively imagination, one can live in the cities and feel like one is in the mountains, and following one's fancies with the clouds, one can convert the dark continent of the south into fairy isles. A great wrong has been committed on the plane tree by the necromancers who regard it as bringing bad luck, saying that when a plane tree grows in the yard, its owner will live abroad ... Most superstitions are like that.

有地上之山水,有画上之山水,有梦中之山水,有胸中之山水。地上者妙在邱壑深邃,画上者妙在笔墨淋漓,梦中者妙在景象变幻,胸中者妙在位置自如。

There are hills and waters on the earth, in paintings, in dreams, and in one's imagination. The beauty of such hills and waters on the earth is in their grace and variety; that in paintings, richness of ink and freedom of the brush; that in dreams, their changefulness; and that in one's imagination, good composition.

鳞虫中金鱼,羽虫中紫燕,可云物类神仙。正如东方曼倩避世金马门,人不得而害之。

Be a goldfish among the fish and a swallow among the birds. These are like Taoist fairies who go through life like the witty Tungfang Manching, safe from harm from those in power.

人须求可入诗,物须求可入画。

So live that your life may be like a poem. Arrange things so that they look like they are in a painting.

昔人云,若无花、月、美人,不愿生此世界。予益一语云,若无翰墨、棋、酒,不必定作人身。

An ancient writer said, "Life would not be worth living if there were no moon, no flowers, and no beautiful women." I might add, "It might not be important to be born a man, if there were no pen and paper, and no chess and wine."

愿在木而为樗,愿在草而为蓍,愿在鸟而为鸥,愿在兽而为廌,愿在虫而为蝶,愿在鱼而为鲲。

That I might be the *shu* among the trees (which is never cut down because of its worthless timber), the *shi* among the grass (which can foretell events), the sea gull among the birds (which merges with the elements), the *chih* among animals (a kind of deer which attacks the guilty one), the butterfly among insects (which flits among flowers), and the *kun* among fish (which has the freedom of the ocean).

庄周梦为蝴蝶,庄周之幸也;蝴蝶梦为庄周,蝴蝶之不幸也。

It was fortunate of Chuangtse to dream of being a butterfly, but a misfortune for the butterfly to dream of being Chuangtse.

假使梦能自主,虽千里无难命驾,可不羡长房之缩地;死者可以晤对,可不需少君之招魂;五岳可以卧游,可不俟婚嫁之尽毕。

That one might control one's dreams! Then one could go anywhere one likes, conjure up the spirits of the past, and set out on a world trip without waiting for the sons and daughters to be married first.

少年人须有老成之识见,老成人须有少年之襟怀。

Young people should have the wisdom of the old, and old people should have the heart of the young.

躬耕吾所不能,学灌园而已矣;樵薪吾所不能,学薙草而已矣。

I cannot hope to be a farmer, but will learn watering flowers; cannot hope to become a woodcutter, but will be contented with pulling out weeds.

高语山林者,辄不善谈市朝事。审若此,则当并废《史》、《汉》诸书而不读矣。盖诸书所载者,皆古之市朝也。

Recluse scholars often disdain to discuss affairs of the government. But history is full of affairs of the government. Should one stop reading history, too? They cannot have meant it.

凡事不宜刻,若读书则不可不刻;凡事不宜贪,若买书则不可不贪;凡事不宜痴,若行善则不可不痴。

A man must not be fastidious about other things, but he must be about reading. He must not be greedy, except in buying books. He should not be a confirmed addict, except in the habit of doing good and helping others.

文名可以当科第,俭德可以当货材,清闲可以当寿考。

To enjoy literary fame can take the place of passing imperial examinations; to manage to live within one's means can take the place of wealth; to lead a life of leisure can well be the equivalent of a long life.

涉猎虽曰无用,犹胜于不通古今;清高固然可嘉,莫流于不识时务。

Random reading and browsing are better than not being acquainted with books at all; it is all right to be detached, but not to be ignorant of the trend of the times.

有山林隐逸之乐而不知享者,渔樵也,农圃也,缁黄也;有园亭姬妾之乐而不能享、不善享者,富商也,大僚也。

There are those who have the beauties of forests and hills before their eyes, but do not appreciate them—the fishermen, woodcutters, peasants, and the black and yellow [Buddhist and Taoist monks]—and others who have gardens, terraces and women, but often fail to enjoy them for lack of time or of culture—the rich merchants and high officials.

清宵独坐,邀月言愁;良夜孤眠,呼蛩语恨。

To sit alone at night and invite the moon to tell it one's sorrows; to sleep alone at night and call to the cricket and pour out one's regrets.

官声采于舆论,豪右之口与寒乞之口俱不得其真;花案定于成心,艳媚之评与寝陋之评概恐失其实。

An official's reputation comes from public opinion, but that of his close associates and of beggars of office should be discounted. The reputation of women should come from real knowledge; the views of fans and superficial critics cannot be trusted.

多情者不以生死易心,好饮者不以寒暑改量,喜读书者不以忙闲作辍。

A true lover does not change with the years; a good drinker does not change with the seasons; a lover of books does not stop reading because of business.

立品须发乎宋人之道学,涉世须参以晋代之风流。

Build one's character on the foundation of the moral teachings of the Sung Neo-Confucianists [twelfth century]; but go through life in the spirit of the Chin romanticists [third and fourth centuries].

豪杰易于圣贤,文人多于才子。

It is easier to be a hero than a sage, and easier to be a writer than a real genius.

风流自赏,只容花鸟趋陪;真率谁知,合受烟霞供养。

In self-contentment, a brilliant man takes his ease with birds and flowers; careless of popular fame, he regards himself as being served by the hilltop clouds.

痛可忍而痒不可忍;苦可耐而酸不可耐。

It is easier to stand pain than to stand an itch; bitter taste is easier to bear than sour.

2　品　格
Personal Character

何谓善人? 无损于世者则谓之善人;何谓恶人? 有害于世者则谓之恶人。

What is a good man? Simply one whose life is useful to the world. And a bad man is simply one whose life is harmful to others.

无善无恶是圣人,善多恶少是贤者,善少恶多是庸人,有恶无善是小人,有善无恶是仙佛。

Those beyond good and evil are sages. Those who have more good than bad in them are distinguished persons. Common men have more evil than good, and the scum and riffraff of society have no good at all. Fairies and buddhas have only good and no evil.

昭君以和亲而显,刘蕡以下第而传,可谓之不幸,不可谓之缺憾。

Some men and women left a name for posterity because they were victims of some adverse circumstances. One can say that they were most unfortunate, but I doubt that one should express regret for them.

为浊富不若为清贫，以忧生不若以乐死。

Be clean and poor rather than be filthy rich; accept death cheerily when it comes rather than be worried about life.

天下唯鬼最富，生前囊无一文，死后每饶楮锭；天下唯鬼最尊，生前或受欺凌，死后必多跪拜。

It is not bad to be a ghost. One who was penniless has a lot of paper money burnt for his benefit and one who was pushed around all his life is worshiped by people on their knees after his death.

富贵而劳悴，不若安闲之贫贱；贫贱而骄傲，不若谦恭之富贵。

Rather lead a poor but leisurely life than be a success and lead a busy one. But better be simple though rich, than be poor and proud.

贫而无诌，富而无骄，古人之所贤也，贫而无骄，富而无诌，今人之所少也，足以知世风之降矣。

The ancients praised those who were proud though poor, and not snobbish though rich. Now in modern days it is difficult to find the poor who are not snobbish and the rich who are not haughty.

文人每好鄙薄富人，然于诗文之佳者，又往往以金玉珠玑锦绣誉之，则又何也？

Scholars often jeer at the rich. Then when they praise a piece of composition, why do they compare it to gold, jade and gems, and brocade?

黑与白交，黑能污白，白不能掩黑；香与臭混，臭能胜香，香不能敌臭，此君子小人相攻之大势也。

Black can besmirch white and a bad odor wipe out a fragrance easily, but not vice versa. This is what happens when a gentleman is confronted by a cad or a sneak.

耻之一字,所以治君子;痛之一字,所以治小人。

Remind a gentleman of shame and threaten a sneak with pain. It always works.

无益之施舍,莫过于斋僧;无益之诗文,莫过于祝寿。

Nothing is more bootless than to give money to the monks, and nothing quite such a waste of time as writing eulogies on the occasion of someone's birthday.

宁为小人之所骂,毋为君子之所鄙;宁为盲主司之所摈弃,毋为诸名宿之所不知。

I would rather be criticized by the rabble than despised by a gentleman, and rather fail at the imperial examinations than be unknown to great scholars.

傲骨不可无,傲心不可有;无傲骨则近于鄙夫,有傲心不得为君子。

A man must have pride in his character [literally "in his bones"], but not in his heart. Not to have pride in character is to be with the common herd, and to have pride in one's heart does not belong to a gentleman.

人非圣贤,安能无所不知。只知其一,惟恐不止其一,复求知其二者,上也;止知其一,因人言始知有其二者,次也;止知其一,人言有其二而莫之信者,又其次也;止知其一,恶人言有其二者,斯下之下矣。

No man can know everything. The best and highest kind of man knows something, but is sure that there is something he does not know and seeks it. Next come those who know one point of view, but admit another point of view when told. Next come those who will not accept it when told, and the lowest are those who know one side of a question and hate to have people tell them the other side.

武人不苟战,是为武中之文;文人不迂腐,是为文中之武。

A military man who does not talk lightly of war is also a cultured man; a cultured man who does not rest with his smug opinions has something of the conqueror's spirit.

文人讲武事,大都纸上谈兵;武将论文章,半属道听途说。

A literary man discussing wars and battles is mostly an armchair strategist; a military man who discusses literature relies mostly on rumors picked up from hearsay.

圣贤者,天地之替身。

A sage speaks for the universe.

天极不难做,只须生仁人君子有才德者二三十人足矣,君一相一冢宰一,及诸路总制抚军是也。

Is it very difficult for Heaven [God] to bring peace to the world? I do not think so. All He needs to do will be to send into this world about two dozen great, upright men—one to be the king, one to be prime minister, one to be crown prince, and the rest to be provincial governors.

予尝谓二氏不可废,非袭夫大养济院之陈言也。盖名山胜境,我辈每思褰裳就之,使非琳宫梵刹,则倦时无可驻足,饥时谁与授餐?忽有疾风暴雨,五大夫果真足恃乎?又或丘壑深邃,非一日可了,岂能露宿以待明日乎?虎豹蛇虺,能保其不为人患乎?又或为士大夫所有,果能不问主人,任我之登陟凭吊而莫之禁乎?不特此也,甲之所有,乙思起而夺之,是启争端也;祖父之所创建,子孙贫力不能修葺,其倾颓之状,反足令山川减色矣,然此特就名山胜境言之耳,即城市之内,与夫四达之衢,亦不可少此一种。客游可作居停,一也;长途可以稍憩,二也;夏之茗,冬之姜汤,复可以济役夫负戴之困,三也。凡此皆就事理言之,非二氏福报之说也。

I think Buddhism and Taoism are most useful and should not be destroyed. For when we visit the famous mountains, it is often difficult to find a good resting place for the tired feet, or have meals and refreshments except at the temples, or to rush into shelter in case of rain. Sometimes a journey takes several days, and one cannot stop in the open overnight without fear of tigers and leopards... But even in cities, it is necessary to have temples, for a stopover in long journeys, for rest in a short one, for having tea in summer, ginger soup in winter, and for a rest for the carriers. This is a practical consideration, and has nothing to do with the theory of retribution.

3　妇女与朋友
Women and Friends

以爱花之心爱美人,则领略自饶别趣;以爱美人之心爱花,则护惜倍有深情。

To love a beautiful woman with the sentiment of loving flowers increases the keenness of admiration; to love flowers with the sentiment of loving women increases one's tenderness in protecting them.

美人之胜于花者,解语也;花之胜于美人者,生香也,二者不可得兼,舍生香而取解语者也。

Women are flowers that can talk, and flowers are women which give off fragrance. Rather enjoy talk than fragrance.

女子自十四五岁至二十四五岁,此十年中,无论燕秦吴越,其音大都娇媚动人,一睹其貌,则美恶判然矣。耳闻不如目见,于此益信。

Girls between fourteen and twenty-five of whatever locality usually have a charming accent, but when you see their faces, there is a great difference between the ugly and the beautiful.

所谓美人者,以花为貌,以鸟为声,以月为神,以柳为态,以玉为骨,以冰雪为肤,以秋水为姿,以诗词为心,吾无间然矣。

For a woman to have the expression of a flower, the voice of a bird, the soul of the moon, the posture of the willow, bones of jade and a skin of snow, the charm of an autumn lake and the heart of poetry—that would indeed be perfect.

花不可见其落,月不可见其沉,美人不可见其夭。种花须见其开,待月须见其满,著书须见其成,美人须见其畅适,方有实际,否则皆为虚设。

Avoid seeing the wilting of flowers, the decline of the moon, and the death of young women. One should wait to see the flowers in bloom after planting them, see the full moon after waiting days for it, and complete writing a book after starting it, and should see to it that a beautiful woman is happy and gay. Otherwise, all the labors are in vain.

闲人之砚固欲其佳,而忙人之砚尤不可不佳;娱情之妾固欲其美,而广嗣之妾亦不可不美。

A scholar's inkstone should be exquisite, but so should a businessman's. A concubine for pleasure should be beautiful, but so should also a concubine for continuing the family line.

看晓妆宜于傅粉之后。

It is good to look at a lady at her morning toilet after she has powdered her face.

昔人云,妇人识字多致诲淫,予谓此非识字之过也。盖识字则非无闻之人,其淫也,人易得而知耳。

There is an ancient saying that women who can read and write are apt to have loose morals. My opinion is that this is not the fault of education, but that when an educated woman has loose morals, the public gets to know about it more quickly.

才子遇才子,每有怜才之心;美人遇美人,必无惜美之意。我愿来世托生为绝代佳人,一反其局而后快。

When a scholar meets another scholar, usually there is a feeling of mutual sympathy, but when one beauty meets another, the sense of tenderness toward beauty is always lacking. May I be born a beautiful woman in the next life and change all that!

予尝欲建一无遮大会,一祭历代才子,一祭历代佳人。俟遇有真正高僧,即当为之。

I propose to hold a grand temple gathering for sacrifices to all the famous beauties and all the great poets of the past, with absolutely free intermingling of the men and women. When I find a first-class monk of real learning, I am going to do it.

一介之士必有密友，密友不必定是刎颈之交。大率虽千百里之遥，皆可相信，而不为浮言所动。闻有谤之者，即多方为之辨析而后已。事之宜行宜止者，代为筹画决断。或事当利害关头，有所需而后济者，即不必与闻，亦不虑其负我与否，竟为力承其事。此皆所谓密友也。

A scholar must have bosom friends. By a bosom friend I do not mean necessarily one who has sworn a pledge of friendship for life and death, but one who has faith in you against rumors, although separated by a thousand miles, and tries every means to explain it away, who will assume the responsibility and make a decision for you, or in case of need make a financial settlement, even without letting you know or worrying whether by so doing he is laying himself open to criticism. This is what I call a bosom friend.

云映日而成霞，泉挂岩而成瀑，所托者异而名亦因之，此友道之所以可贵也。

A cloud becomes multicolored when it reflects the sun, and a mountain current becomes a fall when it passes over a cliff. Things become different from what they associate with. That is why friendship is so valued.

发前人未发之论，方是奇书；言妻子难言之情，乃为密友。

A remarkable book is one which says something never said before; a bosom friend is one who will confide in you all his heartfelt feelings.

天下有一人知己，可以不恨。

One does not live in vain if there is one in this world who truly understands oneself.

对渊博友如读异书,对风雅友如读名人诗文,对谨饬友如读圣贤经传,对滑稽友如阅传奇小说。

To talk with a learned friend is like reading a remarkable book; with a romantic friend, like reading good prose and poetry; with an upright friend, like reading the classics; with a humorous friend, like reading fiction.

乡居须得良朋始佳,若田夫樵子,仅能辨五谷而测晴雨。久且数,未免生厌矣。而友之中,又当以能诗为第一,能谈次之,能画次之,能歌又次之,解觞政者又次之。

It is necessary to have good friends when living in the country. One can get tired of the peasants who talk only of the crops and the weather. Among friends, those who write poetry are the best; next, those good at conversation; next, those who paint; next, those who can sing; and lastly, those who can play wine games.

上元须酹豪友,端午须酹丽友,七夕须酹韵友,中秋须酹淡友,重九须酹逸友。

Drink a toast to cavalier friends during the Lantern Festival [fifteenth of January], to handsome friends during the Dragon Boat Festival [fifth day of fifth moon], to charming friends on the Double Seventh [the seventh of seventh moon], to friends of mild disposition during the Harvest Moon [fifteenth of eighth moon], and to romantic friends on the Double Ninth [ninth day of ninth moon].

求知己于朋友易,求知己于妻妾难,求知己于君臣则尤难之难。

It is easier to find real understanding among friends than among one's wife and mistresses. Between a king and his ministers, such a close understanding is even more rare.

并头联句,交颈论文,宫中应制,历使属国,皆极人间乐事。

Some of the greatest joys of life are: to discuss literature with a friend, to compose tête-à-tête together a poem by providing alternate lines, to sit at the palace examinations, and to be sent abroad as a diplomat to a dependency.

4 宇宙万物
Nature

春者,天之本怀;秋者,天之别调。

Spring is the natural disposition of Heaven [the creator]; autumn is one of its varying moods.

古人以冬为三余,余谓当以夏为三余。晨起者夜之余,夜坐者昼之余,午睡者应酬人事之余。古人诗云:"我爱夏日长",洵不诬也。

The ancient people regarded the winter as the "extra" period of rest of the other three seasons. I think the summer may also be considered to have three "extras" or rest periods: the summer morn is the "extra" of the night, the evening talks are the "extra" of the day's activities, and the siesta is an "extra" period for rest from seeing people. It is indeed true as the poet says, "I love the livelong summer day."

诗文之体得秋气为佳,词曲之体得春气为佳。

Prose and poetry are best when they have the spirit of autumn; drama and love ditties are best when they reflect the mood of spring.

雨之为物,能令昼短,能令夜长。

This thing called rain can make the days short and the nights long.

春雨宜读书,夏雨宜弈棋,秋雨宜检藏,冬雨宜饮酒。

A rainy day in spring is suitable for reading; a rainy day in summer for playing chess; a rainy day in autumn for going over things in the trunks or in the attic; and that in winter for a good drink.

春雨如恩诏,夏雨如赦书,秋雨如挽歌。

A spring rain is like an imperial edict conferring an honor, a summer rain like a writ of pardon, and an autumn rain like a dirge.

春风如酒,夏风如茗,秋风如烟,冬风如姜芥。

Spring wind is like wine, summer wind is like tea, autumn wind is like smoke, and winter wind is like ginger or mustard.

云之为物,或崔巍如山,或潋滟如水,或如人,或如兽,或如鸟毳,或如鱼鳞。故天下万物皆可画,惟云不能画。世所画云,亦强名耳。

The cloud is ever-changeful, sometimes piled up like high cliffs, sometimes translucent like water, and sometimes it resembles human beings or beasts or fish or insects. That is why clouds are most difficult to paint. The so-called paintings of clouds that I have seen are sheer tours de force.

新月恨其易沉,缺月恨其迟上。

One hates the new moon for its declining early and the third-quarter moon for its coming up late.

月下谈禅,旨趣益远;月下说剑,肝胆益真;月下论诗,风致益幽;月下对美人,情意益笃。

This is what the moonlight does: it makes a conversation on Shan (Zen) seem more spiritual and ethereal, a talk about swordsmanship seem more romantic, a discussion of poetry more charming, and a woman more enchanting.

春听鸟声,夏听蝉声,秋听虫声,冬听雪声,白昼听棋声,月下听箫声,山中听松风声,水际听欸乃声,方不虚此生耳。若恶少斥辱,悍妻诟谇,真不若耳聋也。

One does not live in vain to have heard the bird songs in spring, the cicada's song in summer, the insects' chirp in autumn, and the sound of crunching snow in winter, and furthermore, to have heard the sound of chess in daytime, the sound of flute in moonlight, the sound of winds whistling through the pines, and the sound of rippling, lapping water. As for the noise of fighting youths and scolding wives, it were better to be born deaf.

闻鹅声如在白门,闻橹声如在三吴,闻滩声如在浙江,闻骡马项下铃铎声如在长安道上。

The sound of geese makes one think of Nanking, that of creaking oars reminds one of the Kiangsu lake district; the sound of rapids makes one feel like being in Chekiang, and the sound of bells on horses' necks suggests travel on the road to Chang-an [in the northwest].

凡声皆宜远听,惟听琴则远近皆宜。

All sounds are better listened to from a distance, but that of the string instrument *chin* is an exception.

松下听琴,月下听箫,涧边听瀑布,山中听梵呗,觉耳中别有不同。

There is a difference when listening to the *chin* under a pine tree, to a flute under the moonlight, to a waterfall along a stream, and a Buddhist service up in the mountains.

鸟声之最佳者,画眉第一,黄鹂、百舌次之,然黄鹂、百舌,世未有笼而畜之者,其殆高士之俦,可闻而不可屈者耶?

The best bird songs are those of the thrush, and next to them those of the oriole and the blackbird. But the latter two have never been cage birds. Perhaps they have the soul of high-minded scholars—they can be heard, but not kept.

水之为声有四:有瀑布声,有流泉声,有滩声,有沟浍声。风之为声有三:有松涛声,有秋叶声,有波浪声。雨之为声有二:有梧叶、荷叶上声,有承檐溜竹筒中声。

There are four kinds of noise made by water: in a cataract, in a spring, over rapids, and in ditches. Three kinds of noise made by winds: those of "pine surfs" (whistle of winds over pine forests as heard from a distance), of autumn leaves, and of waves. Two kinds of noise made by rains: that of drops on plane leaves and lotus leaves, and of rain water coming down drainpipes into bamboo pails.

目不能自见,鼻不能自嗅,舌不能自舐,手不能自握,惟耳能自闻其声。

The eye cannot see itself, the nose does not smell itself, the tongue cannot taste itself, the hand cannot clasp itself. Only the ear can hear itself.

为月忧云,为书忧蠹,为花忧风雨,为才子佳人忧命薄,真是菩萨心肠。

It shows the heart of Buddha (*misericordia*) to worry about clouds with the moon, about moths with books, about winds and rains with flowers, and to sympathize with beautiful women and brilliant poets about their harsh fate.

花不可以无蝶,山不可以无泉,石不可以无苔,水不可以无藻,乔木不可以无藤萝,人不可以无癖。

It is absolutely necessary for flowers to have butterflies, for hills to have springs, for rocks to be accompanied by moss, for water to have water cress in it, for tall trees to have creepers, and for a man to have hobbies.

赏花宜对佳人,醉月宜对韵人,映雪宜对高人。

See flowers in the company of beautiful women; drink under the moon with charming friends; take a stroll in the snow with high-minded persons.

景有言之极幽而实萧索者,烟雨也;境有言之极雅而实难堪者,贫病也;声有言之极韵而实粗鄙者,卖花声也。

Some moments are exquisite, but really dreary—heavy fog and rain. Some circumstances are said to be poetic, but really hard to bear—poverty and sickness. Some sounds seem very charming on paper, but are really coarse—the cry of flower sellers on the streets.

楼上看山,城头看雪,灯前看月,舟中看霞,月下看美人,另是一番情境。

Things give you a different mood and impression when looked at from a particular place: such as hills seen from a tower, snow seen from the top of a city wall, the moon seen from the lamplight, river haze seen from a boat, and pretty women seen in the moonlight.

玩月之法,皎洁则仰观,朦胧则宜俯视。

A clear moon should be seen looking up; a dark or hazy moon should be seen looking down from a high altitude.

山之光,水之声,月之色,花之香,文人之韵致,美人之姿态,皆无可名状,无可执著,真足以摄召魂梦,颠倒情思。

Such things as the color of mountains, the sound of water, the light of the moon, the fragrance of flowers, the charm of poets, and the expression of beautiful women cannot be put into words, yet they have a power to captivate one's soul and linger in one's memories and dreams.

游玩山水,亦复有缘。苟机缘未至,则虽近在数十里之内,亦无暇到也。

One either has or has not the luck to travel and visit places. Without luck, one has no time to visit the nearest mountain within a few miles of one's home.

镜中之影,着色人物也;月下之影,写意人物也。镜中之影,钩边画也;月下之影,没骨画也。月中山河之影,天文中地理也;水中星月之象,地理中天文也。

Reflections in the mirror are color paintings, forms in the moonlight are drawings in ink. Reflections in the mirror are paintings with sharp contours, while the forms in moonlight are "boneless paintings" (without delineated contours). The hills and rivers in the moon are geography in heaven, while the reflections of the stars and the moon in water are astronomy on earth.

蝶为才子之化身,花乃美人之别号。

The butterfly is the incarnation of a brilliant scholar, and flower is the poetic name of woman.

因雪想高士,因花想美人,因酒想侠客,因月想好友,因山水想得意诗文。

Snow reminds one of a great high-minded scholar; the flower reminds one of a beautiful woman; wine brings up memories of great cavaliers; the moon makes one think of friends; a beautiful landscape makes one think of some good verse or prose.

当为花中之萱草,毋为鸟中之杜鹃。

Be the day lily among grass. Do not be the cuckoo among the birds.

花之宜于目而复宜于鼻者,梅也、菊也、兰也、水仙也、珠兰也、木香也、玫瑰也、腊梅也,余则皆宜于目者也。花与叶俱可观者,秋海棠为最,荷次之,海棠、酴醾、虞美人、水仙又次之。叶胜于花者,止雁来红、美人蕉而已。花与叶俱不足观者,紫薇也、辛夷也。

Flowers which are both pretty and have a good smell are the plum, the chrysanthemum, the [Chinese] orchid, the narcissus, the *Chloranthus inconspicua*, the banksia rose, the rose, and the winter sweet. The others are all for the eye. Among those whose leaves as well as flowers are good to look at, the begonia ranks first, the lotus comes next, and then follow the cherry apple, the *Rubus commersonii* [of the rose family], the red poppy, and the narcissus. The amaranth and the *Musa uranoscopus* [of the banana family] have prettier leaves than flowers. The crape myrtle and the magnolia have nothing to recommend themselves either in leaves or in flowers.

梅令人高,兰令人幽,菊令人野,莲令人淡,春海棠令人艳,牡丹令人豪,蕉与竹令人韵,秋海棠令人媚,松令人逸,桐令人清,柳令人感。

The following flowers create each a mood: the plum flower goes with poetry [which alone of all flowers blooms in pink against a background of snow], the orchid with seclusion [flowering on mountain cliffs content with being unseen], the chrysanthemum with the rustic flavor, the lotus with simplicity of heart, the cherry apple with glamour, the peony with success [power and wealth], the banana and the bamboo with gentlemanly charm, the begonia with seductive beauty, the pine tree with retirement, the plane tree with absence of worry, and the willow with sentimentality.

凡花色之娇媚者,多不甚香;瓣之千层者,多不结实。甚矣,全才之难也,兼之者其惟莲乎!

Most flowers that are pretty have no smell, and those that are a composite do not bear fruit. How rare is a perfect talent! The lotus, however, combines both.

以松花为量,以松实为香,以松枝为尘尾,以松阴为步障,以松涛为鼓吹。山居得乔松百余章,真乃受用不尽。

One can use the pine flower for measurement, its seeds for perfume, its branches for a duster to drive away insects, its big shade for cover, and the wind whistling through it as music. Thus a man living in the country with a hundred pine trees benefits from them in many ways.

笋为蔬中尤物,荔枝为果中尤物,蟹为水族中尤物,酒为饮食中尤物,月为天文中尤物,西湖为山水中尤物,词曲为文字中尤物。

The bamboo shoot is unique among vegetarian food, and so are the following, each in its class: the litchi among fruit, the crab among shellfish, wine among drinks, the moon in the firmament, the West Lake [Hangchow] among hills and waters, and the Sung *tze* [poems of irregular lines written to music] and the *chu* [songs for the opera] in literature.

秋虫春鸟尚能调声弄舌,时吐好音,我辈搦管拈毫,岂可甘作鸦鸣牛喘。

Even autumn insects and spring birds can make melodious songs to please the ear. How can we who write make just noises like the mooing of a cow or the cackling of a crow?

蝉为虫中之夷齐,蜂为虫中之管晏。

The cicada is the retired gentleman among the insects, and the bee is an efficient administrator.

蝇集人面,蚊嘬人肤,不知以人为何物。

A fly rests on a man's face, and a mosquito sucks man's blood. What do these insects take man for?

蛛为蝶之敌国,驴为马之附庸。

The spider is the racial enemy of the butterfly, while the donkey is a satellite of the horse.

物之稚者皆不可厌,惟驴独否。

All babies and the young of animals are lovely, except the donkey colt.

牛与马,一仕而一隐也;鹿与豕,一仙而一凡也。

The horse is a public servant, the cow a retired scholar. The deer belongs to fairyland, the pig to this world.

人则女美于男,禽则雄华于雌,兽则牝牡无分者也。

In human beings, the female is more beautiful than the male. Among the birds, the male is prettier than the female. Among the beasts, there is no difference.

5 房屋与家庭
The House and Home

抄写之笔墨不必过求其佳,若施之缣素,则不可不求其佳;诵读之书籍,不必过求其备,若以供稽考,则不可不求其备;游历之山水,不必过求其妙,若因之卜居,则不可不求其妙。

One need not be too particular about pen and ink when doing copy work, but should be particular when writing for things to be framed up. Also one can have a random collection of books for reading, but should insist on good, adequate reference works. Likewise, what landscape one sees in passing in travel is not too important, but that of the place where you are going to build a house and settle down is of prime importance.

忙人园亭宜与住宅相连,闲人园亭不妨与住宅相远。

A busy man must plan to have his garden next to his house, but a man of leisure can afford to have it some distance away.

园亭之妙,在丘壑布置,不在雕绘琐屑。往往见人家园亭,屋脊墙头,雕砖镂瓦,非不穷极工巧。然未久即坏,坏后极难修葺,是何如朴素之为佳乎?

The essential thing in a garden with terraces is plan and composition, and not ornamental details. I have often seen homes which expended a great deal of effort on such carvings and ornamentations. These are difficult to keep in good condition and costly in repairs. Better have a simpler taste.

艺花可以邀蝶,累石可以邀云,栽松可以邀风,贮水可以邀萍,筑台可以邀月,种蕉可以邀雨,植柳可以邀蝉。

Planting flowers invites the butterflies, and in the same way rocks invite clouds, the pine invites winds, a water pond invites duckweed, a terrace may be said to invite the moon, bananas invite the rain, and willows invite cicadas.

梅边之石宜古,松下之石宜拙,竹傍之石宜瘦,盆内之石宜巧。

Different types of rocks should be selected for different places:

"primitive" ones should be placed with the plum tree, rugged, heavy ones near pines, slender slabs near bamboos, and delicate varieties in a flowerpot or tray.

一日之计种蕉,一岁之计种竹,十年之计种柳,百年之计种松。

In planting trees, so much depends on in how many years you want to see the results. For immediate results, choose bananas; planning for one year, choose bamboos; for ten years, willows; and for a hundred years, pine trees.

一恨书囊易蛀,二恨夏夜有蚊,三恨月台易漏,四恨菊叶多焦,五恨松多大蚁,六恨竹多落叶,七恨桂荷易谢,八恨薜萝藏虺,九恨架花生刺,十恨河豚多毒。

There are ten kinds of worries or things to look out for: (1) Moths in book bags. (2) Mosquitoes on summer nights. (3) A leaky terrace. (4) Dry chrysanthemum leaves. (5) Big ants near pines. (6) Too many fallen leaves of bamboos. (7) Too quick wilting of lotus flowers. (8) Snakes near creepers. (9) Thorns on a trellis of flowers. (10) Being poisoned from eating globefish.

窗内人于窗纸上作字,吾于窗外观之极佳。

It is wonderful to see from the outside a man writing characters on window paper from the inside.

冰裂纹极雅,然宜细不宜肥。若以之作窗栏,殊不耐观也。

Latticework is all right, but it should consist of fine lines and spaces, and not made with big ones. It would not look nice in windows.

养花胆瓶,其式之高低大小须与花相称,而色之浅深浓淡又须与花相反。

The vases used for arranging flowers should be chosen so that their size and shape agree with the flowers but their dark or light shades of color contrast with them.

虽不善书,而笔砚不可不精;虽不业医,而验方不可不存;虽不工弈,而楸枰不可不备。

Certain things must be provided in the home: good pens and ink stone, although the owner himself is not a calligraphist; a home book of medical recipes, although not a doctor; and a chessboard although he may not play.

居城市中,当以画幅当山水,以盆景当苑囿,以书籍当朋友。

A man living in the city must make scrolls of painting serve as a natural landscape, have flower arrangements in pots serve as a garden, and have books serve as his friends.

如何是独乐乐,曰鼓琴;如何是与人乐乐,曰奕棋;如何是与众乐乐,曰马吊。

To amuse oneself, play the *chin*, to amuse oneself with a friend, play chess, and to have general entertainment, play *matiao* [a game of cards, ancestor of mahjong].

宜于耳复宜于目者,弹琴也,吹萧也;宜于耳不宜于目者,吹笙也,攌管也。

Musical instruments that are good to listen to and to look at playing are the *chin* and the *shiao* [a flute]; those good to listen to, but not to look at playing are the *sheng* [small reed organ held close to the mouth] and the *kuan* [oboe-like instrument, but simpler].

天下器玩之类,其制日工,其价日贱,毋惑乎民之贫也。

The quality of things made, vessels, utensils, and toys, has steadily improved in these years, while their prices have steadily gone down. It must be that the artisans are becoming poorer.

镜不幸而遇嫫母,砚不幸而遇俗子,剑不幸而遇庸将,皆无可奈何之事。

When a good mirror meets an ugly owner, a good inkstone meets a vulgar person, and a good sword finds itself in the hands of a common general, there is nothing these things can do about it.

6 读书与文学
Reading and Literature

古今至文,皆血泪所成。

All literary masterpieces of the ancients and moderns were written with blood and tears.

文章是案头之山水,山水是地上之文章。

Literature is landscape on the desk; landscape is literature on the earth.

善读书者,无之而非书。山水亦书也,棋酒亦书也,花月亦书也。善游山水者,无之而非山水。书史亦山水也,诗酒亦山水也,花月亦山水也。

A good reader regards many things as books to read wherever he

goes; a good landscape, chess and wine, and flowers and the moon are all books to be read. A good traveler also sees a landscape [a picture] in everything: in history, in poems and wining parties, and in flowers and the moon.

读书最乐,若读史书则喜少怒多,究之,怒处亦乐处也。

Generally, reading is a pleasure. But reading history, more often than not, makes one gripped with sadness or anger. But even that feeling of sadness or anger is a luxury.

读经宜冬,其神专也;读史宜夏,其时久也;读诸子宜秋,其致别也;读诸集宜春,其机畅也。

Winter is good for reading the classics, for one's mind is more collected. Summer is good for reading history, for one has plenty of time. The autumn is good for reading the ancient philosophers, because of the great diversity of thought and ideas. Finally, spring is suitable for reading literary works, for in spring one's spirit expands.

经传宜独坐读,史鉴宜与友共读。

The classics should be read by oneself while alone (for reflection). History should be read together with friends (for discussion of opinions).

少年读书如隙中窥月,中年读书如庭中望月,老年读书如台上玩月,皆以阅历之浅深为所得之浅深耳。

The benefit of reading varies directly with one's experience in life. It is like looking at the moon. A young reader may be compared to one seeing the moon through a single crack, a middle-aged reader seems to see it from an enclosed courtyard, and an old man seems to see it from an open terrace, with a complete view of the entire field.

不独诵其诗读其书是尚友古人,即观其字画亦是尚友古人处。

It is not only through reading that we make friends with ancient authors; even in looking at their manuscripts, we have the same feeling.

著得一部新书,便是千秋大业;注得一部古书,允为万世宏功。

Next to the author of a good book is the man who makes a good commentary on it.

延名师训子弟,入名山习举业,丐名士代捉刀,三者都无是处。

To ask a famous scholar to be tutor for young children, to discuss official promotions and examinations at a mountain retreat, and to ask a famous writer to be the ghost for your compositions—these things are utterly wrong.

大家之文,吾爱之慕之,吾愿学之;名家之文,吾爱之慕之,吾不敢学之。学大家而不得,所谓刻鹄不成尚类鹜也;学名家而不得,则是画虎不成反类犬矣。

One can admire and try to imitate the writing of great thinkers, but not that of a famous writer. One can fail and yet not make too bad a mistake in the first case, but the result may be disastrous in the second.

方外不必戒酒,但须戒俗;红裙不必通文,但须得趣。

Monks need not abstain from wine, but only from being vulgar;

red skirts [women] need not master literature, but they should have good taste.

能读无字之书，方可得惊人妙句；能会难通之解，方可参最上禅机。

One who can read the wordless book of life should be able to write striking lines; one who understands the truth which is difficult to express by words is qualified to grasp the highest Shan wisdom.

读书不难，能用为难；能用不难，能记为难。

The difficulty is not in reading books, but in applying the truths to life, and the greater difficulty is in remembering them.

《水浒传》是一部怒书，《西游记》是一部悟书，《金瓶梅》是一部哀书。

Among the classics of fiction, the *Shuihu* [about a band of rebels in times of a bad government] is a book of anger, the *Shiyuchi* [a religious allegory and story of adventure] is a book of spiritual awakening, and the *Chinpingmei* [*Hsimen Ching and His Six Wives*], a book of sorrow.

貌有丑而可观者，有虽不丑而不足观者；文有不通而可爱者，有虽通而极可厌者。此未易与浅人道也。

There are faces that are ugly but interesting, and others that are pretty but dull. There are, too, books that are not well written, but utterly fascinating, and others that are well written, but extremely dull. This is difficult to explain to superficial critics.

创新庵不若修古庙，读生书不若温旧业。

It is more profitable to reread some old books than to read new ones, just as it is better to repair and add to an old temple than to build one entirely new.

作文之法,意之曲折者宜写之以显浅之词,理之显浅者宜运之以曲折之笔,题之熟者参之以新奇之想,题之庸者深之以关系之论,至于窘者舒之使长,缛者删之使简,俚者文之使雅,闹者摄之使静,皆所谓裁制也。

The secret of composition lies in this: Try to express difficult points clearly and avoid the obvious and superficial. Commonplace subjects must be illuminated with fresh thoughts, and commonplace themes must be shown to have deeper implications. As to amplifications, tightening up, weeding out overwriting and common, overused expressions, these are matters of revision.

先读经后读史,则论事不谬于圣贤;既读史复读经,则观书不徒为章句。

First study the classics, then history. Then one has a deeper central point of view. Then one can go back to the classics again, when one will not be satisfied with merely beautiful phrases.

古人云:"诗必穷而后工。"盖穷则语多感慨易于见长耳。若富贵中人,既不可忧贫叹贱,所谈者不过风云月露而已,诗安得佳? 苟思所变,计惟有出游一法。即以所见之山川风土物产人情,或当疮痍兵燹之余,或值旱涝灾祲之后,无一不可寓之诗中。借他人之穷愁以供我之咏叹,则诗亦不必待穷而后工也。

The ancient people say: "A man becomes a better poet after he has tasted poverty." That is because from poverty and hardships, one gains depth and experience. People who are rich and well-to-do do not taste all aspects of life, and they can only write about the winds and the clouds, and the moon and the dew. As a substitute for personal experience, they might go about and watch the sufferings of the common people, especially in times of war and famine and in that way acquire a vicarious experience of life.

二十三

华阳散稿自序
Dreams, Interesting and Otherwise
Preface to *Huayang Essays*

史震林(Shih Chenlin)

　　我生如戏,嬉笑怒骂,皆戏具耳。我生如梦,语言文字,皆梦呓耳。诗文之道有四:理、事、情、景而已。理有理趣,事有事趣,情有情趣,景有景趣。趣者,生气与灵机也。做无趣之梦,串无趣之戏,岂不负有趣之天,虚有趣之地乎哉? 搭不三不四之人,作不深不浅之揖,吃不冷不热之饼,说不痛不痒之话。小人之描画君子,虽为无礼,不为无趣也。余生也晚,未见古人;余才也鲁,未见奇书。矢口为诗,信笔为文,理事情景,四无一趣。人之所嗤,鬼之所笑,此中有泪,哭之者其谁也? 风有时而逆,列子之御无趣矣。月有时而晦,太白之邀无趣矣。花有时而萎,南华之蝶无趣矣。槐有时而枯,南柯之蚁无趣矣。此中有泪,哭之者又谁也? 墨耕琴庄者,趣士也。游趣园,拈趣笔,吟趣事;与有趣之人,爱无趣之我;挥有趣之金,刻无趣之文,是犹玉勾词客之刻余《西青散记》。余将毁之,震亭藏之,而祝融氏厌其无趣,起而焚之。人莫能嗤,鬼莫能笑,此中有泪,哭之者又谁也? 墨耕琴庄喟然叹曰:"嗟乎,梦为生,梦为旦,未必无趣也;梦为生而忽净,梦为旦而忽丑,亦未必无趣也。至于争无趣之蜗角,竞无趣之蝇头,梦不成梦,戏不成戏,此中尚有泪乎,哭之者谁?"且游华阳第八洞天第一福地可也。

Our life is like a play as we stomp about the stage, laughing with joy or shouting in a rage. It is like a dream in which we write and talk like somnambulists. After all, there are only four things which are the contents of literature: ideas, human reactions, events, and scenes. There are curious ideas, interesting events, fascinating human reactions, and arresting scenes. The curious interest in all these is the center and foundation of all life and literature. Would it not be a sin against this curious heaven and curious earth to go on dreaming uninteresting dreams and acting in dull plays? But we do: we make meaningless bows to witless persons, eat tasteless food, and engage in helpless conversations. Now this may be a little unkind to say of the gentlemen, but that very scene of their doing so is interesting and curious.

I was born late and never saw the ancients, and with my limitations of knowledge have never read the "extraordinary books." I write both poetry and prose just as I feel, unable, I am afraid, to reveal what is of curious interest in ideas or events, or human reactions or scenes. They deserve the snoring of humans and the laughter of ghosts. There are tears in these. Who will cry over them?

Sometimes the winds are rough and Liehtse [reputed to be able to ride the winds] would find no interest in them. Sometimes the moon is dark and Li Po would find no interest in inviting it for company. Sometimes the flowers are withered and Chuangtse's butterflies would find no interest in flitting about. And sometimes the locust tree is dried up and the ants would find no interest in its southern bough. [1] There

---

[1] A reference to "Southern Bough Record," a Rip Van Winkle type of short story, depicting what a man saw in his dream of a visit to the kingdom of the ants, with its king and queen and nobles and their pompous vanity.

are tears in these. Again who will cry over them?

Ink-Farmer is an interesting person. He lives in an interesting garden, wields an interesting pen, writes interesting verse, makes interesting friends, but loves the uninteresting me. He is going to spend his most interesting money to publish my uninteresting book. It reminds me of Wu Chensheng who published my *West-Green Random Notes* over my protests. Another friend, Tsao Chenting, kept a stock of copies. But the God of Fire thought it a most uninteresting book and destroyed it. There was then no need for humans to snort or ghosts to laugh. There are tears in these. Again who will cry over them? But Ink-Farmer said with a sigh, "I do not think it is so bad after all to dream of being a young man or a pretty lady, nor so deplorable to dream of being a young man and find oneself a middle-aged person, or of being a pretty lady and find oneself a clown. What is deadening would be to spend one's time fighting over uninteresting pennies and amassing uninteresting small gains. Will there still be tears left in these dreams? And again who will cry over them?"

Let's go and visit the blessed spot of the Huayang Caves, No. 8.

二十四

贫贱行乐之法
How to Be Happy though Poor[①]

李笠翁(Li Liweng)

穷人行乐之方,无他秘巧,亦止有退一步法。我以为贫,更有贫于我者;我以为贱,更有贱于我者;我以妻子为累,尚有鳏寡孤独之民,求为妻子之累而不能者;我以胼胝为劳,尚有身系狱廷,荒芜田地,求安耕凿之生而不可得者。以此居心,则苦海尽成乐地。如或向前一算,以胜己者相衡,则片刻难安,种种桎梏幽囚之境出矣。

一显者旅宿邮亭,时方溽暑,帐内多蚊,驱之不出,因忆家居时堂宽似宇,簟冷如冰,又有群姬握扇而挥,不复知其为夏,何遽困厄至此!因怀至乐,愈觉心烦,遂致终夕不寐。一亭长露宿阶下,为众蚊所啮,几至露筋,不得已而奔走庭中,俾四体动而弗停,则啮人者无由厕足;乃形则往来仆仆,口则赞叹嚣嚣,一似苦中有乐者。显者不解,呼而讯之,谓:"汝之受困,什伯于我,我以为苦,而汝以为乐,其故维何?"亭长曰:"偶忆某年,为仇家所陷,身系狱中。维时亦当暑月,狱卒防予私逸,每夜拘挛手足,使不得动摇,时蚊蚋之繁,倍于今夕,听其自啮,欲稍稍规避而不能,以视今夕之奔走不息,四体得以自如者,奚啻仙凡人鬼之别乎!以昔较今,是以但见其乐,不知其苦。"显者听之,不觉爽然自失。

---

① 原文节选自李笠翁的《闲情偶寄》。——编者注

The art of being happy though poor consists in one phrase, to think "it could be worse." I am poor and humble but there are people poorer and more humble than myself. I have a big family to support, but there are people living alone and without children, and widows and orphans. I have to work hard on a farm, but there are people without a farm, or who would rather work hard on their farm like me but cannot because they are sitting in jail. It is a way of thinking, or of looking at it. The same situation may look like hell to one and like paradise to another. On the other hand, always to want to compare oneself with one's betters will breed a state of mind conducive only to one's own misery.

I remember the story of a high official who was traveling abroad. It was summer and his bed was full of mosquitoes inside the net. He thought of his own spacious hall at home, where the summer mat was cooling to the body and many maids would attend to his comforts. The more he thought, the more miserable he felt. He was not able to sleep a wink. Then he saw a man walking about in the court of the inn, seemingly quite happy with himself. He was puzzled and inquired how he seemed to be so happy with the mosquitoes around and was not bothered at all. The man replied, "I once had an enemy and was put in jail. It was summer and the jail was full of vermin. But my hands and feet were tied to prevent me from escape. It was terrible to be bitten by insects and mosquitoes and not be able to do anything about it. There are mosquitoes now. But I move about and they can't touch me. In fact, it makes me happy to feel just the freedom of the limbs alone." The man saw one side of it and the other man saw the other side. The rich man felt quite lost when he heard the story.

二十五

随时即景就事行乐之法
The Arts of Sleeping,
Walking, Sitting and Standing^①

李笠翁（Li Liweng）

行乐之事多端，未可执一而论。如睡有睡之乐，坐有坐之乐，行有行之乐，立有立之乐，饮食有饮食之乐，盥栉有盥栉之乐，即祖裼裸裎、如厕便溺，种种秽亵之事，处之得宜，亦各有其乐。苟能见景生情，逢场作戏，即可悲可涕之事，亦变欢娱。如其应事寡才，养生无术，即征歌选舞之场，亦生悲戚。兹以家常受用，起居安乐之事，因便制宜，各存其说于左。

睡

有专言法术之人，遍授养生之诀，欲予北面事之。予讯益寿之功，何物称最？颐生之地，谁处居多？如其不谋而合，则奉为师，不则友之可耳。

其人曰："益寿之方，全凭导引；安生之计，惟赖坐功。"予曰："若是，则汝法最苦，惟修苦行者能之。予懒而好动，且事事求乐，未可以语此也。"其人曰："然则汝意云何？试言之，不妨互为印证。"予曰："天地生人以时，动之者半，息之者半。动则旦，而息则暮也。苟劳之以日，而不息之以夜，则旦旦而伐之，其死也，可立而待矣。吾人养生亦以时，扰之以半，静之以半，扰则行起坐立，而静则睡也。如其劳我以经营，而不逸我以寝处，则岌岌乎殆哉！其年也，不堪指屈矣。若是，则养生之诀，当以善睡居先。睡能还精,睡能养气,睡能健脾益胃,睡能坚骨壮筋。如其不信,试以无疾之人与有疾之人,合而验之。人本无疾,而劳之以夜,使累夕不得安眠,则眼眶渐落而精气日颓,虽未即病,而病之情形出矣。患疾之人,久而不寐,则病势日增;偶一沉酣,则其醒也,必有油然勃然之势。是睡,非睡也,药也;非疗一疾之药,及治百病,救万民,无试不验之神药也。兹欲从事导引,并力坐功,势必先遣睡魔,使无倦态而后可。予忍弃生平最效之药,而试未必果验之方哉?"其人艴然而去,以予不足教也。予诚不足教哉!但自陈所得,实为有见而然,与强辩饰非者稍别。前人睡诗云:"花竹幽窗午梦长,此中与世暂相忘。华山处士如容见,不觅仙方觅睡方。"近人睡诀云:"先睡心,后睡眼。"此皆书本唾余,请置弗道,道其未经发明者而已。睡有睡之时,睡有睡之地,睡又有可睡可不睡之人。请条晰言之。由戌至卯,睡之时也。未戌而睡,谓之先时,先时者不详,谓与疾作思卧者无异也。过卯而睡,谓之后时,后时者犯忌,谓与长夜不醒者无异也。且人生百年,夜居其半,穷日行乐,犹苦不多,况以睡梦之有余,而损宴游之不足乎?有一名士善睡,起必过午,先时而访,未有能晤之者。予每过其居,必俟良久而后见。一日闷坐无聊,笔墨具在,乃取旧诗一首,更易数字而嘲之曰:"吾在此静睡,起来常过午;便活七十年,止当三十五。"同人见之,无不绝倒。此虽谑浪,颇关至理。是当睡之时,止有黑夜,舍此皆非其候矣。然而午睡之乐,倍于黄昏,三时皆所不宜,而独宜于长夏。非私之也,长夏之一日,可抵残冬之二日;长夏之一夜,不敌残冬之半夜。使止息于夜,而不息于昼,是以一分之逸,敌四分之劳,精力几何,其能堪此?况暑气铄金,当之未有不倦者。倦极而眠,犹饥之得食,渴之得饮,养生之计,未有善于此者。午餐之后,略逾寸晷,俟所食既消,而后徘徊近榻。又勿有心觅睡,觅睡得睡,其为睡也不甜。必先处于有事,事未毕而忽倦,睡乡之民自来招我。桃源、天台诸妙境,原非有意造之,皆莫知其然而然者。予最爱旧诗中,有"手倦抛书午梦长"一句。手书而眠,意不在睡;抛书而寝,则又意不在书,所谓莫知其然而然也。睡中三昧,惟此得之。此论睡之时也。睡又必先择地。地之善者有二:曰静,曰凉。不静之地,止能睡目不能睡耳,耳目两岐,岂安身之善策乎?不凉之地,止能睡魂不能睡身,身魂不附,乃养生之至忌也。至于可睡可不睡之人,则分别于"忙闲"二字。就常理而论之,则忙人宜睡,闲人可以不必睡。然使忙人假寐,止能睡眼不能睡心,心不睡而眼睡,犹之未尝睡也。其最不受用者,在将觉未觉之一时,忽然想起某事未行,某人未见,皆万万不可已者,睡此一觉,未免失事妨时,想到此处,便觉魂趋梦绕,胆怯心惊,较之未睡之前,更加烦躁,此忙人之不宜睡也。闲则眼未阖而心先阖,心已开而眼未开;已睡较未睡为乐,已醒较未醒更乐,此闲人之宜睡也。然天地之间,能有几个闲人?必欲闲而始睡,是无可睡之时矣。有暂逸其心以妥梦魂之法:凡一日之中,急切当行之事,俱当于上半日告竣,有未竣者,则分遣家人代之,使事事皆有着落,然后寻床觅枕以赴黑甜,则与闲人无别矣。此言可睡之人也。而尤有吃紧一关未经道破者,则在莫行歹事。"半夜敲门不吃惊",始可于日间睡觉,不则一闻剥啄,即是逻倅到门矣。

行

贵人之出,必乘车马。逸则逸矣,然于造物赋形之义,略欠周全。有足而不用,与无足等耳,反不若安步当车之人,五官四体皆能适用。此贫士骄人语。乘车策马,曳履拖裳,一般同是行人,止有动静之别。使乘车策马之人,能以步趋为乐,或经山水之胜,或逢花柳之妍,或遇戴笠之贫交,或见负薪之高士,欣然止驭,徒步为欢,有时安车而待步,有时安步以当车,其能用足也,又胜贫士一筹矣。至于贫士骄人,不在有足能行,而在缓急出门之可恃。事属可缓,则以安步当车;如其急也,则以疾行当马。有人亦出,无人亦出;结伴可行,无伴亦可行。不似富贵者假足于人,人或不来,则我不能即出,此则有足若无,大悖谬于造物赋形之义耳。兴言及此,行殊可乐!

坐

从来善养生者,莫过于孔子。何以知之?知之于"寝不尸,居不容"二语。使其好饰观瞻,务修边幅,时时求肖君子,处处欲为圣人,则其寝也,居也,不求尸而自尸,不求容而自容;则五官四体,不复有舒展之刻。岂有泥塑木雕其形,而能久长于世者哉?"不尸"、"不容"四字,绘出一幅时哉圣人,宜乎崇祀千秋,而为风雅斯文之鼻祖也。吾人燕居坐法,当以孔子为师,勿务端庄而必正襟危坐,勿同束缚而为胶柱难移。抱膝长吟,虽坐也,而不妨同于箕踞;支颐丧我,行乐也,而何必名为坐忘?但见面与身齐,久而不动者,其人必死。此图画真容之先兆也。

立

立分久暂,暂可无依,久当思傍。亭亭独立之事,但可偶一为之,旦旦如是,则筋骨皆悬而脚跟如砥,有血脉胶凝之患矣。或倚长松,或凭怪石,或靠危栏作轼,或扶瘦竹为筇;既作羲皇上人,又作画图中物,何乐如之!但不可以美人作柱,虑其础石太纤,而致栋梁皆仆也。

There are many ways of enjoying life that are hard to hold down to any one theory. There are the joys of sleeping, of sitting, of walking, and of standing up. There is the pleasure in eating, washing up, hairdressing, and even in such lowly activities as going about naked and barefooted, or going to the toilet. In its proper place, each can be enjoyable. If one can enter into the spirit of fun and take things in his stride anywhere any time, one can enjoy some things over which others may weep. On the other hand, if one is a crude person and awkward in meeting life or taking care of one's health, he can be the saddest person amidst song and dance. I speak here only of the joys of daily living and of the ways in which advantage may be taken of the commonest occupations.

The Art of Sleeping

There was a yogi who traveled about, teaching the secrets of conservation of life force and of prolonging life, and he wanted to teach me. I asked him what he could do to attain longevity and where such blessings were to be found. I thought it would be fine if his methods agreed with my way of thinking, and if not, I could at least befriend him.

This man told me that the secret of longevity lay in controlled breathing, and peace of mind was to be sought through séance. I said to him, "Your ways are hard and forced, and only people like you can practice it. I am lazy and like motion. I seek joy in everything. I am afraid it is not for me."

"What is your way then?" he asked. "I should like to hear it and we can compare notes."

And this is what I said to him:

In the natural scheme of things, it is meant for man to spend half his time in activity and half at rest. In the day, he sits, moves, or stands, and at night he rests. If a man labors by day and does not rest by night and continues this day after day, you can get ready and wait for his funeral to pass by. I try to keep my health by dividing half my time in rest and half my time in activity. If something troubles me and prevents me from sleep, there's the danger signal. I should count my remaining years on my fingers!

In other words, the secret of good health lies in a good and restful sleep. One who sleeps well restores his energy, revitalizes his inner system, and tones up his muscles. Compare a sick man with a healthy person. A man who is not permitted to rest will get sick; his eyes become sunken, and all kinds of symptoms appear. A sick man becomes worse without sleep. But after a good sleep, he wakes up full of eagerness for life again. Is not sleep the infallible miracle drug, not just a cure for an illness but for a hundred, a cure that saves a thousand lives? To seek health by controlled breathing and the hard exercises of yoga would only involve great concentration and effort to keep awake instead! Would I throw away the best medicine in the world for an untested formula?

The man left in anger and I did not argue with him.

An ancient poem goes, "After a long, sound sleep in bamboo-shaded quiet, I feel so far removed from the day's turmoil. If the hermit of Huashan comes to visit me, I shall not ask for the secret of becoming an immortal, but of sleeping well." A modern saying goes, "First rest your mind, then rest your eyes."

There is a proper time and a proper place for sleep, and there are certain sleeping habits which should be avoided. To be specific one should rest between 9 p.m. and 8 a.m. To go to bed before nine is too early; it is a bad sign to be craving for sleep like a sick person. To sleep after eight in the morning is bad for health, like all oversleeping. Where would be the time left for other pleasures? I know a friend who never gets up before noon, and anyone visiting him before noon is kept waiting. One day I sat miserably in his parlor waiting, and with ink and brush ready, I playfully parodied an ancient poem and wrote as follows:

I am busying sleeping,
Throughout the whole morn.
If I live to seventy,
Five and thirty are gone.

Although it was one in fun, it is close to the truth. One should only sleep at night as a rule. The pleasure of an afternoon nap is understandable, but it should be reserved only for summer when the day is long and the night is short. It is natural that one tires easily in the heat, and it is as good for a man to sleep when tired as to drink when thirsty. This is common sense. The best time is after lunch. One should wait a while until the food is partly digested and then leisurely stroll toward the couch. Do not tell yourself that you are determined to get a nap. In that way, the mind is tense and the sleep will not be sound. Occupy yourself with something first and before it is finished, you are overcome with a sense of fatigue and the sandman calls. The never-never land cannot be chased down. I love that line in a poem which says, "Dozing off, the book slips out of my hand." Thus sleep comes without his artifice or knowledge. This is the secret of the art of sleeping.

Next, one must consider the place, which should be cool and quiet. If it is not quiet, the eyes rest but not the ears. If it is too hot, the soul rests but not the body, and body and soul are at loggerheads. This goes against the principle of good health.

Lastly, we will consider the sleeper himself. Some people are busy and others have plenty of time. Logically, the man of leisure needs little sleep; it is the busy man who needs it most of all. But often the busy man cannot sleep well. He rests his eyes in sleep but not his mind. In fact, he gets no rest from sleep at all. The worst of it is to think of something during the half-awake hours of the morning and suddenly remember something he hasn't done or someone he hasn't seen. It is very, very important! He must not sleep another wink or something will be spoiled! That very thought drives away all sleep. He becomes tense and gets up more keyed up than before. The man of leisure rests his mind before his eyes are shut, and his mind wakes up refreshed before his eyes are open, happy to slumber and happier to wake up. Such is the sleep of the man of leisure.

Yet in this world how many such men are there? All men cannot lead a life with nothing to do. Therefore a method must be found. It is best to dispose of the urgent business of the day in the morning, and delegate to others those things that are not finished. Then one knows that everything is in order and under control. He can afford to seek the pillow and go for that slumber which is described as the "dark, sweet village." He will then sleep as well as the man of leisure.

Another thing: to enjoy a perfect sleep requires a peaceful conscience. Such a man will not be "frightened when there is a knock on the door at midnight," as the saying goes. He will not mistake the peckings of chickens in the barnyard for policemen's footsteps!

The Art of Walking

The rich man will go out only in a horse and carriage. It may be called a comfort and a luxury, but it can hardly be said that it fulfills the intention of God in giving man a pair of legs. He who does not use his legs is *ipso facto* deprived of the use of his legs. On the other hand, a man who uses his legs is giving exercise to his entire body. That is why an ancient poor scholar① boasted that "a leisurely stroll is as good as a drive." Now to drive or to go on foot are both methods of transportation or locomotion. A man who is used to driving or riding on horseback can learn to enjoy the pleasures of a walk. Perhaps he comes upon a beautiful view or beautiful flowers on the way, or stops to talk with a peasant in his palm hat or meets a recluse philosopher turned woodcutter in the deep mountains. Sometimes one might enjoy a drive, and sometimes a walk. Surely this is better than the obstinacy of

---

① Yen Cho, of the third century B. C. He was a Diogenes who refused gifts of money and power from a king.

that proud scholar of ancient days!

What the poor man can be truly proud of is not the fact that he uses his legs, but that he does not depend on others for going anywhere. If he is not in a hurry, he can go slowly, and if he is, he breaks into a run. He does not have to wait for someone else, and he is not dependent on the carriage, unlike the rich man who is helpless when the driver is not there. The poor man has fulfilled the intentions of God in giving him legs to walk with. It makes me happy just to think of this.

The Art of Sitting

No one knows the art of living better than Confucius. I know this from the statement that he "did not sleep like a corpse [with straight legs] and did not sit like a statue." If the Master had been completely absorbed in keeping decorum, intent on appearing like a gentleman at all hours and being seen as a sage at all times, then he would have had to lie down like a corpse and sit like a statue. His four limbs and his internal system would never have been able to relax. How could such a stiff wooden statue expect to live a long life? Because Confucius did not do this, the statement describes the ease of the Master in his private life, which makes him worthy of worship as the father of all cultured gentlemen. We should follow Confucius's example when at home. Do not sit erect and look severe as if you were chained or glued to the chair. Hug your knee and sing, or sit chin in hand, without honoring it with the phrase of "losing oneself in thought" [as Chuangtse said]. On the other hand, if a person sits stiffly for a long time, head high and chest out, this is a premonition that he is heading for the grave. He is sitting for his memorial portrait!

The Art of Standing

Stand straight, but do not do it for long. Otherwise, all leg muscles will become stiff and circulation will be blocked up. Lean on something! —On an old pine or a quaint rock, or on a balcony or on a bamboo cane. It makes one look like one is in a painting. But do *not* lean on a lady! The foundation is not solid and the roof may come down!

二十六

说　韵
On Charm in Women[1]

李笠翁（Li Liweng）

古云："尤物足以移人。"尤物维何？媚态是已。世人不知，以为美色，乌知颜色虽美，是一物也，乌足移人？加之以态，则物而尤矣。如云美色即是尤物，即可移人，则今时绢做之美女，画上之娇娥，其颜色较之生人，岂止十倍，何以不见移人，而使之害相思成郁病耶？是知"媚态"二字，必不可少。媚态之在人身，犹火之有焰，灯之有光，珠贝金银之有宝色，是无形之物，非有形之物也。惟其是物而非物，无形似有形，是以名为"尤物"。尤物者，怪物也，不可解说之事也。凡女子，一见即令人思，思而不能自己，遂至舍命以图，与生为难者，皆怪物也，皆不可解说之事也。

吾于"态"之一字，服天地生人之巧，鬼神体物之工。使以我作天地鬼神，形体吾能赋之，知识我能予之，至于是物而非物，无形似有形之态度，我实不能变之化之，使其自无而有，复自有而无也。态之为物，不特能使美者愈美，艳者愈艳，且能使老者少而媸者妍，无情之事变为有情，使人暗受笼络而不觉者。女子一有媚态，三四分姿色，便可抵过六七分。试以六七分姿色而无媚态之妇人，与三四分姿色而有媚态之妇人同立一处，则人止爱三四分而不爱六七分，是态度之于颜色，犹不止一倍当两倍也。试以二三分姿色而无媚态之妇人，与全无姿色而止有媚态之妇人同立一处，或

---

① 　原文节选自李笠翁的《闲情偶寄》。——编者注

与人各交数言,则人止为媚态所惑,而不为美色所惑,是态度之于颜色,犹不止于以少敌多,且能以无而敌有也。今之女子,每有状貌姿容一无可取,而能令人思之不倦,甚至舍命相从者,皆"态"之一字之为祟也。是知选貌选姿,总不如选态一着之为要。

态自天生,非可强造。强造之态,不能饰美,止能愈增其陋。同一颦也,出于西施则可爱,出于东施则可憎者,天生、强造之别也。相面、相肌、相眉、相眼之法,皆可言传,独相态一事,则予心能知之,口实不能言之。口之所能言者,物也,非尤物也。噫,能使人知,而能使人欲言不得,其为物也何知!其为事也何知!岂非天地之间一大怪物,而从古及今,一件解说不来之事乎?

诘予者曰:既为态度立言,又不指人以法,终觉首鼠,盍亦舍精言粗,略示相女者以意乎?予曰:不得已而为言,止有直书所见,聊为榜样而已。向在维扬,代一贵人相妾。靓妆而至者不一其人,始皆俯首而立,及命之抬头,一人不作羞容而竟抬;一人娇羞腼腆,强之数四而后抬;一人初不即抬,及强而后可,先以眼光一瞬,似于看人而实非看人,瞬毕复定而后抬,俟人看毕,复以眼光一瞬而后俯,此即"态"也。

记曩时春游遇雨,避一亭中,见无数女子,妍媸不一,皆踉跄而至。中一缟衣贫妇,年三十许,人皆趋入亭中,彼独徘徊檐下,以中无隙地故也;人皆抖擞衣衫,虑其太湿,彼独听其自然,以檐下雨侵,抖之无益,徒现丑态故也。及雨将止而告行,彼独迟疑稍后,去不数武而雨复作,乃趋入亭。彼则先立亭中,以逆料必转,先踞胜地故也。然臆虽偶中,绝无骄人之色。见后人者反立檐下,衣衫之湿,数倍于前,而此妇代为振衣,姿态百出,竟若天集众丑,以形一人之媚者。自观者视之,其初之不动,似以郑重而养态;其后之故动,似以徜徉而生态。然彼岂能必天复雨,先储其才以俟用乎?其养也,出之无心,其生也,亦非有意,皆天机之自起自伏耳。当其养态之时,先有一种娇羞无那之致现于身外,令人生爱生怜,不俟娉婷大露而后觉也。斯二者,皆妇人媚态之一斑,举之以见大较。噫,以年三十许之贫妇,止为姿态稍异,遂使二八佳人与曳珠顶翠者皆出其下,然则态之为用,岂浅鲜哉!

人问:圣贤神化之事,皆可造诣而成,岂妇人媚态独不可学而至乎?予曰:学则可学,教则不能。人又问:既不能教,胡云可学? 予曰:使无态之人与有态者同居,朝夕薰陶,或能为其所化;如蓬生麻中,不扶自直,鹰变成鸠,形为气感,是则可矣。若欲耳提而面命之,则一部《廿一史》,当从何处说起? 还怕愈说愈增其木强,奈何!

There is an ancient saying that "the power of exotic beauty fascinates." Exotic beauty means charm, although it has been commonly misunderstood as referring to "good looks" merely. Good looks, it should be understood, can never move us unless it has charm, and only then does the beauty become fascinating and exotic. People who think that all beauties can fascinate people need only stop to think why all the silk dolls and pictures of women can never move one, although probably their faces are ten times more beautiful than living women. Charm in a person is like the flame in a fire, the light in a lamp, and the luster in jewels. It is something invisible and yet seemingly palpable, something which can be seen and yet has no definite shape or body. That is why charm is always mysterious—why a woman with charm is regarded as being exotic, for to be exotic is to be exciting and mystifying, to be that which people cannot quite understand. There are women who make people fall in love with them at first sight, who once seen are never forgotten, and who make men risk all they have, glory, wealth, and even their own lives, in order to possess them. Such is the strange power of women's fascination, something which is elusive and defies all explanation.

Of all the things that I admire the creator of the universe for, and of all the mysteries of the universe, the charm of personality ranks the greatest. If I were God, I could give my creatures bodily shape and wisdom and knowledge, but I could not give them this something which is invisible and yet seemingly palpable, which exists and yet has no bodily shape, is seen for a moment and disappears again—namely, charm. For charm not only enhances beauty and attraction in women; it can make the old appear young, the ugly beautiful, and the dull become exciting. For silently and secretly it fascinates a man without his being aware of it. A girl who has only a third-grade facial beauty is as fascinating as another one who has better looks, if she has only charm. Take two girls, one who has only ordinary third-grade "looks" but has charm, and the other who has no charm but has better "looks," and put them side by side. People will like the third-grade and not the second-grade beauty. Or again, take a moderately good-looking woman without charm and another who has charm but is totally deficient in good looks and put them together and let people exchange a few words with each of them. People will fall in love with the one who has charm and not with the one who has merely good looks, which goes to prove that charm can substitute for a total absence of good looks. There are today girls who are otherwise common-looking, yet who can fascinate men even to the point of making them risk their lives for them. The secret lies solely in this one word "charm."

Charm is something which comes naturally to a person and directly grows out of her personality. It is not something which can be copied from others, for charm imitated is beauty spoiled. To knit her eyebrows was beautiful in Shishih, because it was natural to her, but would be actually disgusting if Tungshih were to assume the same pose, because she was born differently. It is possible to lay down rules for judging a person's face and skin and eyebrows and eyes by certain standards, but as for this thing called "charm," it is something that is immediately felt, but cannot be analyzed or put into words; for in its elusiveness lies its exciting power and fascination...

I shall give a few examples of what I saw to show my meaning. I was once in Yangchow, trying to pick a concubine for a certain official. There were rows of women in beautiful dresses and of different types. At first they stood all with their heads bent, but when they were ordered to hold their heads up, one of them just raised her head and stared blandly at me, and another was terribly shy and would not hold her head up until she had been bidden to do so several times. There was one, however, who would not look up at first but did so after some persuasion, and then she first cast a quick glance as if she was looking and yet not looking at me before she held her head up, and again she cast another glance before she bent her head again. This is what I call charm.

I also remember that on a certain spring day, a number of people including myself were taking shelter in a pavilion to avoid a spring shower. Many girls and women, both ugly and beautiful ones, made a dash for the place. There was one woman in a white dress, however, about thirty years old, who stood by under the eaves outside the pavilion, seeing that there was no more room inside. The other women were all shaking their dresses, but there she stood, calm and poised under the eaves, without bothering to do so, because she knew that, exposed as she was, to shake her dress would only make her looking ridiculous. Then the shower stopped and people rushed out only to rush back again when the shower came again. They found her quietly standing inside the pavilion, for she had anticipated it. She did not show an air of self-satisfaction; on the other hand, when she saw the other women standing outside with their dresses all wet, she did her best to wipe the water off their shoulders and sleeves, revealing then her infinite charm of movement as if God had ordained this crowd of ugly women to come there with their fussiness in order to show off her beauty to greater advantage. As an observer, I saw it as perfect; in the beginning she showed her charm by her poise when she was standing outside, and then she showed her charm in movement when she was helping the others. But the whole thing came naturally, for she could not have planned it. Her former poise and charm were just as natural as her subsequent activity. She had revealed this inner charm already when she was standing outside the pavilion, quiet and reserved and just natural self, a charm which was just as effective and suitable to the circumstances of the time as her later movements and activity...

Some readers may ask: Is it true that charm can never be taught, for we say that one can even learn to be a saint or sage? I can only say in reply that charm can be learned, but cannot be taught. If it again be asked: Why can't it be taught if it can be learned? My reply is that people without charm can learn it by living together with people who have it. They will acquire it by daily example and contagion, like reeds learning to grow straight in a field of hemp. It comes gradually and naturally by a kind of invisible influence. To lay down so many rules for acquiring charm would be futile and indeed only make confusion worse confounded.

二十七

秋声诗自序
Sound Mimicry
Preface to *Autumn Sounds* (*A Collection of Poems*)①

林嗣环（Lin Tsehuan）

彻呆子当正秋之日,杜门简出,毡有针,壁有衷甲,苦无可排解者。然每听谣诼之来,则濡墨吮笔而为诗,诗成,以"秋声"名篇。

适有数客至,不问何人,留共醉,酒酣,令客各举似何声最佳。一客曰:"机声,儿子读书声佳耳。"予曰:"何言之庄也?"又一客曰:"堂下呵驺声,堂后笙歌声何如?"予曰:"何言之华也?"又一客曰:"姑妇楸枰声最佳。"曰:"何言之玄也?"一客独嘿嘿,乃取大杯满酌而前曰:"先生喜闻人所未闻,仆请数言为先生抚掌,可乎? 京中有善口技者。会宾客大宴,于厅事之东北角,施八尺屏障,口技人坐屏障中,一桌、一椅、一扇、一抚尺而已。众宾团坐。少顷,但闻屏障中抚尺二下,满堂寂然,无敢哗者。遥遥闻深巷犬吠声,便有妇人惊觉欠伸,摇其夫语猥亵事。夫呓语,初不甚应,妇摇之不止,则二人语渐间杂,床又从中戛戛。既而儿醒,大啼。夫令妇抚儿乳,儿含乳啼,妇拍而呜之。夫起溺,妇亦抱儿起溺。床上又一大儿醒,猬猬不止。当是时,妇手拍儿声,口中呜声,儿含乳啼声,大儿初醒声,床声,夫叱大儿声,溺瓶中声,溺桶中声,一齐凑发,众妙毕备。满座宾客无不伸颈侧目,微笑默叹,以为妙绝也。既而夫上床寝,妇又呼大儿溺,

---

① 本文也常被称为《口技》。——编者注

毕,都上床寝。小儿亦渐欲睡,夫齁声起,妇拍儿亦渐拍渐止。微闻有鼠
作作索索,盆器倾侧,妇梦中咳嗽之声。宾客意少舒,稍稍正坐。忽一人
大呼:'火起!'夫起大呼,妇亦起大呼。两儿齐哭。俄而百千人大呼,百千
儿哭,百千狗吠。中间力拉崩倒之声,火爆声,呼呼风声,百千齐作;又夹
百千求救声,曳屋许许声,抢夺声,泼水声。凡所应有,无所不有。虽人有
百手,手有百指,不能指其一端;人有百口,口有百舌,不能名其一处也。
于是宾客无不变色离席,奋袖出臂,两股战战,几欲先走。而忽然抚尺一
下,群响毕绝。撤屏视之,一人、一桌、一椅、一扇、一抚尺而已。"

嘻! 若而人者,可谓善画声矣。遂录其语,以为秋声序。

During the autumn days, Che Aitzu [Lin Tsehuan] used to lock himself up indoors, and often he felt restless and did not know what to do. But whenever he heard of gossip and anecdotes, he dipped his pen in ink and wrote some poems. When these poems were collected together, he called them "autumn sounds." One day several of his friends dropped in to see him, and he asked them to stay and have a drink. He asked his guests to say what sounds they liked best respectively. "The sounds of the loom and the spinning wheel and of children reciting their lessons," said one of them. "What a good father!" said I. "The sounds of scolding footmen outside and of music and singing in the inner court," said another. "So you are given to luxuries," I commented. "The sounds of mother-in-law and daughter-in-law playing chess," said a third. "How romantic!" A friend who had remained hitherto silent, advanced with a large cup filled with wine and said:

"May I tell you something you never heard of before? There is a great imitator of sounds in the capital. On festive days, he sets up a screen eight feet high in the northeastern corner of the hall, and sits behind the screen with nothing except a table, a chair, a fan, and a sounding board. The guests sit around. By and by from behind the screen are heard two taps with the sounding board, which is the signal for silence. At first, they hear a dog barking far away in some alleyway. Then a woman wakes up and yawns; she tries to wake up her husband and says lewd things to him. The husband at first makes no reply but mumbles in his sleep. The woman keeps on jerking him, when the conversation between the two becomes clearer and clearer, and there is a creaking of the bed. Then the baby wakes up. The husband asks the woman to feed the baby, and while the baby is sucking and crying, the woman pats the baby and coos it to silence. Meanwhile, the husband has got up and is clearing himself, while the mother is also trying to make the baby urinate. This, however, wakes up the older child, who begins to cry vociferously. There is then started an immense confusion of sounds—of the woman patting the baby with her hand and cooing, the baby crying and sucking, the older child just waking up, the bed creaking, the husband scolding the older child, and the sounds of discharge in the night pot and the wooden pail. While the guests listen amazed with outstretched necks at this medley of realistic sounds, they hear the husband going to bed again. The wife then asks the older child to get up and clear himself also, and when this is done, they all get ready to go to sleep again. The baby is falling asleep. The husband begins to snore, and the rhythm of the wife patting her baby becomes slower and slower until it stops entirely. Then they hear a mouse going about the room and overturning things on the floor, while the woman coughs in her sleep. While the listeners begin to sit back and take it more easily, they suddenly hear a loud cry, 'Fire! Fire!' The husband gets up and shouts, the wife screams, and both children begin to cry. Very soon it seems there are hundreds of people shouting, hundreds of children crying, and hundreds of dogs barking, while through and above all this are heard the sounds of structures falling, fire cracking, wind blowing, water pouring, and men struggling and crying for help in a general pandemonium. The sounds are so real that the listeners' faces turn, their knees shake, and they almost take to their heels. But all of a sudden, a tap is heard and all sounds cease. When the screen is taken away, they see nothing but a table, a chair, a fan, and a sounding board."

Indeed here is a great painter of sounds. I set down my friend's words and let this serve as the preface to the *Autumn Sounds*.

二十八

大明湖说书
Beautiful Singing[①]

刘　鹗（Liu Ao）

"不是。这人叫黑妞，是白妞的妹子。他的调门儿都是白妞教的，若比白妞，还不晓得差多远呢！他的好处人说得出，白妞的好处人说不出；他的好处人学的到，白妞的好处人学不到。你想，这几年来，好顽耍的谁不学他们的调儿呢？就是窑子里的姑娘，也人人都学，只是顶多有一两句到黑妞的地步。若白妞的好处，从没有一个人能及他十分里的一分的。"说着的时候，黑妞早唱完，后面去了。

这时满园子里的人，谈心的谈心，说笑的说笑。卖瓜子、落花生、山里红、核桃仁的，高声喊叫着卖，满园子里听来都是人声。正在热闹哄哄的时节，只见那后台里，又出来了一位姑娘，年纪约十八九岁，装束与前一个毫无分别，瓜子脸儿，白净面皮，相貌不过中人以上之姿，只觉得秀而不媚，清而不寒，半低着头出来，立在半桌后面，把梨花简丁当了几声，煞是奇怪：只是两片顽铁，到他手里，便有了五音十二律以的。又将鼓捶子轻轻的点了两下，方抬起头来，向台下一盼。那双眼睛，如秋水，如寒星，如宝珠，如白水银里头养着两丸黑水银，左右一顾一看，连那坐在远远墙角子里的人，都觉得王小玉看见我了；那坐得近的，更不必说。就这一眼，满园了里便鸦雀无声，比皇帝出来还要静悄得多呢，连一根针吊在地下都听

得见响!

王小玉便启朱唇,发皓齿,唱了几句书儿。声音初不甚大,只觉入耳有说不出来的妙境:五脏六腑里,像熨斗熨过,无一处不伏贴;三万六千个毛孔,像吃了人参果,无一个毛孔不畅快。唱了十数句之后,渐渐的越唱越高,忽然拔了一个尖儿,像一线钢丝抛入天际,不禁暗暗叫绝。那知他于那极高的地方,尚能回环转折。几啭之后,又高一层,接连有三四叠,节节高起。恍如由傲来峰西面攀登泰山的景象:初看傲来峰削壁干仞,以为上与天通;及至翻到傲来峰顶,才见扇子崖更在傲来峰上;及至翻到扇子崖,又见南天门更在扇子崖上:愈翻愈险,愈险愈奇。那王小玉唱到极高的三四叠后,陡然一落,又极力骋其千回百折的精神,如一条飞蛇在黄山三十六峰半中腰里盘旋穿插,顷刻之间,周匝数遍。从此以后,愈唱愈低,愈低愈细,那声音渐渐的就听不见了。满园子的人都屏气凝神,不敢少动。约有两三分钟之久,仿佛有一点声音从地底下发出。这一出之后,忽又扬起,像放那东洋烟火,一个弹子上天,随化作千百道五色火光,纵横散乱。这一声飞起,即有无限声音俱来并发。那弹弦子的亦全用轮指,忽大忽小,同他那声音相和相合,有如花坞春晓,好鸟乱鸣。耳朵忙不过来,不晓得听那一声的为是。正在撩乱之际,忽听霍然一声,人弦俱寂。这时台下叫好之声,轰然雷动。

停了一会,闹声稍定,只听那台下正座上,有一个少年人,不到三十岁光景,是湖南口音,说道:"当年读书,见古人形容歌声的好处,有那'余音绕梁,三日不绝'的话,我总不懂。空中设想,余音怎样会得绕梁呢?又怎会三日不绝呢?及至听了小玉先生说书,才知古人措辞之妙。每次听他说书之后,总有好几天耳朵里无非都是他的书,无论做什么事,总不入神,反觉得'三日不绝',这'三日'二字下得太少,还是孔子'三月不知肉味','三月'二字形容得透彻些!"

"No, this one is Dark Maid, Fair Maid's younger sister. She learned all her singing from Fair Maid... One can admire Dark Maid's singing and say why, but Fair Maid's singing just sweeps you along.

Dark Maid's art can be imitated, but Fair Maid's art cannot. For some years, people have been trying to learn her style, including the singsong girls; one could reach the level of Dark Maid at best, but no one could come anywhere near Fair Maid." Meanwhile, Dark Maid had disappeared behind the stage.

At this time, the garden was full of people, talking and chatting amid the cries of vendors of melon seeds, peanuts, wild plums, and walnuts. While the garden was filled with all this din of human noise, there appeared on the stage a maid of eighteen or nineteen, dressed just like her sister. She had a small, oval face, fair in complexion, slightly better-looking than the average, and there was an air of pleasant refinement without cold dignity. With a slightly bent head, she came forward and stood behind the table, and gave a light shake to her sounding boards used for keeping rhythm. Strange to say, in her hands, these two stupid metal pieces seemed to be filled with a strange, rich rhythm. She then tapped the drum lightly, and looked up at her audience. The light of her eyes was like that of an autumn lake, and had the cold splendor of a midnight star. As she turned them about, everyone in the audience, including those sitting in the remote corners, thought she was looking at him. That look of hers alone laid a spell on those present. The hall became as quiet as if the emperor had appeared. You could hear a pin drop to the floor.

Little Jade opened her red lips, showing her white teeth, and began leisurely a few bars. At first, it was quiet and low, making the audience feel that there was something extremely satisfying about it. It was as if all their bowels had been ironed over with a warm iron and set at ease, or as if they had just eaten *ginseng*, so that every single one of the 36,000 pores on their body was glowing with joy. After a dozen lines, the pitch gradually rose higher and higher, until all of a sudden it shot high up like a steel wire reaching a height that made everyone aghast with amazement. Who would think that after lingering there for a second with a few turns and flourishes, it would go higher, and holding it suspended for a moment with a few turns, again higher she would soar, and this would go on three or four times until she was caroling in the clouds? It was like a man climbing the Taishan Mountains: when he started out, he thought that rocky Aolai Peak was in cloudy regions, and when he had reached Aolai Peak, he began to see the Fan Rocks, and when he had reached the latter, the vision of Nantienmen opened up before his eyes. The higher he went, the stranger and more awesome the view became. When Little Jade had reached the top, suddenly she let it go and took a swoop downward, and it was like a flying eagle winding its way from the heavens down the thirty-six peaks of Huangshan. Backward and forward she carried her song, until gradually it sank lower and lower, reaching the depth of inaudibility. In that spell of quiet, everyone held his breath. After a moment, a voice rose as if from underground, and this time, it clamored forth straight up and broke out into an orgy of sounds, like detonating fireworks that shot into the sky and spread out into lines of fire of different colors. And in its ascent, it was met by a symphony of other sounds, and the *pipa* players began to use all fingers in quick succession, the noise of the accompaniment waxing and waning in perfect harmony with the singer's voice. It was as if we were transported to a garden of spring flowers and caroling birds, filling the air with swift, changing, competing melodies. All of a sudden, the singing and the instrumental music stopped, followed by a thundering applause from the audience.

When the din of applause had died down, a young man of about thirty in the audience said with a Hunan accent: "I used to read an ancient book, saying that 'the melodies remain in the air for three days,' and found it difficult to understand. Now I begin to understand. After listening to Little Jade's singing, my ears hear nothing but her haunting melodies for days, whatever I do and wherever I go. When Confucius said that music made him 'forget the taste of meat for three months,' it must have been something like this..."

二十九

小港渡者
The Ferryman's Wisdom

周　容（Chou Yung）

庚寅冬，予自小港欲入蛟川城，命小奚以木简束书从。时西日沉山，晚烟萦树，望城二里许，因问渡者："尚可得南门开否？"渡者熟视小奚，应曰："徐行之，尚开也；速进，则阖。"予愠为戏。趋行及半，小奚仆，束断书崩，啼，未即起。理书就束，而前门已牡下矣。予爽然思渡者言近道。

In the winter of 1650, I was going into the city of Chiaochuan from the Little Harbor, accompanied by a boy carrying a big load of books, tied with a cord and strengthened with a few pieces of board.

It was toward sunset and the country was covered with haze. We were about a mile from the city.

"Will we be in time to get into the city before the gates are closed?" I asked the ferryman.

"You will if you go slowly. But if you run, you will miss it," replied the ferryman, casting a look at the boy.

But we walked as fast as possible. About halfway, the boy fell down. The cord broke and the books fell on the ground. The boy sat crying. By the time we had retied the package and reached the city gate, it was already closed.

I thought of the ferryman. He had wisdom.

三十

自立说
A Thought on Immortality

张士元（Chang Shihyuan）

凡物莫不有死。草木鸟兽昆虫，有朝生而暮死者，有春夏生而秋冬死者，有十年百年千年而死者。虽有迟速，相去曾几何时？

惟人亦然。方其生时，劳之以所为，淫之以所好，汩之以所思，其经营不已，若无复有尽期者。及其气散而死，则髐然不能肉其白骨，与草木鸟兽昆虫之变灭何异乎？

君子知之，故不以形体之有无为生死，而以志气之消长为生死。吾今日形体无恙，而志气已竭，斯为死矣；吾志气配乎道义，发乎文章，且与天地同流，而奚有于形体乎？

故简策所载古圣贤人虽死已久矣，而其辉光如日星之烂然，盖其人至今存也。然则死而不死，亦在人之自为之而已。虽然，自古及今，生人皆死；而其不死者，乃天下一人，千百年一人也。士宜何如自立哉！

All living things in this universe die. Among the plants, birds, beasts, and insects, some are born in the morning and die at eve, some have a life span of a year, and some last ten, or hundred or a thousand years. But they all die. The difference is merely one of length of time.

The same is true of man. When he is living, he labors and occupies himself with something and worries and plans as if he were going to live forever. But when his spirit is dispersed and he dies, he cannot even grow enough flesh to cover his white bones. Death comes to him exactly as it comes to the plants and birds and beasts and insects.

A gentleman is aware of this fact. He therefore does not regard life and death as depending upon the existence or nonexistence of bodily form, but rather upon the growth or decay of his spirit of life. When a man is perfectly well in his body but his vital spirit is gone, he may well be regarded as dead. If, however, one's life spirit is developed to find expression in principles of truth and justice or in literature, it becomes then a part of the great stream of life of this universe. He is then freed from this dependence on a material body.

We find in the classics and history the ancient wise men who died long ago but whose light shines through the ages like the stars and the sun. I may truly say that these men are still living with us. Therefore, whether man is mortal or immortal depends entirely upon the man himself. However, all men die and few there are indeed who have become immortal. A scholar should make up his mind and rely on himself.

三十一

九喜榻记
The Nine-blessings Couch

丁雄飞（Ting Shiungfei）

年来息交绝游，一味静坐，觉广厦俱属长物，得一方床结跏趺，足矣。一日过友人斋，一榻坚好，抚而爱之。友人爰举以赠，大慰夙怀，移置心太平庵中。檀香一线，素帷下垂，湛然深广，身世两忘。因念前哲来瞿塘先生，长年学道，万念尽捐，每一入枕，甜寝自如，有九喜焉，因以名榻。予今日亦次予之喜于榻左。一喜多藏书；二喜闺人习笔墨；三喜不能饮；四喜不解奕；五喜为世所弃；六喜得名师；七喜携眷属居山水间；八喜无病；九喜年未五十，家务尽付儿子，翛然世外。百年之内，前有来先生，后有不肖，俱于榻结欢喜缘，榻于是乎传矣。先生之所谓喜，亦附于末：一喜生中华；二喜丁太平；三喜为儒闻道；四喜父母兄俱寿考；五喜婚嫁早毕；六喜无妾；七喜寿已逾六十花甲之外；八喜赋性简淡宽缓；九喜无恶疾。

Since my retirement last year, I have stopped all social activities and am doing a great deal of sitting quietly by myself. I have thought that what I really need is a good couch on which to take up my sitting with crossed legs like a Buddhist monk, all else being unnecessary luxury. One day I saw a good, firm couch in the place of one of my friends and loved it. My friend forthwith gave it to me as a present. I was delighted with it and had it put in the center of Peaceful Mind Hall. With a coil of burning incense, and letting the curtains down, I feel it is so spacious and comfortable that I seem to have left the world far behind me. I thought of Mr. Lai Chutang, generations ago, who after long years of study of Taoism had been able to dismiss all worries from his mind. With such a peaceful mind he always had a perfect sleep, and he counted his blessings, which were nine in number, and called his bed by that name. Today I have counted my blessings, too, while resting in bed. They are as follows: I am happy that (1) I have a good collection of books; (2) that I have a wife who loves reading and writing; (3) that I cannot drink; (4) that I do not understand chess; (5) that nobody wants me; (6) that I have found a famous master; (7) that I am able to live with my family in such beautiful surroundings; (8) that I am free from sickness; and (9) that though I am still under fifty, I am able to delegate all matters to my sons and live like a free bird. Thus I am able to take after the example of Mr. Lai, who lived less than a hundred years ago, and both of us have found our happiness in a couch. This couch shall go down to posterity as "the Nine-blessings Couch."

I note also here that what Mr. Lai called his nine blessings were the following: (1) that he was born in China; (2) that he lived in times of peace; (3) that as a Confucianist he came to hear the teachings of Tao; (4) that both his parents and his elder brother lived a long life; (5) that his children's marriages were early arranged and completed; (6) that he had no concubine; (7) that he had already reached beyond the age of sixty; (8) that he was born of a mild, easygoing disposition; and (9) that he suffered from no ugly disease.

三十二

淮安舟中寄舍弟墨
To Brother Mo, Written on a Boat at Huaian[①]

郑板桥（Cheng Panchiao）

以人为可爱，而我亦可爱矣；以人为可恶，而我亦可恶矣。东坡一生觉得世上没有不好的人，最是他好处。愚兄平生谩骂无礼，然人有一才一技之长，一行一言之美，未尝不啧啧称道。囊中数千金，随手散尽，爱人故也。至于缺厄敧危之处，亦往往得人之力。好骂人，尤好骂秀才。细细想来，秀才受病，只是推廓不开，他若推廓得开，又不是秀才了。且专骂秀才，亦是冤屈。而今世上那个是推廓得开的？年老身孤，当慎口过。爱人是好处，骂人是不好处。东坡以此受病，况板桥乎！老弟亦当时时劝我。

If one loves other people, he himself becomes worthy of love; if one hates other people, he himself deserves hatred. The best point about (Su) Tungpo is that he felt all his life that there was no bad man in this world. I, your foolish elder brother, have all my life criticized people without mincing words, but whenever someone has one good point or special ability, or said one good word or done one good deed, I have never failed to praise it with all my heart. It is because I love people that whenever I have several thousand dollars, I must use it all. And when I am in need of help, other people have often helped me. I

---

① 原文出自郑板桥的《板桥家书》。——编者注

always love criticizing people, particularly the government graduates. But, come to think about it, the trouble with the graduates is that they are so bound up with themselves. On the other hand, if they were not so bound up with themselves, they wouldn't be graduates. But I think it is unfair to criticize the graduates alone—who nowadays are not bound up with themselves? I am an old man now and living alone. I must watch out for this habit of mine. It is good to love people, and a bad habit to criticize people. Su Tungpo suffered on account of this habit. ①
And certainly a person like myself should be more careful than he. You must also often remind me of this point, old brother.

---

① He was exiled to a southern district because he could not help making fun of Wang Anshih who was in power.

三十三

潍县寄舍弟墨第四书
Fourth Letter to Brother Mo from Weihsien

郑板桥（Cheng Panchiao）

凡人读书,原拿不定发达。然即不发达要不可以不读书,主意便拿定也。科名不来,学问在我,原不是折本的买卖。愚兄而今已发达矣,人亦共称愚兄为善读书矣,究竟自问胸中担得出几卷书来? 不过挪移借贷,改窜添补,便尔钓名欺世。人有负于书耳,书亦何负于人哉!

昔有人问沈近思侍郎如何是救贫的良法,沈曰:读书。其人以为迂阔,其实不迂阔也。东投西窜,费时失业,徒丧其品,而卒归于无济,何如优游书史中,不求获而得力在眉睫间乎! 信此言,则富贵,不信,则贫贱,亦在人之有识与有决并有忍耳。

When a man goes to school, he cannot be certain that he will become an official. But whether he becomes an official or not, he should not forget the true object of study. If one fails in the examinations, the knowledge gained still remains his own and it should not be regarded as a losing investment. I, for instance, have become successful and am reputed to have a good knowledge of books. But when I ask myself, I cannot say how many books I have really absorbed into my heart. All we do usually is to borrow from one book and adapt from others, thus gaining a reputation by cheating. The scholars owe a debt to the books, while the books owe nothing to them.

Formerly someone asked Shen Chinsze what to do to avoid poverty, and his reply was to read books. The man thought Shen's advice was impractical, but it is practical. A man loses his character by rushing about and attending to worthless affairs and in the end gains nothing. It would be better for him to wander about in the land of books and history, without any object of seeking benefit, but suddenly coming upon some truth before his very eyes. Who believes in this advice will become successful and who does not will remain poor. It all depends on whether one has the wit to realize it and whether he has persistence.

气韵与形似·集古
Rhythmic Vitality and Verisimilitude

六法者何？一、气韵生动是也；二、骨法用笔是也；三、应物象形是也；四、随类赋彩是也；五、经营位置是也；六、传移模写是也。

——谢赫《古画品录》

What are the six laws of painting? They are：（1）rhythmic vitality, （2）skeletal pattern and basic strokes, （3）verisimilitude, or likeness to objects, （4）details belonging to particular objects, （5）composition, and （6）copying models and spontaneous variations.

—Shieh Ho (c. 479—501) in *Ku Huapin Lu*

论画以形似，见与儿童邻。

——苏东坡《书鄢陵王主簿所画折枝》

Those who judge paintings by fidelity to objects speak on the mental level of a child.

—Su Tungpo (1037—1101) in a poem

古之画，或能移其形似而尚其骨气，以形似之外求其画，此难可与俗人道也。今之画纵得形似而气韵不生，以气韵求其画，则形似在其间矣。

——张彦远《历代名画记》

Some ancient painters might be lacking in accuracy of form, but they had the bones and spirit. One has to judge such paintings apart from accuracy of form. This is something difficult to explain to the uncultivated. On the other hand, some modern paintings have accuracy of form, but no rhythmic vitality. The proper approach is through aiming at rhythmic vitality which governs factual resemblance.

—Chang Yenyuan (c. 860—890) in *Litai Shuhua Chi* ①

今人或寥寥数笔，自矜高简；或重床迭屋，一味颟顸。动曰不求形似，岂知古人所云不求形似者，不似之似也，彼繁简失宜者乌可同年语哉。

——王绂《书画传习录》

Many modern painters draw a few simple lines, or else let themselves go unashamedly and pile up things on the silk without rhyme or reason by saying, "I am not concerned with the question of whether the painting resembles objects or not." These people do not understand that "not insisting on verisimilitude" implies that one should rather try to suggest resemblance to the things without formal resemblance. Those painters who merely cover up a painting with lines and blotches like furniture laid topsy-turvy in storage have no right to discuss it.

—Wang Fu (1362—1416) in *Shuhua Chuanshi Lu*

迁翁（倪瓒）之妙会在不似处，其不似正是潜移造化而与天游，此神骏灭没处也。近人只在求似，愈似所以愈离，可与言此者鲜矣。

——恽寿平《瓯香馆画跋》

The strange beauty of "Cranky Old Man" lies not in his fidelity to

---

① 这里张彦远的生卒年有误，应该为 815 年至 907 年。*Shuhua* 疑为当时拼写有误。——编者注

form, but rather in his disregard for it. It is where he departs from it that he enters into the spirit of the creation, like a celestial steed lost in the clouds. Many modern painters try to aim at accuracy of form, and the more they try the farther away they get from the spirit of things.

—Yun Shouping (1633—1690) in *Oushiang Kuan Huapa*

凡用笔,先求气韵,次采体要,然后精思。若形势未备,便用巧密精思,必失其气韵也。

——韩拙《山水纯全集》,引自余绍宋《画法要录》

In a painting, aim first at the general concept of rhythmic vitality, and then the filling in of actual forms. Then weigh and consider. But if one has not a clear idea of the general developing movements and starts to think about the laborious details, one will have lost the rhythmic vitality already.

—Han Chuo of Sung (eleventh to twelfth centuries) in *Shanshui Chunchuan Chi*, quoted in *Huafa Yaolu* by Yu Shaosung, a contemporary

喜工整而恶荒率,喜华丽而恶质朴,喜软美而恶瘦硬,喜细致而恶简浑,喜浓缛而恶雅澹,此常人之情也。艺术之胜境,岂仅以表相而定之哉?若夫以纤弱为娟秀,以粗犷为苍浑,以板滞为沉厚,以浅薄为淡远,又比比皆是也。舍气韵骨法之不求,而斤斤于此者,盖不达乎文人画之旨耳。

——陈师曾《文人画之价值》

It is human nature to prefer careful workmanship to slipshod work, the decorative to the simple and unadorned, the graceful to the rugged and the fine details to suggestions of all-round atmosphere, and the brilliant-colored to the subdued. The best in art can never go by such crude standards. On the other hand, there are many who mistake the ingenious and clever for true beauty, the boldly and crassly assertive for true strength, the immature and childish for true depth, and the awkward and superficial for true detachment of spirit. To neglect the first laws of rhythmic vitality and general conception in favor of such trite characteristics is to misunderstand the true meaning of a literary man's painting.

　　—Chen Yinchuo[1](contemporary) in "The Value of Literary Man's Painting"

---

① 此处疑是林语堂误译为陈寅恪(陈师曾之弟)。——编者注

第三编

古典诗词

责　子
Unworthy Sons

陶渊明（Tao Yuanming）

白发被两鬓,肌肤不复实。

虽有五男儿,总不好纸笔。

阿舒已二八,懒惰固无匹。

阿宣行志学,而不爱文术。

雍端年十三,不识六与七。

通子垂九龄,但觅梨与栗。

天运苟如此,且进杯中物。

My temples are gray, my muscles are no longer full.

Five sons have I, and none of them likes school.

Ah-shu is sixteen and as lazy as lazy can be.

Ah-hsüan is fifteen and no taste for reading has he.

Thirteen are Yung and Tuan, yet they can't tell six from seven.

A-t'ung wants only pears and chestnuts—in two years he'll be eleven.

Then, come! Let me empty this cup, if such be the will of heaven.

石壕吏
The Bailiff of Shihhao

杜 甫（Tu Fu）

暮投石壕村，有吏夜捉人。

老翁逾墙走，老妇出门看。

吏呼一何怒！妇啼一何苦！

听妇前致词："三男邺城戍。

一男附书至，二男新战死。

存者且偷生，死者长已矣！

室中更无人，惟有乳下孙。

有孙母未去，出入无完裙。

老妪力虽衰，请从吏夜归。

急应河阳役，犹得备晨炊。"

夜久语声绝，如闻泣幽咽。

天明登前途，独与老翁别。

I came to Shihhao village and stayed that eve.

A bailiff came for press-gang in the night.

The old man, hearing this, climbed o'er the wall,

And the old woman saw the bailiff at the door.

Oh, why was the bailiff's voice so terrible,

And why the woman's plaint so soft and low?

"I have three sons all at the Niehch'eng post.

And one just wrote a letter home to say

The other two had in the battle died.

Let those who live live on as best they can,

For those who've died are dead for evermore.

Now in the house there's only grandson left;

For him his mother still remains—without

A decent petticoat to go about.

Although my strength is ebbing weak and low,

I'll go with you, bailiff, in the front to serve.

For I can cook breakfast for the army, and

I'll march and hurry to the Hoyang front."

—So spake the woman, and in the night, the voice

Became so low it broke into a whimper.

And in the morning ere I resumed my way,

I said good-bye to her old man alone.

琵琶行
The Sound of the *Pipa* on the Water

白居易（Po Chuyi）

浔阳江头夜送客，枫叶荻花秋瑟瑟。

主人下马客在船，举酒欲饮无管弦。

醉不成欢惨将别，别时茫茫江浸月。

忽闻水上琵琶声，主人忘归客不发。

寻声暗问弹者谁，琵琶声停欲语迟。

移船相近邀相见，添酒回灯重开宴。

千呼万唤始出来，犹抱琵琶半遮面。

转轴拨弦三两声，未成曲调先有情。

弦弦掩抑声声思，似诉平生不得志。

低眉信手续续弹，说尽心中无限事。

轻拢慢捻抹复挑，初为《霓裳》后《六幺》。

大弦嘈嘈如急雨，小弦切切如私语。

嘈嘈切切错杂弹，大珠小珠落玉盘。

间关莺语花底滑，幽咽泉流冰下难。

冰泉冷涩弦凝绝，凝绝不通声暂歇。

别有幽愁暗恨生，此时无声胜有声。

银瓶乍破水浆迸，铁骑突出刀枪鸣。

曲终收拨当心画，四弦一声如裂帛。

东船西舫悄无言，唯见江心秋月白。

沉吟放拨插弦中，整顿衣裳起敛容。

自言本是京城女，家在虾蟆陵下住。

十三学得琵琶成，名属教坊第一部。

曲罢曾教善才服，妆成每被秋娘妒。

五陵年少争缠头，一曲红绡不知数。

钿头银篦击节碎，血色罗裙翻酒污。

今年欢笑复明年，秋月春风等闲度。

弟走从军阿姨死，暮去朝来颜色故。

门前冷落鞍马稀，老大嫁作商人妇。

商人重利轻别离，前月浮梁买茶去。

去来江口守空船，绕船月明江水寒。

夜深忽梦少年事，梦啼妆泪红阑干。

我闻琵琶已叹息，又闻此语重唧唧。

同是天涯沦落人，相逢何必曾相识！

我从去年辞帝京，谪居卧病浔阳城。

浔阳地僻无音乐，终岁不闻丝竹声。

住近湓江地低湿，黄芦苦竹绕宅生。

其间旦暮闻何物？杜鹃啼血猿哀鸣。

春江花朝秋月夜，往往取酒还独倾。

岂无山歌与村笛？呕哑嘲哳难为听。

今夜闻君琵琶语，如听仙乐耳暂明。

莫辞更坐弹一曲，为君翻作《琵琶行》。

感我此言良久立，却坐促弦弦转急。

凄凄不似向前声，满座重闻皆掩泣。

座中泣下谁最多？江州司马青衫湿。

One night I was sending a friend off to the riverbank at Kiukiang. ① It was autumn and maple leaves and reed flowers swooped and flicked and snapped in the wind. I dismounted to find my friend already in the boat. We had a drink, but missed music. It was a dismal parting and I was going on my way. At this time, the river was flooded with a hazy moonlight. Suddenly there came over the water the sound of a *pipa*. I changed my mind and told my friend to delay starting a bit. We were curious to find out where the music came from and learned that it was from a player in another boat. The *pipa* had stopped and we hesitated a while as to how to approach and invite the player to come over. We then moved our boat over near to the other boat and introduced ourselves, begging to have the pleasure of seeing the player, for we were going to warm up some more wine, relight the lamps, and have dinner again. It was after repeated pleading that she came out, and when she did, she half covered her face with the instrument.

She adjusted the strings and plucked a few notes, but even before the melody began, we were struck with its languorous tone. And as she went along, with her head bent, the sounds were soft and muted, sad and plaintive and meditative, as if she were telling the story of her frustrated life. I felt that there was a long story behind it. Gently she scraped or plucked the strings, and I recognized the melody of "Nichang," followed by that of "Liuyao." The notes gathered up speed, those from the lower strings falling like fast raindrops and those from the higher trailing like whispers, and these were mingled together, giving the effect of marbles of different sizes falling into a jade plate. Then the melody was like orioles chirping and chattering in

---

① This is the same district where the poet built his mountain lodge in Lushan.

trees after a rain, while a covered spring gurgled below. And the water seemed to freeze suddenly as the sound of the strings came to a stop. It seemed that she could not go on and we held our breath in that moment of silence. When it started again, it broke out like water rushing forth from a broken silver vase, and again it was like the clash and clang of battle of men on horseback. When it was finished, she took out the stop in the center, and rattled her fingers across all four strings, making a sound like the tearing of silk. The people in both boats were struck speechless, and only a white haze hung over the middle of the river. Quietly she put back the finger caps in their place among the strings, and readjusted her dress and made a slight gesture of rising from her sitting position as a form of courtesy.

She then told us her story. She was born in the capital, but is now making her home at the Hamoling [Frog Hill]. She said that she had begun to learn playing the *pipa* from the age of thirteen at the Court of Musicians No. 1. ① She often won high praise from her professors and was the envy of many girls. Oh, she was very popular. Every time she played, she received she did not know how many pieces of silk for presents. And she could afford to break silver brooches and hair ornaments, and her blood-red skirt was often splashed with wine. It was that kind of gay life she had in her youth year after year. Then her younger brother went into the army and her elder sister died. In time she lost her youthful glamour and now carriages rarely appeared in front of her establishment. When she was in her thirties, what could

---

① A government institution for training musicians and actors and actresses.

she do but marry a businessman?① The merchant was too busy attending to business and had left upriver a month ago to buy tea. So she was left alone on the boat, facing the cold water and the silent moon all by herself. Sometimes she cried herself to sleep, thinking of the days of her youth.

I was already saddened by her music, and now after I heard her story, I clicked my tongue in pity. And this I said to her: "We are both travelers in this wide world. We do not need to have met before to be friends. I was demoted from the emperor's court last year and sent down here to Kiukiang. The hardest thing here is to hear good music. Sometimes for a whole year I go without the sound of woodwind or of strings. The place is on low-lying ground and near the river, and houses are surrounded with rushes and wild bamboos. What can one hear except the song of cuckoos and the sad cries of monkeys? To be sure, there are folk songs and country pipes, but it rather grates on one's ears. So it is quite an agreeable surprise to hear your *pipa* tonight; it's like fairy music which my ears have missed for a long time. Come on, stay a while and play some more for me while I write this poem in your honor."

She felt greatly touched, standing there listening to what I said. Then she sat down again and played for me. And the notes fell fast, and they were sad and cut into one's heart. All who heard it shed tears, and the one who shed most was myself, for my black gown was wet.

---

① This line is considered by the Chinese readers as one of the saddest lines and is often quoted. One day, three centuries later, Su Tungpo was matching quotations from poetry with a famous courtesan. "What about the end [of a courtesan's life]?" asked Tungpo. The courtesan, Chintsao, quoted this line, and then was struck with its pathos and decided to become a nun. Marrying a businessman was considered an anticlimax for an educated lady.

寻隐者不遇
Failing to Meet a Hermit

贾　岛（Chia Tao）

松下问童子，言师采药去。
只在此山中，云深不知处。

I asked the boy beneath the pines,

He said, "The master's gone alone,

Herb-picking somewhere on the mount,

Cloud-hidden, whereabouts unknown."

行　宫
Country Palace

元　稹（Yuan Chen）

寥落古行宫，宫花寂寞红。
白头宫女在，闲坐说玄宗。

Here empty is the country palace, empty like a dream,
In loneliness and quiet the red imperial flowers gleam,
Some white-haired, palace chambermaids are chatting,
Chatting about the dead and gone Hsüanchuang regime.

饮湖上初晴后雨
West Lake

苏东坡（Su Tungpo）

水光潋滟晴方好，山色空蒙雨亦奇。
欲把西湖比西子，淡妆浓抹总相宜。

The light of water sparkles on a sunny day;
And misty mountains lend excitement to the rain.
I like to compare the West Lake to "Miss West",
Pretty in a gay dress, and pretty in simple again.

七

和文与可洋川园池三十首·望云楼
Cloud Gazing Tower

苏东坡（Su Tungpo）

阴晴朝暮几回新，已向虚空付此身。
出本无心归亦好，白云还似望云人。

Through rain and shine, alternate night and day,
Drifting at will and stopping as it may,
The cloud has made the universe its home,
And like the cloud's so is the gazer's way.

八

和子由渑池怀旧
Nostalgia—In Response to Tseyu's Poem①

苏东坡(Su Tungpo)

人生到处知何似? 应似飞鸿踏雪泥。

泥上偶然留指爪,鸿飞那复计东西。

老僧已死成新塔,坏壁无由见旧题。

往日崎岖还记否,路长人困蹇驴嘶。

To what can human life be likened?

Perhaps to a wild goose's footprint on snow;

The claws' imprint is accidentally left,

But carefree, the bird flies east and west.

---

① 林语堂仅译了该诗的前半部分,后半部分未译。——编者注

水调歌头·明月几时有
Mid-Autumn Festival,
to the Tune of Shuitiaoket'ou

苏东坡（Su Tungpo）

明月几时有？把酒问青天。不知天上宫阙，今夕是何年。我欲乘风归去，又恐琼楼玉宇，高处不胜寒。起舞弄清影，何似在人间！

转朱阁，低绮户，照无眠。不应有恨，何事长向别时圆？人有悲欢离合，月有阴晴圆缺，此事古难全。但愿人长久，千里共婵娟。

How rare the moon, so round and clear!

　　With cup in hand, I ask of the blue sky,

"I do not know in the celestial sphere

　　What name this festive night goes by?"

I want to fly home, riding the air,

But fear the ethereal cold up there,

　　The jade and crystal mansions are so high!

Dancing to my shadow,

　　I feel no longer the mortal tie.

She rounds the vermilion tower,

Stoops to silk-pad doors,

　　Shines on those who sleepless lie.

Why does she, bearing us no grudge,

  Shine upon our parting, reunion deny?

But rare is perfect happiness—

The moon does wax, the moon does wane,

  And so men meet and say goodbye.

I only pray our life be long,

  And our souls together heavenward fly!

江城子·十年生死两茫茫
A Dream, to the Tune of Chiangch'engtse

苏东坡（Su Tungpo）

十年生死两茫茫。不思量,自难忘。千里孤坟,无处话凄凉。纵使相逢应不识,尘满面,鬓如霜。

夜来幽梦忽还乡。小轩窗,正梳妆。相顾无言,惟有泪千行。料得年年肠断处,明月夜,短松冈。

Ten years have we been parted:

The living and the dead—

    Hearing no news,

    Not thinking

    And yet forgetting nothing!

I cannot come to your grave a thousand miles away

To converse with you and whisper my longing;

And even if we did meet

    How would you greet

        My weathered face, my hair a frosty white?

Last night I dreamed I had suddenly returned to our old home

And saw you sitting there before the familiar dressing table,

We looked at each other in silence,

With misty eyes beneath the candle light.

May we year after year

    In heartbreak meet,

    On the pine-crest,

    In the moonlight!

临江仙·夜归临皋
To Linkao at Night,
to the Tune of Linchiangsien

苏东坡(Su Tungpo)

夜饮东坡醒复醉,归来仿佛三更。家童鼻息已雷鸣。敲门都不应,倚杖听江声。

长恨此身非我有,何时忘却营营! 夜阑风静縠纹平。小舟从此逝,江海寄余生。

After a drink at night, Tungpo wakes up and gets drunk again.

By the time I come home it seems to be midnight.

The boy servant is asleep snoring like thunder

And does not answer the door.

Resting on a cane I listen to the murmur of the river

And feel with a pang that I am not master of my own life.

When can I stop this hustling about?

The night is late, the air is calm,

And the water a sheen of unruffled light.

Let me take a small boat down the river hence

To spend beyond the seas the remainder of my days.

丑奴儿
"In My Young Days"

辛弃疾（Hsin Ch'ichi）

少年不识愁滋味，爱上层楼。爱上层楼，为赋新词强说愁。
而今识尽愁滋味，欲说还休。欲说还休，却道天凉好个秋！

In my young days,

   I had tasted only gladness,

But loved to mount the top floor,

But loved to mount the top floor,

   To write a song pretending sadness.

And now I've tasted,

   Sorrow's flavors, bitter and sour,

And can't find a word,

And can't find a word,

   But merely say, "What a golden autumn hour!"

十三

声声慢
Forlorn

李清照（Li Chingchao）

寻寻觅觅，冷冷清清，凄凄惨惨戚戚。乍暖还寒时候，最难将息。三杯两盏淡酒，怎敌他晚来风急！雁过也，正伤心，却是旧时相识。

满地黄花堆积，憔悴损，如今有谁堪摘？守着窗儿，独自怎生得黑！梧桐更兼细雨，到黄昏、点点滴滴。这次第，怎一个愁字了得！

So dim, so dark,
  So dense, so dull,
    So damp, so dank,
      So dead!
The weather, now warm, now cold,
  Makes it harder
    Than ever to forget!
How can a few cups of thin wine
  Bring warmth against
    The chilly winds of sunset?
I recognize the geese flying overhead：
  My old friends,
    Bring not the old memories back!

Let fallen flowers lie where they fall.

    To what purpose

        And for whom should I decorate?

By the window shut,

    Guarding it alone,

        To see the sky has turned so black!

And the drizzle on the kola nut

    Keeps on droning:

        Pit-a-pat, pit-a-pat!

Is this the kind of mood and moment

    To be expressed

        By one word "sad"?

慵庵铭

Inscription on the Hall of Idleness

白玉蟾(Po Yüchien)

丹经慵读,道不在书;

藏经慵览,道之皮肤。

至道之要,贵乎清虚;

何谓清虚?终日如愚。

有诗慵吟,句外肠枯;

有琴慵弹,弦外韵孤;

有酒慵饮,醉外江湖;

有棋慵奕,意外干戈;

慵观溪山,内有画图;

慵对风月,内有蓬壶;

慵陪世事,内有田庐;

慵问寒暑,内有神都。

松枯石烂,我常如如。

谓之慵庵,不亦可乎?

I'm too lazy to read the Taoist classics, for Tao doesn't reside in
  the books;

Too lazy to look over the sutras, for they go no deeper in Tao than
  its looks.

The essence of Tao consists in a void, clear and cool,

But what is this void except being the whole day like a fool?

Too lazy am I to read poetry, for when I stop, the poetry will be
gone;

Too lazy to play on the *chin*, for music dies on the string where
it's born;

Too lazy to drink wine, for beyond the drunkard's dream there are
rivers and lakes;

Too lazy to play chess, for besides in the pawns there are other
stakes;

Too lazy to look at the hills and streams, for there is a painting
within my heart's portals;

Too lazy to face the wind and the moon, for within me is the Isle
of the Immortals;

Too lazy to attend to worldly affairs, for inside me are my hut and
my possessions;

Too lazy to watch the changing of the seasons, for within me are
heavenly processions.

Pine trees may decay and rocks may rot; but I shall always remain
what I am.

Is it not fitting that I call this the Hall of Idleness?

葬花吟
Taiyu Predicting Her Own Death

曹雪芹（Tsao Shuehchin）

花谢花飞花满天，红消香断有谁怜？

游丝软系飘春榭，落絮轻沾扑绣帘。

闺中女儿惜春暮，愁绪满怀无释处。

手把花锄出绣帘，忍踏落花来复去。

柳丝榆荚自芳菲，不管桃飘与李飞。

桃李明年能再发，明年闺中知有谁？

三月香巢已垒成，梁间燕子太无情！

明年花发虽可啄，却不道人去梁空巢已倾。

一年三百六十日，风刀霜剑严相逼，

明媚鲜妍能几时，一朝漂泊难寻觅。

花开易见落难寻，阶前愁杀葬花人。

独倚花锄泪暗洒，洒上空枝见血痕。

杜鹃无语正黄昏，荷锄归去掩重门。

青灯照壁人初睡，冷雨敲窗被未温。

怪奴底事倍伤神？半为怜春半恼春：

怜春忽至恼忽去，至又无言去未闻。

昨宵庭外悲歌发，知是花魂与鸟魂？

花魂鸟魂总难留，鸟自无言花自羞。

愿侬此日生双翼,随花飞到天尽头。

天尽头,何处有香丘?①

未若锦囊收艳骨,一抔净土掩风流。

质本洁来还洁去,强于污淖陷渠沟。

尔今死去侬收葬,未卜侬身何日丧?

侬今葬花人笑痴,他年葬侬知是谁?

试看春残花渐落,便是红颜老死时。

一朝春尽红颜老,花落人亡两不知!

Fly, fly, ye faded and broken dreams

    Of fragrance, for the spring is gone!

Behold the gossamer entwine the screens,

    And wandering catkins kiss the stone.

Here comes the maiden from out her chamber door,

    Whose secret no one shall share.

She gathers the trodden blossoms lingeringly,

    And says to them her votive prayer.

I smell the scent of elm seeds and the willow

    Where once did blush the peach and pear.

When next they bloom in their new-made spring dress,

    She may be gone—no one knows where.

Sweet are the swallows' nests, whose labors of love

    This spring these eaves and girders grace.

Next year they'll come and see the mistress's home—

    To find her gone—without a trace.

The frost and cutting wind in whirling cycle

---

① 此句林语堂无对应译文,后面两句的语义也有所省略。——编者注

Hurtle through the seasons' round.

How but a while ago these flowers did smile

　　Then quietly vanished without a sound.

With stifled sobs she picks the wilted blooms,

　　And stands transfixed and dazed hourlong,

And sheds her scalding tears which shall be changed

　　Into the cuckoo's heartbreak song.

But the cuckoo is silent in the twilight eve,

　　And she returns to her lone home.

The flickering lamp casts shadows upon the wall,

　　And night rain patters, bed unwarmed.

Oh, ask not why and wherefore she is grieved.

　　For loving spring, her heart is torn

That it should have arrived without warning,

　　And just as noiselessly is gone.

I heard last night a mournful wail and I knew

　　It was the souls of parting flowers,

Harried and reluctant and all in a rush,

　　Bidding their last farewell hours.

Oh, that I might take winged flight to heaven,

　　With these beauties in my trust!

'Twere better I buried you undefiled,

　　Than let them trample you to dust.

Now I take the shovel and bury your scented breath,

　　A-wondering when my turn shall be.

Let me be silly and weep atop your grave,

　　For next year who will bury me?

Oh, look upon these tender, fragile beauties,

Of perfumed flesh and bone and hair.
The admirer shan't be there when her time is up,
    And the admired shall no longer care.

半半歌
The Half-and-Half Song

李密庵（Li Mi-an）

看破浮生过半，半之受用无边：
半中岁月尽幽闲，半里乾坤宽展。
半郭半乡村舍，半山半水田园；
半耕半读半经廛，半士半民姻眷。
半雅半粗器具，半华半实庭轩；
衾裳半素半轻鲜，肴馔半丰半俭。
童仆半能半拙，妻儿半朴半贤；
心情半佛半神仙，姓字半藏半显。
一半还之天地，让将一半人间；
半思后代与沧田，半想阎罗怎见？
酒饮半酣正好，花开半吐偏妍；
帆张半扇免翻颠，马放半缰稳便。
半少却饶滋味，半多反厌纠缠；
百年苦乐半相参，会占便宜只半。

By far the greater half have I seen through
This floating life—ah, there's the magic word—
This "half"—so rich in implications.

It bids us taste the joy of more than we

Can ever own. Halfway in life is man's

Best state, when slackened pace allows him ease.

A wide world lies halfway 'twixt heaven and earth;

To live halfway between the town and land,

Have farms halfway between the streams and hills;

Be half-a-scholar, and half-a-squire, and half

In business; half as gentry live,

And half related to the common folk;

And have a house that's half genteel, half plain,

Half elegantly furnished and half bare;

Dresses and gowns that are half old, half new,

And food half epicure's, half simple fare;

Have servants not too clever, nor too dull;

A wife who is not too ugly, nor too fair.

—So then, at heart, I feel I'm half a Buddha,

And almost half a Taoist fairy blest.

And have a name half-known and half obscure.

One half myself to Father Heaven I

Return; the other half to children leave—

Half thinking how for my posterity

To plan and provide, and yet minding how

To answer God when the body's laid at rest.

He is most wisely drunk who is half drunk;

And flowers in half-bloom look their prettiest;

As boats at half-sail sail the steadiest,

And horses held at half-slack reins trot best.

Who half too much has, adds anxiety;

But half too little, adds possession's zest.

Since life's of sweet and bitter compounded,

Who tastes but half is wisest and cleverest.

尼姑思凡
The Mortal Thoughts of a Nun[①]

小尼姑年方二八，

正青春被师父削去了头发。

只因俺父好看经，俺娘亲爱念佛，

暮礼朝参，每日里佛殿上烧香供佛；

生下我来疾病多，

因此上把奴家舍入在空门为尼寄活。

与人家追荐亡灵，

不住口地念着弥陀。

只听得钟声法号，

不住手地击磬摇铃，

击磬摇铃，擂鼓吹螺，

平白地与那地府阴司做功课。

念几声南无佛哆旦哆萨摩诃的般若波罗。

念几声弥陀，咿！恨一声媒婆；

念几声娑婆诃，哎、叫，叫一声没奈何；

念几声哆旦哆，唉，怎知我感叹还多！

越思越想，反添愁闷，不免到回廊下散步一回，多少是好。

---

① 　原文根据林语堂的译文回译节选，林语堂在翻译过程中多有删减。——编者注

绕回廊散闷则个，
绕回廊散闷则个！

来此已是大雄宝殿，看那两旁的罗汉塑得好庄严也！

又只见那两旁罗汉塑得来有些傻角；
一个儿抱膝舒怀，口儿里念着我；
一个儿手托香腮，心儿里想着我；
一个儿眼倦开，朦胧地觑看我；
惟有布袋罗汉笑呵呵，他笑我时光挫、光阴过，
有谁人，有谁人肯娶我这年老婆婆？
降龙的恼着我；伏虎的恨着我；
那长眉大仙愁着我，说我老来时有什么结果！

佛前灯做不得洞房花烛，
香积厨做不得玳筵东阁，
钟鼓楼做不得望夫台，
草蒲团做不得芙蓉，芙蓉软褥。
哎呀天啊！不由人心热如火！

我把袈裟扯破，埋了藏经，
弃了木鱼，丢了铙钹。
从今后把钟鼓楼佛殿远离却，
下山去寻找一个年少哥哥。
凭他打我，骂我，说我，笑我，
一心不愿成佛，
不念弥陀般若波罗！

A young nun am I, sixteen years of age;
My head was shaven in my young maidenhood.

For my father, he loves the Buddhist sutras,
And my mother, she loves the Buddhist priests.

Morning and night, morning and night,
I burn incense and I pray, for I
Was born a sickly child, full of ills.
So they sent me here into this monastery.

Amitabha! Amitabha!
Unceasingly I pray.
Oh, tired am I of the humming of the drums and the tinkling of
　　the bells;
Tired am I of the droning of the prayers and the crooning of the
　　priors;
The chatter and the clatter of unintelligible charms,
The clamor and the clangor of interminable chants,
The mumbling and murmuring of monotonous psalms.
Prajnaparamita, Mayura-sutra,
　　Saddharmapundarika—
　　　Oh, how I hate them all!
While I say Mitabha,
　　I sigh for my beau.
While I chant saparah,
　　My heart cries, "Oh!"
While I sing tarata,

My heart palpitates so!

Ah, let me take a stroll,
Let me take a stroll!

(*She comes to the Hall of the Five Hundred Lohans*, *where are clay figures of the Buddhist saints*, *known for their distinctive facial expressions*.)

Ah, here are the Lohans,
　　What a bunch of silly, amorous souls!
Every one a bearded man!
　　How each his eyes at me rolls!

Look at the one hugging his knees!
　　His lips are mumbling my name so!
And the one with his cheek in hand,
　　As though thinking of me so!
That one has a pair of dreamy eyes,
　　Dreaming dreams of me so!

But the Lohan in sackcloth!
　　What is he after,
With his hellish, heathenish laughter?
　　With his roaring, rollicking laughter,
Laughing at me so!
　　—laughing at me, for
When beauty is past and youth is lost,

Who will marry an old crone?

When beauty is faded and youth is jaded,

   Who will marry an old, shriveled cocoon?

The one holding a dragon,

   He is cynical;

The one riding a tiger,

   He is quizzical;

And that long-browed handsome giant,

   He seems pitiful,

For what will become of me when my beauty is gone?

These candles of the altar,

   They are not for my bridal chamber.

These long incense containers,

   They are not for my bridal parlor.

And the straw prayer cushions,

   They cannot serve as quilt or cover.

Oh, God!

Whence comes this burning, suffocating ardor?

   Whence comes this strange, infernal, unearthly ardor?

I'll tear these monkish robes!

   I'll bury all the Buddhist sutras;

I'll drown the wooden fish,

   And leave all the monastic putras!

I'll leave the drums,

I'll leave the bells,

 And the chants,

  And the yells,

And all the interminable, exasperating, religious chatter!

I'll go downhill, and find me a young and handsome lover—

Let him scold me, beat me!

 Kick or ill-treat me!

I will *not* become a buddha!

I will *not* mumble mita, prajna, para!

十八

咏怅集·集古
A Chinese Fantasia: The Song of Life①

诏问山中何所有赋诗以答·陶弘景

山中何所有,岭上多白云。

只可自怡悦,不堪持赐君。

Tao Hungching②:

O tell me, friend, what thy hill lodge has got?

Why, clouds around the passes, quite a lot!

They are just for my own enjoyment, but

To make thee presents—unfortunately not!

遣兴词·辛幼安

醉里且贪欢笑,要愁那得工夫。

近来始觉古人书,信着全无是处。

Shin Yu-an:

One drunk is a free dispenser of his smiles,

---

① 此处仅节选部分内容。——编者注

② This man is counted as one of the Taoist "fairies" and is reported to have ascended bodily to heaven. He lived from 452 to 536.

Forgotten all injustice, all men's guiles.

Of late have I just come to realize,

Spurn bookish wisdom and your ambition's wiles.

观物吟·邓青阳

人生天地常如客,何独乡关定是家。

争似区区随所寓,年年处处看梅花。

Teng Chingyang:

We are but passing guests from who knows where.

Say not thy home is here, thy home is there.

It suits me well wherever I may be;

The flowers bloom here, there and everywhere.

渔翁歌·张君寿

郎提密网截江围,妾把长竿守钓矶。

满载鲂鱼都换酒,轻烟细雨又空归。

Chang Chunshou

He casts his nets mid-stream his haul to take;

She drops her line and waits her catch to make.

When all the day's catch is changed again for wine,

They row the boat homeward in showers' wake.

行香子·苏东坡

清夜无尘,月色如银,酒斟时须满十分。浮名浮利,虚苦劳神,叹隙中驹,石中火,梦中身。

虽抱文章,开口谁亲,且陶陶乐尽天真。几时归去,作个闲人,对一张琴、一壶酒、一溪云。

Su Tungpo[①]:

O the clear moon's speckless, silvery night!

When filling thy cup, be sure to fill it quite!

Strive not for frothy fame or bubble wealth:

    A passing dream—

      A flashing flint—

        A shadow's flight!

O what is knowledge, fine and superfine?

To innocent and simple joys resign!

When I go home, I'll carry on my back

    A load of clouds—

      A sweet-toned *chin*[②]—

        A pot of wine.

乐住辞 · 中峰和尚

水竹之居,吾爱吾庐,石磷磷乱砌阶除。

    轩窗随意,小巧规矩,却也清幽,也潇洒,也宽舒。

阆苑瀛洲,金谷陵楼,算不如茅舍清幽。

    野花绣地,莫也风流,也宜春,也宜夏,也宜秋。

短短横墙,矮矮疏窗,忔渣儿小小池塘。

    高低叠障,绿水边旁,也有些风,有些月,有些凉。

懒散无拘,此乐何如,倚栏杆临水观鱼。

    风花雪月,赢得工夫,好炷些香,说些话,读些书。

---

①   This is the single one poem that I love best in all Chinese poetry.

②   A string instrument.

日用家常,竹几藤床,靠眼前水色山光。

　　客来无酒,清话何妨? 但细烹茶,热烘盏,浅烧汤。

净扫尘埃,惜尔苍苔,任门前红叶铺阶。

　　也堪图画,还也奇哉,有数株松,数竿竹,数枝梅。

花木栽培,取次教开,明朝事天自安排。

　　知他富贵几时来? 且优游,且随分,且开怀。

酒熟堪酌,客至堪留,更无荣无污无忧。

　　退后一步,着甚来由,但倦时眠,渴时饮,醉时讴。

顿脱尘羁,深处幽栖,兀腾腾绝虑忘机。

　　绳床草枕,竹榻柴扉。却也无忧,也无喜,也无悲。

万事俱休,名利都勾,罢攀援永绝追求。

　　溪山作伴,云水为俦,但乐清闲,乐自在,乐优游。

Chungfeng:

I love my bamboo hut, by water included,

Where rockery o'er stone steps protruded;

A quiet, peaceful study, small but fine:

　　Which is so cozy—

　　　　So delightful—

　　　　　　So secluded!

No marble halls, no vermilion towers

Are quite so good as my secluded bowers.

The lawn embroidered so with buttercups

　　Greets me in rain—

　　　　Or in shine—

　　　　　　Or in showers.

A short, low wall, with windows hid by trees;

A tiny, little pond myself to please;

And there upon its shady, rocky banks:

  A pretty maid—

    A little moon—

      A little breeze!

And how about a quiet life leading?

From balcony watch the fish in water feeding.

And earn from moon and flowers a leisure life:

  Have friendly chats—

    Some incense—

      And some reading?

For household use, some furniture decrepit.

'Tis enough! The hills and water so exquisite!

When guests arrive, to make it just perfect:

  Put on the kettle—

    Brew the tea—

      And sip it!

O sweep thy yard, but spare the mossy spots!

Let petals bedeck thy steps with purple dots

As in a painting. What's more wonderful:

  Some pine trees—

    And bamboos—

      And apricots!

Let bloom in order pear and peach and cherry!

The morrow lies in the gods' lap—why worry?

Who knows but what and when our fortune is?

   And so be wise—

      Be content—

         Be merry!

When friend arrives that thou hast so admired,

As by some idle nothing in common inspired,

Ask him so stay for a good, carefree half-day:

   And drink when happy—

      Sing when drunk—

         Sleep when tired.

A quiet home, far from the hustling crowd;

Let no trivialities thy mind becloud.

Gay and contented, being disenchanted,

   And not be fussy—

      Nor selfish—

         Nor be proud.

Obey God's will, and wait on Heaven's pleasure.

Thy purity of heart alone do treasure.

Enough the library and the court of flowers

   To lead a life of peace—

      And contentment—

         And leisure.

第四编

传奇散文

莺莺传
Passion (Or the Western Room)[①]

元　稹（Yuan Chen）

　　唐贞元中，有张生者，性温茂，美风容，内秉坚孤，非礼不可入。或朋从游宴，扰杂其间，他人皆汹汹拳拳，若将不及，张生容顺而已，终不能乱。以是年二十三，未尝近女色。知者诘之，谢而言曰："登徒子非好色者，是有凶行。余真好色者，而适不我值。何以言之？大凡物之尤者，未尝不留连于心，是知其非忘情者也。"诘者识之。

　　无几何，张生游于蒲。蒲之东十余里，有僧舍曰普救寺，张生寓焉。适有崔氏孀妇，将归长安，路出于蒲，亦止兹寺。崔氏妇，郑女也。张出于郑，绪其亲，乃异派之从母。是岁，浑瑊薨于蒲。有中人丁文雅，不善于军，军人因丧而扰，大掠蒲人。崔氏之家，财产甚厚，多奴仆。旅寓惶骇，不知所托。先是，张与蒲将之党有善，请吏护之，遂不及于难。十余日，廉使杜确将天子命以总戎节，令于军，军由是戢。

　　郑厚张之德甚，因饰馔以命张，中堂宴之。复谓张曰："姨之孤嫠未亡，提携幼稚，不幸属师徒大溃，实不保其身。弱子幼女，犹君之生，岂可比常恩哉！今俾以仁兄礼奉见，冀所以报恩也。"命其子，曰欢郎，可十余岁，容甚温美。次命女："出拜尔兄，尔兄活尔。"久之，辞疾。郑怒曰："张

---

①　林语堂根据元稹之诗对原文有所增补，创译与改编成分较大，使之更符合英语诗学习惯，如开篇增添的细节描写以及元稹的回忆、篇中增添的大量细节描写以及人物话语等。——编者注

兄保尔之命。不然,尔且掳矣,能复远嫌乎?"久之,乃至。常服睟容,不加新饰,垂鬟接黛,双脸销红而已。颜色艳异,光辉动人。张惊,为之礼。因坐郑旁,以郑之抑而见也,凝睇怨绝,若不胜其体者。问其年纪。郑曰:"今天子甲子岁之七月,终于贞元庚辰,生年十七矣。"张生稍以词导之,不对。终席而罢。

张自是惑之,愿致其情,无由得也。崔之婢曰红娘,生私为之礼者数四,乘间遂道其衷。婢果惊沮,腆然而奔。张生悔之。翼日,婢复至。张生乃羞而谢之,不复云所求矣。婢因谓张曰:"郎之言,所不敢言,亦不敢泄。然而崔之姻族,君所详也。何不因其德而求娶焉?"张曰:"余始自孩提,性不苟合。或时纨绮间居,曾莫流盼。不为当年,终有所蔽。昨日一席间,几不自持。数日来,行忘止,食忘饱,恐不能逾旦暮。若因媒氏而娶,纳采问名,则三数月间,索我于枯鱼之肆矣。尔其谓我何?"婢曰:"崔之贞慎自保,虽所尊不可以非语犯之,下人之谋,固难入矣。然而善属文,往往沈吟章句,怨慕者久之。君试为喻情诗以乱之,不然则无由也。"张大喜,立缀《春词》二首以授之。是夕,红娘复至,持彩笺以授张曰:"崔所命也。"题其篇曰《明月三五夜》,其词曰:"待月西厢下,迎风户半开。拂墙花影动,疑是玉人来。"张亦微喻其旨,是夕,岁二月旬有四日矣。崔之东有杏花一株,攀援可逾。

既望之夕,张因梯其树而逾焉。达于西厢,则户半开矣。红娘寝于床。生因惊之。红娘骇曰:"郎何以至?"张因绐之曰:"崔氏之笺召我也。尔为我告之。"无几,红娘复来,连曰:"至矣!至矣!"张生且喜且骇,必谓获济。及崔至,则端服严容,大数张曰:"兄之恩,活我之家,厚矣!是以慈母以弱子幼女见托。奈何因不令之婢,致淫逸之词。始以护人之乱为义,而终掠乱以求之。是以乱易乱,其去几何? 诚欲寝其词,则保人之奸,不义。明之于母,则背人之惠,不祥。将寄于婢仆,又惧不得发其真诚。是用托短章,愿自陈启。犹惧兄之见难,是用鄙靡之词,以求其必至。非礼之动,能不愧心? 特愿以礼自持,无及于乱!"言毕,翻然而逝。张自失者久之,复逾而出,于是绝望。

数夕,张生临轩独寝,忽有人觉之。惊骇而起,则红娘敛衾携枕而至,抚张曰:"至矣,至矣!睡何为哉?"并枕重衾而去。张生拭目危坐久之,犹疑梦寐。然而修谨以俟。俄而红娘捧崔氏而至,至则娇羞融冶,力不能运支体,曩时端庄,不复同矣。是夕,旬有八日也。斜月晶莹,幽辉半床。张生飘飘然,且疑神仙之徒,不谓从人间至矣。有顷,寺钟鸣,天将晓,红娘促去。崔氏娇啼宛转,红娘又捧之而去,终夕无一言。张生辨色而兴,自疑曰:"岂其梦邪?"及明,睹妆在臂,香在衣,泪光荧荧然,犹莹于茵席而已。是后又十余日,杳不复知。张生赋《会真诗》三十韵,未毕,而红娘适至,因授之,以贻崔氏。自是复容之。朝隐而出,暮隐而入,同安于曩所谓西厢者,几一月矣。张生常诘郑氏之情,则曰:"我不可奈何矣。"因欲就成之。

无何,张生将之长安,先以情喻之。崔氏宛无难词,然而愁怨之容动人矣。将行之再夕,不可复见,而张生遂西下。数月,复游于蒲,会于崔氏者又累月。崔氏甚工刀札,善属文。求索再三,终不可见。往往张生自以文挑,亦不甚睹览。大略崔之出人者,艺必穷极,而貌若不知;言则敏辩,而寡于酬对。待张之意甚厚,然未尝以词继之。时愁艳幽邃,恒若不识,喜愠之容,亦罕形见。异时独夜操琴,愁弄凄恻。张窃听之。求之,则终不复鼓矣。以是愈惑之。

张生俄以文调及期,又当西去。当去之夕,不复自言其情,愁叹于崔氏之侧。崔已阴知将诀矣,恭貌怡声,徐谓张曰:"始乱之,终弃之,固其宜矣。愚不敢恨。必也君乱之,君终之,君之惠也。则殁身之誓,其有终矣。又何必深感于此行?然而君既不怿,无以奉宁。君常谓我善鼓琴,向时羞颜,所不能及。今且往矣,既君此诚。"因命拂琴,鼓《霓裳羽衣序》,不数声,哀音怨乱,不复知其是曲也。左右皆歔欷,崔亦遽止之,投琴,泣下流连,趋归郑所,遂不复至。明旦而张行。

明年,文战不胜,张遂止于京。因贻书于崔,以广其意。崔氏缄报之词,粗载于此。曰:

捧览来问,抚爱过深,儿女之情,悲喜交集。兼惠花胜一合,口脂五寸，致耀首膏唇之饰。虽荷殊恩，谁复为容？睹物增怀，但积悲叹耳。伏承使于京中就业。进修之道，固在便安。但恨僻陋之人，永以遐弃。命也如此，知复何言！自去秋已来，常忽忽如有所失。于喧哗之下，或勉为语笑，闲宵自处，无不泪零。乃至梦寐之间，亦多感咽。离忧之思，绸缪缱绻，暂若寻常。幽会未终，惊魂已断。虽半衾如暖，而思之甚遥。一昨拜辞，倏逾旧岁。长安行乐之地，触绪牵情。何幸不忘幽微，眷念无斁。鄙薄之志，无以奉酬。至于终始之盟，则固不忒。

鄙昔中表相因，或同宴处。婢仆见诱，遂致私诚。儿女之心，不能自固。君子有援琴之挑，鄙人无投梭之拒。及荐寝席，义盛意深，愚陋之情，永谓终托。岂期既见君子，而不能定情，致有自献之羞，不复明侍巾帻。没身永恨，含叹何言！倘仁人用心，俯遂幽眇，虽死之日，犹生之年。如或达士略情，舍小从大，以先配为丑行，以要盟为可欺，则当骨化形销，丹诚不泯，因风委露，犹托清尘。存没之诚，言尽于此。临纸呜咽，情不能申。千万珍重！珍重千万！

玉环一枚，是儿婴年所弄，寄充君子下体所佩。玉取其坚润不渝，环取其终始不绝。兼乱丝一絇，文竹茶碾子一枚。此数物不足见珍，意者欲君子如玉之真，弊志如环不解。泪痕在竹，愁绪萦丝。因物达情，永以为好耳。心迹身遐，拜会无期。幽愤所钟，千里神合。千万珍重！春风多厉，强饭为嘉。慎言自保，无以鄙为深念。

张生发其书于所知，由是时人多闻之。所善杨巨源好属词，因为赋《崔娘诗》一绝云："清润潘郎玉不如，中庭蕙草雪销初。风流才子多春思，肠断萧娘一纸书。"河南元稹亦续生《会真诗》三十韵。诗曰：

微月透帘栊，萤光度碧空。遥天初缥缈，低树渐葱茏。
龙吹过庭竹，鸾歌拂井桐。罗绡垂薄雾，环珮响轻风。
绛节随金母，云心捧玉童。更深人悄悄，晨会雨蒙蒙。
珠莹光文履，花明隐绣龙。瑶钗行彩凤，罗帔掩丹虹。

言自瑶华浦,将朝碧玉宫。因游洛城北,偶向宋家东。

戏调初微拒,柔情已暗通。低鬟蝉影动,回步玉尘蒙。

转面流花雪,登床抱绮丛。鸳鸯交颈舞,翡翠合欢笼。

眉黛羞偏聚,唇朱暖更融。气清兰蕊馥,肤润玉肌丰。

无力慵移腕,多娇爱敛躬。汗流珠点点,发乱绿葱葱。

方喜千年会,俄闻五夜穷。留连时有恨,缱绻意难终。

慢脸含愁态,芳词誓素衷。赠环明运合,留结表心同。

啼粉流宵镜,残灯远暗虫。华光犹苒苒,旭日渐瞳瞳。

乘鹜还归洛,吹箫亦上嵩。衣香犹染麝,枕腻尚残红。

冪冪临塘草,飘飘思渚蓬。素琴鸣怨鹤,清汉望归鸿。

海阔诚难渡,天高不易冲。行云无处所,萧史在楼中。

张之友闻之者莫不耸异之,然而张志亦绝矣。稹特与张厚,因征其词。张曰:"大凡天之所命尤物也,不妖其身,必妖于人。使崔氏子遇合富贵,乘宠娇,不为云,不为雨,为蛟为螭,吾不知其所变化矣。昔殷之辛、周之幽,据百万之国,其势甚厚。然而一女子败之。溃其众,屠其身,至今为天下僇笑。予之德不足以胜妖孽,是用忍情。"于时坐者皆为深叹。

后岁余,崔已委身于人,张亦有所娶。适经所居,乃因其夫言于崔,求以外兄见。夫语之,而崔终不为出。张怨念之诚,动于颜色。崔知之,潜赋一章,词曰:"自从消瘦减容光,万转千回懒下床。不为旁人羞不起,为郎憔悴却羞郎。"竟不之见。后数日,张生将行,又赋一章以谢绝云:"弃置今何道,当时且自亲。还将旧时意,怜取眼前人。"自是,绝不复知矣。时人多许张为善补过者。予常于朋会之中,往往及此意者,夫使知者不为,为者不惑。

贞元岁九月,执事李公垂宿于予靖安里第,语及于是。公垂卓然称异,遂为《莺莺歌》以传之。崔氏小名莺莺,公垂以命篇。

Whenever Yuan Chen stopped at an inn at Pucheng on his official travels, the sound of the nearby monastery bells, especially when heard in his bed at dawn, always touched him to the quick and made him feel young and romantic again. He was in his forties, a conventionally happy husband, a popular poet, and a high official who had his many ups and downs. He should have been able to forget, or at least calmly reflect on, a love affair which happened so long ago. But he surprised himself. Twenty years had passed, and the tolling of those monastery bells in the early hours presaging the break of dawn, their familiar pitch and rhythm, still evoked in him a mood of infinite sadness, awaked some deep, hidden emotion, intimate as life itself, and a sense of the strange pathos and beauty of life which even his poetic pen could only suggest. As he lay in bed, he recalled the sight of the pale sky with its dim, shimmering stars, the suffocating emotions associated with it, the strong perfumes, and the vision of a smile that was half a smile on the face of the girl who was his first love.

Yuan was then a young man of twenty-two, on his way to seek literary honors at the capital. According to his own story, he had never fallen in love before and had never had an affair with a woman, for as a brilliant and highly sensitive young man, he had set his mark high. He was not particularly jovial or sociable, and the common, good-looking girls about whom his young friends raved left him untouched, although he confessed that when he saw a girl of distinguished looks or talent, he was deeply moved.

In the days of the Tang Empire, scholars set out to the capital months or even half a year before the national examinations, and took the chance to travel and see the country. His time was his own. When he passed Pucheng, at the bend of the Yellow River, he stopped to see

Yang who was a schoolmate of his. Yang urged him to stop over, and he did. They often walked to the Puchiu Temple about three miles east of the city, where the hillsides were covered with plum blossoms in winter. The weather was cold, but crisp, sunny, and dry. Here one obtained a view of the wide expanse of the river and the distant Taipo mountains to the south, which rose on the other side.

Yuan was so enamoured of the place that he made arrangements with the monastery to stay in one of the guest rooms provided for pilgrims. The temple had been built about fifty years before the Empress Wu and was laid out on a grand scale, with glazed yellow roofs and gilt decorations. It was large enough to accommodate over a hundred pilgrims during the crowded spring season. There were cheaper rooms for peasants and their families, and some elegant suites in special courtyards reserved for the more important guests. Yuan chose a room in the northwestern corner for its quiet and seclusion. The tall trees at the back cast a cool green light over the court, while a covered corridor in front with its many hexagonal windows afforded glimpses of the great river and the mountains beyond. The room and the furniture were simple, but comfortable. Yuan was delighted, and with the few volumes of poetry which he always kept in his light luggage, he felt comfortably settled for a short and delightful vacation.

"You are romantic to choose a place like this," said Yang.

"Romantic about what?"

"The moon, the flowers, the snow, and the wind-swept hills. This is an ideal place for romance."

"Don't be silly. If I wanted to seek pleasures, I would go to the capital. No, I am going to be a monk and bury myself in books for a few weeks here."

Yang knew that his friend was highly temperamental, sensitive, and self-willed, and he let him have his way.

He had not been there a day before he discovered that on the west adjoining the temple wall there was a villa of some rich family, with a big orchard of flower and fruit trees at the back which he could see from his back window. The dark-tiled roofs, partly hidden by an apricot tree stretching across the wall, revealed a spacious building of several courtyards. He found out from the servant that the villa was part of the temple property and was occupied by a family by the name of Tsui. The father of the family, who was now dead, had been a patron of the temple and a great friend of the abbot, and used to come and live there whenever he wanted to get away from the city. After the father died, the family came to live there permanently because the widow, Mrs. Tsui, was a timid woman and said she felt safe there. The abbot permitted them to do so, partly because of their personal friendship and partly because the villa had been built by a large donation from the deceased father.

On the third night, the young man heard the sound of distant music, sweet and sad and low, played on a seven-stringed instrument. Heard in the silence of the night at a monastery, it was strangely exciting.

The next morning, his curiosity aroused, he walked around the temple grounds and found there was a wall enclosing the villa so that he could not see much of the inside. A stream ran along the front of the house, which was set farther back than the temple, and the gate was reached by a charming red-painted bridge. The door was closed, and there was a sign of mourning in the form of a diagonal cross of white paper, old and torn, pasted over the red circle of the gate. A separate path ran for about fifty yards down and joined the main road at the temple outer gate. The air was fragrant with the many plum flowers in full bloom and a small stream ran from the inside garden through an opening in the wall and fell into the stream in front with the sound of frolicking children. Yuan was fascinated. He kept thinking of the family which lived in such beautiful seclusion and the player of the sweet melody he had heard the night before, who had never allowed herself to be seen. On coming back, he realized that the part adjoining his court was the back of the house.

He would not have paid more attention to his unknown neighbor had not something happened in the second week of his arrival. There was rumor of looting and riots in the city. General Hun Chan had died, and the ill-disciplined soldiery had taken the occasion of the funeral to stage a riot. They looted the shops and carried away women from the people's homes. The next morning, things seemed to get worse. Some of the soldiers, having looted the city, came toward the river. The village nearby was full of foot-loose ragged troops. Just before noon, when he was sitting in a rattan chair with his feet upon a table and a volume of Meng Haojan on his lap, he heard feminine voices and hurrying steps passing the corridor in front. He went out to see what had happened. He was the more surprised because his room was at the end of the passage. There was a door which was usually locked and which he had not noticed before. The door was now open and a middle-aged woman, about forty, and two girls were hurrying along the winding corridor toward the main temple rooms as fast as their feet could carry them. The woman, richly dressed, walked in front, while the daughter, who was about seventeen or eighteen, and a maid followed behind. The daughter wore a simple, old dark blue dress and her hair was down, gathered at the back with a large clasp. He was sure that it was she who played the music. The precipitate manner of the women showed that they were in fear of some trouble.

Rather enjoying the excitement, and attracted by the sight of the young girlish figure, Yuan hurried forward and followed them. There was a hubbub among the monks and the servants. A woman whose husband had been killed defending his daughter was weeping and telling her story. The young girl, careless of others looking on, stood by and listened attentively. She had a mass of beautiful black hair, a white neck, an unusually small mouth, and her face was slender and small. Her mother looked terribly anxious and worried, evidently afraid that the soldiers might come to their house, for it was believed that they were wealthy. The abbot came out and told them that in case of emergency he would provide a safe hiding place for them. The rabble soldiers, out for loot mainly, would not dare to desecrate the temple.

"Mother, I won't worry," said the daughter in a calm, but chirping girlish voice. "We must stay in the house. It will invite robbery to abandon it. Time enough when necessary to escape through the back door and run into the temple." The morning sun cast a white light over her pointed nose and high forehead, which was the only thing unfeminine about her, if it is true that brains and good looks should not go together in a woman. The mother listened to her advice. She seemed to rely a good deal on her daughter's judgment.

Being young, and cavalierly willing to help a young girl, Yuan went up to the abbot and said with a correct and decorous countenance, not looking at the girl, that under the circumstances it would be wise to take all precautionary measures for the ladies' protection. He said he had a friend who knew the regional commander well, and who would be willing to go and ask for the commander's protection. All they would need would be half a dozen well-armed guards stationed outside the house.

"That is sensible," said the girl, directing a pleading look at him. The mother asked the young man's name, and Yuan introduced himself.

Delighted at the chance to know the family, Yuan said he would call on his friend Yang immediately. In the evening, he came back with six soldiers and a formal notice signed by the regional commander, warning the rabble off the Tsui house. As a matter of fact, the sight of the red vests of these guards was enough to deter any straggling ragamuffins from venturing into the villa.

Happy with his success, Yuan hoped to win a smile of gratitude from the charming young lady who had looked at him so pleadingly that morning. He went expectantly into an elegantly furnished parlor, but only the mother came out to see him. She said many pleasant things in appreciation of the trouble he had taken, and Yuan thought that being able to secure such official influence must have raised him in the mother's regard. But he could not obtain another glimpse of the girl and he returned to the temple, disappointed.

In a few days, the regional commander's own army arrived, order was restored in the city, and the guards were withdrawn. Mrs. Tsui invited Yuan to dinner in the central parlor, which gave the occasion an atmosphere of great formality.

"I wish to thank you for all that you have done for us," said the mother, "and I want to introduce you properly to my family."

She called to a boy about twelve, whose name was Huanlang (Joy) and bade him make his formal bow to his "elder brother."

"He is my only son," said Mrs. Tsui with a big smile, and then she called, "Inging, come out and thank the gentleman who has saved our lives."

The girl was long in coming out. Yuan thought that she was shy because this was to be a formal introduction, and girls of high families would hardly think of sitting at the same table with a strange young man. The mother called again impatiently and repeatedly, "Inging, I am asking you to come out. Mr. Yuan has saved your life and your mother's life. Is this the time to follow conventions?"

The daughter came out at last and made her bow, shyly, yet proudly. She wore a simple, tight-fitting dress, with a neat but modest makeup. Like a well-educated girl of a highly born family, she took a seat next to her mother silently, giving Yuan the distinct impression that seeing her at all was a rare privilege.

According to custom, Yuan asked her mother, "How old is your daughter?"

"She was born under the present emperor, in the year *chiatse*. She is seventeen."

Though this was a home dinner and Yuan was the only guest, the daughter was perhaps overconscious of the young man's presence. She maintained a correct and distant manner throughout the whole dinner. Yuan tried several times to guide the conversation to familiar topics— her deceased father and her younger brother's studies—but he could not draw her into conversation. Any ordinary girl, even the most virtuous and least coquettish, would look and feel differently in a young man's presence, and her face and manner would show it. But this charming girl was a riddle to him, like a sphinx or a fairy princess who could not be touched by ordinary human emotions. Was she completely rigid and virtuous—which Yuan could not believe—or was that cold exterior a mask for deep passions within? Or was it an extra reserve adopted by girls brought up in the severe Confucian training?

In the course of the dinner, Yuan learned that the widow's maiden name was Cheng, the same as his own mother's, and being of the same clan branch, she was, in fact, an aunt by relationship. The mother was visibly elated at the discovery and she proposed a toast to the clan nephew. Only then did the daughter's face soften into a suggestion of a smile.

Yuan was both piqued and attracted by the girl's attitude. He had never yet met a girl who was so proud and reserved, and so difficult to approach. The more he fought against his feelings, the more he was fascinated by her and desired her.

He tried every excuse to call on the family, first to pay his return call, and then to talk with the younger brother. He made his presence felt in the family, and Inging must certainly have seen him, for girls of rich families observed and heard a great deal from behind the latticed partitions. But she was as shy as a deer at the approach of a beast of prey. Once he saw her playing in the twilight with her younger brother in the back garden, but upon seeing him, she darted off and disappeared. Oriole, Oriole, he cried, what an elusive oriole!

One day, he chanced upon the maid alone, on the path leading from the house to the outer gate. The maid, whose name was Rose (Hungniang), was a simple, direct girl, pretty and attractive in her own way, and wise in the ways of the world. Yuan took the opportunity to inquire after her young mistress. His face was crimson and Rose smiled a knowing smile.

"Tell me, is your mistress engaged?"

"No. Why do you ask?"

"Well, we are cousins, and I am interested to know more about her. We have been introduced, as you know, but I have never had a chance to talk with her. I should be so happy to have such an opportunity."

Rose was silent, and merely looked at him.

"Tell me, why does she avoid me?"

"How do I know?"

"She seems such a wonderful girl, so refined and well-behaved—I admire her greatly," Yuan said at last.

"Oh, I see. Why don't you ask to see her through the mother?"

"You do not understand. She hardly says a word when her mother is around. Is there a chance of my seeing her alone? Since seeing her, I have not been able to think of anything else."

"I see what you mean," said the maid. She covered her mouth in laughter and started to run away.

"Rose, Rose!" he called after her. When she stopped, he said, "Rose, I beg you. You must help me."

The maid looked at him steadily and said sympathetically, "I would not dare to bring such a message. She is very stern and proper. She has never spoken to a young man. Mr. Yuan, you are a gentleman and you have done a service to the family. I like you. I will tell you a secret. She reads and writes poems, and often sits before her books, lost in thought. You may write a poem to her. That will be the only way to open her heart to you, if there is any way at all. And you'd better thank me for the advice." She winked at him coquettishly.

The next day, Yuan sent a poem through the maid.

Green light suffuses the silent, deep courtyard;

The twittering oriole is silent, too, hidden in the shade.

The shut-out lover sees only flower petals

Floating out with the garden stream, and feels lost.

I watched the declining moon at dawn,

My soul lost in thought of thy lovely face,

And trembled with the fainting hope

Of a kindly gesture, a gracious smile.

That evening, Rose brought back a poem by Inging, which was entitled, "Full Moon Light."

Some one waits in the moonlit night

In the western room, with the door ajar,

Across the wall, the flower shadows move—

Ah, perhaps my love has come!

That was February the fourteenth. Yuan was overjoyed. It was a clear invitation to a secret rendezvous. An appointment by night was more than he had hoped for.

On the sixteenth, he followed the hint in the poem and climbed over the wall by the apricot tree and peeped inside. He found, indeed, that the door of the western room was left open. He climbed down and went into the room.

Rose was sleeping in the bed and he waked her. The maid was surprised. "Why do you come here? What do you want?" she asked.

"She asked me to come," Yuan explained. "Please go and tell her that I am here."

Soon Rose came back and whispered to him, "She is coming!"

Yuan waited ten minutes in unbearable suspense. When Inging

appeared, there was a mixture of excitement and confusion in her face, but her deep, black eyes were veiled in mystery. The momentary wave of bashfulness passed and she said, rather stiffly, "I have asked you to come, Mr. Yuan, because you said you wanted to see me. I am grateful for what you have done to protect my mother and our family, and I want to thank you personally. I am glad that we are cousins, but I am surprised that you sent such a love poem through the maid. I could not, and would not, expose it to my mother, for it would be unfair to you, and I thought I had better personally see you to ask you to stop this." She paused in confusion. It sounded very much like a rehearsed speech.

Yuan was aghast. "But, Miss Tsui, I was only asking to have a talk with you. And I came because of that poem you sent me."

"Yes, I invited you," she replied resolutely. "I took the risk and I did it gladly. But you would be wrong to think I am making an appointment for anything improper. Do not misunderstand."

Her voice shook with suppressed emotion. She turned and left hurriedly.

The disappointment and shame made Yuan angry. He could not believe it, could not understand it! Why should she write that obviously suggestive poem, instead of sending a simple reply through the maid, and then take the trouble to come and lecture him? Or had she changed her mind only at the last moment, afraid of what she was about to do? What womanly caprice! He could not understand women. Now she appeared to him more like a marble-cold princess than ever. His love almost turned into hatred because he thought she was making fun of him.

Two nights later, Yuan was asleep in his bed when he felt some one shaking him in the dark. He sat up and lighted the lamp. Rose was standing before him.

"Get up. She is coming," she whispered, and left the room.

Yuan sat up in bed, rubbing his eyes, not quite sure that he was awake. Quickly he threw a robe around himself and sat up and waited.

Soon the maid brought Inging into the room. The girl's face was flushed, shy, uncertain, and she looked as though she was leaning on her maid for support. All her pride and haughty self-control was gone. She did not apologize, nor explain. He hair was let down over her shoulders, and she looked at him with a deep, dark look in her wonderful eyes. No explanation was necessary.

Yuan's heart palpitated. This sudden surrender of herself to her own free will in his room was even more surprising than her cold repudiation of him on the previous occasion. But all his anger had dissolved at the sight of the girl he loved.

The maid had brought a pillow and, quickly depositing it on the bed, she withdrew. The first thing the girl did was put the light out, still without uttering a word. Yuan walked up to her and, feeling the warmth of her body close to his, he took her in his arms. Just as quickly, the girl's lips found his, and he felt a quiver go over her whole body and heard her quick intake of breath. Again without a word, she sank softly on the bed in a natural gesture, as if her legs were too weak to support her.

Too soon he heard the matin bells of the temple. Dawn was breaking and Rose came to urge her mistress to leave. Inging got up and dressed in the pale light of the dawn. After adjusting her hair roughly with her hand, she left with the maid, a languorous expression on her face. The door closed without a sound. She had not spoken all night. He had done all the talking and when he spoke of his adoration for her, she answered only with sighs and the warm, wet pressure of her lips.

Yuan sat up suddenly and wondered if it had not all happened in a dream. But her strong perfume still lingered in his room and he saw the rouge marks on the towel. Yes, it was real. This sphinx-like girl, who had seemed so aloof and impassive, had given way to a passion beyond her self-control. Was it passion—or was it love? She had come to him shamelessly. He remembered the intense emphasis with which she had said previously, "You would be wrong to think I am making an appointment for anything improper. Do not misunderstand." What did she mean by that? It was enough that she had come. He had not believed it possible only the day before.

He had never known such happiness; he was transported into a new world, with unknown frontiers of beauty and delirious happiness before him. He waited hourly for the coming night when, like a luminous pearl or warm, glowing jade she would again transform his humble room into heaven, by the magic of her love. She had made no sign that she would come again the following night.

It is entirely believable that the girl had decided to come to him in a moment of passion. It is also possible that after the first night, she wanted to take time to think over the romance which she had so rashly begun. Yuan stopped trying to figure out women. Night after night he waited, with the blood pounding in his veins, hoping for another visit from the fairy princess. Was this suspense another caprice of the girl? Had she come to him merely to satisfy her whim and desire?

He sat alone in his room every night. He had bought coils of incense, in preparation for her visit, and he watched the cold cinders fall silently into the container. He tried to take his mind off what seemed to be vain, hopeless waiting by reading a light romance—for he could not read anything serious, prepared to sit up at the slightest noise of footsteps or the faintest creak of the door. Once he went to test the passage door like a thief, but it was firmly locked.

During the first few days, he avoided going to her home, for having had a secret meeting with her, he thought it would be wise to show himself in the house as little as possible. After the third day, however, he could not stand it any longer and he called on the mother. She was as cordial as usual and asked him to stay for lunch. Inging came to the table, again with that cold, correct look on her face, which would not betray their intimacy by so much as a gesture. He waited for a sign, but the girl was a master in the art of deception. When he looked boldly at her, her eyelids did not even flicker. He thought that perhaps her mother's suspicion had been aroused and she was being extra careful. There *had* to be some reason for her silence.

Two weeks passed uneventfully. He did not mention the affair to Yang, and when his friend asked him to stay overnight, he always insisted on returning to the temple, for fear of missing her visit. He could not tear himself away from the place. He composed a poem of sixty lines, recording his strange experience of meeting a fairy, and telling of the heights of his ecstasy and the depths of his longing. "And the seas were wide and the clouds were high, and the fairy did not return."

One evening, past midnight, as if in answer to his prayer, he heard the passage door creak. Quickly he rushed to open it and found Rose standing there. She confided to him that her young mistress had

had a key made for the lock so that they could meet in the western room. She had arranged it so that the padlock would appear to be in place, but he could push it open and reach the western room by a short passage. Even in his delirium, Yuan was impressed with the cunning and audacity of his lover's meticulous plans for their meeting.

After that, Inging came to meet him in the western room every other night, or as often as she could get away, and she always sent a message through the maid when she could not. She nearly always came after midnight and returned to her room before dawn.

Yuan was deliriously happy. The girl opened her heart to him, loved him passionately, and they pledged to be true to one another no matter what happened. It was difficult to believe that there was so much love in her small body. Inging had a mature mind and was interested in all that he was doing or planning to do. They lay together in the dark and talked in whispers, for there was the danger of discovery even though Yuan's ears were always on the alert. On the other hand, she never showed the slightest regret for what she had done. The only explanation for her conduct, when he asked her, was a passionate kiss and a murmur, "I cannot help it, I love you so."

"What if your mother finds out?" He asked her once.

"Then she will have to make you her son-in-law," replied Inging with a smile. Her nerves were as good as her brains.

"I will speak to your mother when the time comes," Yuan said, and Inging did not press the question further.

The time of parting had to come. Yuan told Inging that he must leave for the capital. Inging was not surprised, but remarked calmly, "Go if you must. But the capital is only a few days' journey from here. You will come back in the summer. I want you to." She was so sure of herself.

The night before his departure, he was fully prepared for their usual rendezvous, but for some reason Inging did not come.

He returned in late summer for a short visit, just before the autumn imperial examinations. There was no indication that Inging's mother knew about the affair. She was as cordial as usual and invited him to stay at their house. Perhaps she had an idea that she might marry her daughter to him.

Yuan was pleased with the idea of seeing Inging in the daytime. They had a wonderful week together. She had lost her shyness before him and sometimes he could see her playing with her younger brother, tying blades of grass into a boat to sail down a small stream in their back garden. He was very happy about their secret love.

Yuan's happiness did not escape Yang. When Yang came to visit his friend at Inging's home, he sensed the situation without being told.

"What is going on here, Weichih?" Yang remarked, calling him by his courtesy name, and Yuan smiled.

The mother saw it, too. The day before Yuan left, she asked Inging about the young man, and the girl said with a wholehearted confidence, "He will come back. He has to go and take the imperial examinations."

That evening, they had an opportunity to be alone. Yuan looked miserable and sad, sighing at her side, but Inging had full confidence in his love. There was another side to her character. The girl who trembled in his embrace was clear-headed and unsentimental in a crisis. She did not utter useless words. Calmly, she said to him, "Do not look as if this were good-bye forever. I shall be waiting."

The mother gave Yuan a farewell dinner, and after supper he asked Inging to play the *chin* for him. He had once chanced to find her playing the music alone, but when she discovered that he was listening, she had stopped and refused to continue, in spite of his pleading. That night, however, she consented. Seated before the instrument, with her curls hanging over her bent head, she struck notes slowly and pensively, the "Prelude to the Cloud Cape Dance". Yuan sat entranced, absorbed in the beautiful player and her exquisite melody. Suddenly she lost control and broke off and dashed inside. Her mother called her, but she did not come out again.

The lovers only saw each other once more. Yuan failed at the examinations. Perhaps he was too ashamed of himself to come back and ask for her hand, but she was waiting for him and there was nothing to prevent him from paying her a visit. At first he sent her letters; then the intervals between them became greater. The capital was only a few days away, but Inging could always find reasons for his delay, and she never gave up hope.

At this time, Yang came to see Inging and her mother rather frequently. The mother spoke to Yang about Yuan, for he was an older man and married, and she showed him Yuan's letters. Yang knew something was wrong. He had an idea that his friend was leading a new life in the capital, for Chang-an was full of distractions. He sent Yuan a letter, and the reply only increased his worries. The girl persuaded her mother to put the best complexion upon the matter and assured her that he was hiding until he passed the examinations the following autumn. Then he would surely come.

Spring had come round and summer was approaching. One day

Inging received a poem from Yuan, phrased in the most equivocal language. He spoke of their past happiness and his longing for her, yet the meaning between the lines was clear. It was a poem of farewell. He sent her some gifts and spoke of his torture in their yearlong separation, comparing it to that of the Cowherd and the Spinning Maid in Heaven, who were permitted to meet across the Milky Way only once a year. But, he went on, "Alas! In this yearlong separation, who knows what may happen on the other side of the Milky Way? My future course is as uncertain as that of the clouds, and how can I be sure that you will be as pure as snow? When a peach flower blooms in spring, who is to prevent admirers from plucking its rosy petals? I am happy that I was the first to receive your favor, but who will be the lucky one to take the prize? Ah, a year to wait, and how long will it seem before another year is out? Rather than endure this endless waiting, would it not be better to part forever?"

Read carefully, what the poem implied was utter nonsense—it was an outright, unjustifiable insult on the girl's character. When Yang saw Inging with the letter lying in her hand, her eyes were swollen. Yuan must have gone out of his mind, or he was simply trying to extricate himself from the situation. What was there to prevent him from coming to see her if he loved her? And he did not have to impute to her what he was guilty of himself. Yang made up his mind.

"Miss Tsui, I am going to Chang-an on some business. I shall look him up, and shall be glad to take a letter for you."

Inging looked at him. "Will you?" she asked calmly. Yang was surprised by the matter-of-fact tone in which she said it. "And don't worry about me. I am all right," she added. "Tell him I am all right."

Yang went back and packed up for the trip to Chang-an which he had really undertaken for the girls' sake. He would like to find out what was happening and perhaps give Yuan a piece of his mind. As a man of honor, Yuan should have married her, though Inging was the last girl to demand it of him. He would have liked to bring Yuan back if it were possible.

Three days later, he set out for the capital. He brought with him a letter from Inging which he gave to Yuan. It was as sincere and to the point as it was dignified in her self-defense:

"I am delighted to receive your last letter and touched by your loving remembrance. I am excited and happy to receive the box of hair ornaments and the five inches of rouge. I appreciate these thoughtful gifts, but of what use would they be to me in your absence? They bring you closer to me and only increase my longing to see you. I am glad that you are well and able to pursue your studies at the capital, and I am only sorry for myself, shut up in this small town. There is no use grieving about Fate. I am prepared to take what it has in store for me. I miss you so much since your departure in autumn. I try to appear happy and gay when there is company, but when I am alone, I cannot restrain my tears. I have dreamed often of you and we are so happy together like old times, and then I wake up, clinging to the half-warm quilt with a sense of desolation. I feel you are so far away from me.

"A year has passed since you were gone. I am grateful beyond words that in a gay city like Chang-an, you have not forgotten your old sweetheart entirely. But I shall always be true to our promise. We were formally introduced by my mother, but under the circumstances I lost my self-control and completely surrendered myself to you. You know that after our first night together, I swore I would never love anyone but you, and we would be true to each other for life. That was my hope and our promise to each other. If you keep your promise, all is well, and I shall be the happiest woman in the world. But if you discard the old for the new and think of our love as a casual affair, I shall love you still, but shall go down to my grave with an eternal regret. It is all up to you, and I have nothing further to say.

"Take good care of yourself, please. I am sending you a jade ring, which I wore in my childhood, hoping it will serve as a souvenir of our love. Jade is a symbol of integrity, and the circle of the ring signifies continuity. I am also sending a strand of silk threads and a tear-stained bamboo tea roller. These are simple things but they carry the hope that your love will be as spotless as jade and as continuous as the ring. The tear stains on the bamboo and the skein of threads will be reminders of my love and my tangled feelings for you. My heart is near you, but my body is far away. If thinking would help, I would be hourly by your side. This letter carries with it my ardent longing and my desperate hope that we may meet again. Take good care of yourself, and don't worry about me."

"Well?" Yang watched his friend's face turn from red to white while reading the letter. After a pause, Yang said, "Why don't you come and see her?"

Yuan stammered some excuse about his studies and his being unhappy with himself. Yang saw through it all.

"You are not doing right by her," declared Yang. "Tell me what is the matter."

"I am not ready to marry. I have my scholastic career to attend to. It is true, I had an affair with her. She came to me—I do not think that a youthful folly should interfere with my career."

"Youthful folly?"

"Yes. Don't you think that when a young man has done something he should have not done, the only thing to do is to end it?"

Yang was angry. "It may be a youthful folly to you. But what about the girl who writes you that letter?"

Yuan's face showed great embarrassment. "A young man can make mistakes, can't he? And he shouldn't waste his time with women. He should—"

"Weichih," said Yang, "if you have changed your mind, don't try to moralize about it. Let me tell you what I think. I think you are the most moralistic and the most selfish person I have known."

Yang was convinced his friend was not being honest with him, that there was some other reason. He stayed at the capital for about a week and had time to learn what Yuan was doing. He was having an affair with a Miss Wei of a very rich family. In utter disgust, Yang returned to Pucheng.

He had a difficult job in breaking the news to the girl. He was afraid it would hurt her terribly. He told the mother first.

"Well," asked Inging, when she saw him, "have you brought a letter for me?"

Yang remained silent. He couldn't say it, and while he was trying to find words, he saw the girl's countenance change. In that moment he saw the deep, dark eyes of Inging become bright and penetrating, like those of a woman who understands not only her situation, but all life and eternity; or like one who has been forsaken not by one lover, but by ten. Her eyes burned, and Yang instinctively lowered his lashes.

"Well," he said finally, "that poem he sent you was a poem of farewell."

Inging stood there motionless and speechless for a full five seconds. Yang was afraid she was going to collapse. But something proud and hard was in her words as she said, "So be it!" She turned abruptly to leave the room. Just as she reached the chamber door, Yang heard her hysterical laughter. Her mother rushed after her, and for five minutes Yang could still hear that laughter inside.

Yang was greatly worried, but the next day he found out from the mother, to his great relief, that the girl was all right, that she had been proud and silent as a queen after the moments of hysteria. She had given her consent to marriage with a cousin of her mother's family, by the name of Cheng, who had been soliciting the match for some time. The following spring, Inging and Cheng were married.

One day, Yuan came to her home and asked to see her, as a distant cousin. Inging refused to see him, but as Yuan was preparing to go away, she stepped out from behind the screen.

"Why do you come to bother me? I waited for you and you did not return. There is nothing to be said between us. I have got over it, and you should, too. Go away!"

Yuan left without a word, and Inging collapsed on the floor in a heap.

浮生六记
Six Chapters of a Floating Life[①]

沈　复（Shen Fu）

闺房记乐

余生乾隆癸未冬十一月二十有二日，正值太平盛世，且在衣冠之家，居苏州沧浪亭畔，天之厚我，可谓至矣。东坡云："事如春梦了无痕"，苟不记之笔墨，未免有辜彼苍之厚。

因思《关雎》冠三百篇之首，故列夫妇于首卷，余以次递及焉。所愧少年失学，稍识之无，不过记其实情实事而已。若必考订其文法，是责明于垢鉴矣。

余幼聘金沙于氏，八龄而夭；娶陈氏。陈名芸，字淑珍，舅氏心馀先生女也。生而颖慧，学语时，口授《琵琶行》，即能成诵。四龄失怙；母金氏，弟克昌，家徒壁立。芸既长，娴女红，三口仰其十指供给；克昌从师，修脯无缺。一日，于书簏中得《琵琶行》，挨字而认，始识字；刺绣之暇，渐通吟咏，有"秋侵人影瘦，霜染菊花肥"之句。

余年十三，随母归宁，两小无嫌，得见所作，虽叹其才思隽秀，窃恐其福泽不深；然心注不能释，告母曰："若为儿择妇，非淑姊不娶。"母亦爱其柔和，即脱金约指缔姻焉。此乾隆乙未七月十六日也。

---

① 原著虽为"六记"，然只存"四记"，此仅选其中的第一记《闺房记乐》及其对应译文。——编者注

是年冬,值其堂姊出阁,余又随母往。

芸与余同齿而长余十月,自幼姊弟相呼,故仍呼之曰淑姊。

时但见满室鲜衣,芸独通体素淡,仅新其鞋而已。见其绣制精巧,询为己作,始知其慧心不仅在笔墨也。

其形削肩长项,瘦不露骨,眉弯目秀,顾盼神飞,唯两齿微露,似非佳相。一种缠绵之态,令人之意也消。

索观诗稿,有仅一联,或三四句,多未成篇者,询其故,笑曰:"无师之作,愿得知己堪师者敲成之耳。"余戏题其签曰"锦囊佳句",不知夭寿之机此已伏矣。

是夜送亲城外,返,已漏三下,腹饥索饵,婢妪以枣脯进,余嫌其甜。芸暗牵余袖,随至其室,见藏有暖粥并小菜焉。余欣然举箸,忽闻芸堂兄玉衡呼曰:"淑妹速来!"芸急闭门曰:"已疲乏,将卧矣。"玉衡挤身而入,见余将吃粥,乃笑睨芸曰:"顷我索粥,汝曰'尽矣',乃藏此专待汝婿耶?"芸大窘避去,上下哗笑之。余亦负气,挈老仆先归。

自吃粥被嘲,再往,芸即避匿,余知其恐贻人笑也。

至乾隆庚子正月二十二日花烛之夕,见瘦怯身材依然如昔,头巾既揭,相视嫣然。合卺后,并肩夜膳,余暗于案下握其腕,暖尖滑腻,胸中不觉怦怦作跳。让之食,适逢斋期,已数年矣。暗计吃斋之初,正余出痘之期,因笑调曰:"今我光鲜无恙,姊可从此开戒否?"芸笑之以目,点之以首。

廿四日为余姊于归,廿三国忌不能作乐,故廿二之夜即为余姊款嫁,芸出堂陪宴。余在洞房与伴娘对酌,拇战辄北,大醉而卧;醒则芸正晓妆未竟也。

是日亲朋络绎,上灯后始作乐。廿四子正,余作新舅送嫁,丑末归来,业已灯残人静;悄然入室,伴妪盹于床下,芸卸妆尚未卧,高烧银烛,低垂粉颈,不知观何书而出神若此。因抚其肩曰:"姊连日辛苦,何犹孜孜不倦耶?"

芸忙回首起立曰:"顷正欲卧,开橱得此书,不觉阅之忘倦。《西厢》之名闻之熟矣,今始得见,真不愧才子之名,但未免形容尖薄耳。"

余笑曰:"唯其才子,笔墨方能尖薄。"

伴妪在旁促卧,令其闭门先去。遂与比肩调笑,恍同密友重逢;戏探其怀,亦怦怦作跳,因俯其耳曰:"姊何心春乃尔耶?"芸回眸微笑,便觉一缕情丝摇人魂魄;拥之入帐,不知东方之既白。

芸作新妇,初甚缄默,终日无怒容,与之言,微笑而已。事上以敬,处下以和,井井然未尝稍失。每见朝暾上窗,即披衣急起,如有人呼促者然。余笑曰:"今非吃粥比矣,何尚畏人嘲耶?"芸曰:"曩之藏粥待君,传为话柄。今非畏嘲,恐堂上道新娘懒惰耳。"

余虽恋其卧而德其正,因亦随之早起。自此耳鬓相磨,亲同形影,爱恋之情有不可以言语形容者。

而欢娱易过,转瞬弥月。时吾父稼夫公在会稽幕府,专役相迓,受业于武林赵省斋先生门下。先生循循善诱,余今日之尚能握管,先生力也。

归来完姻时,原订随侍到馆;闻信之余,心甚怅然,恐芸之对人堕泪,而芸反强颜劝勉,代整行装,是晚但觉神色稍异面已。临行,向余小语曰:"无人调护,自去经心!"

及登舟解缆,正当桃李争妍之候,而余则恍同林鸟失群,天地异色。到馆后,吾父即渡江东去。

居三月,如十年之隔。芸虽时有书来,必两问一答,半多勉励词,余皆浮套语,心殊怏怏。每当风生竹院,月上蕉窗,对景怀人,梦魂颠倒。

先生知其情,即致书吾父,出十题而遣余暂归,喜同戍人得赦。

登舟后,反觉一刻如年。及抵家,吾母处问安毕,入房,芸起相迎,握手未通片语,而两人魂魄恍恍然化烟成雾,觉耳中惺然一响,不知更有此身矣。

时当六月,内室炎蒸,幸居沧浪亭爱莲居西间壁,板桥内一轩临流,名曰"我取",取"清斯濯缨,浊斯濯足"意也;檐前老树一株,浓阴覆窗,人面俱绿,隔岸游人往来不绝,此吾父稼夫公垂帘宴客处也。禀命吾母,携芸消夏于此,因暑罢绣,终日伴余课书论古,品月评花而已。芸不善饮,强之可三杯,教以射覆为令。自以为人间之乐无过于此矣。

一日,芸问曰:"各种古文,宗何为是?"余曰:"《国策》、《南华》取其灵快,匡衡、刘向取其雅健,史迁、班固取其博大,昌黎取其浑,柳州取其峭,庐陵取其宕,三苏取其辩,他若贾、董策对,庾、徐骈体,陆贽奏议,取资者不能尽举,在人之慧心领会耳。"

芸曰:"古文全在识高气雄,女子学之恐难入殼;唯诗之一道,妾稍有领悟耳。"

余曰:"唐以诗取士,而诗之宗匠必推李、杜。卿爱宗何人?"

芸发议曰:"杜诗锤炼精纯,李诗激洒落拓;与其学杜之森严,不如学李之活泼。"

余曰:"工部为诗家之大成,学者多宗之,卿独取李,何也?"

芸曰:"格律谨严,词旨老当,诚杜所独擅;但李诗宛如姑射仙子,有一种落花流水之趣,令人可爱。非杜亚于李,不过妾之私心宗杜心浅,爱李心深。"

余笑曰:"初不料陈淑珍乃李青莲知己。"

芸笑曰:"妾尚有启蒙师白乐天先生,时感于怀,未尝稍释。"

余曰:"何谓也?"

芸曰:"彼非作《琵琶行》者耶?"

余笑曰:"异哉!李太白是知己,白乐天是启蒙师,余适字三白,为卿婿,卿与'白'字何其有缘耶?"

芸笑曰:"白字有缘,将来恐白字连篇耳。"(吴音呼"别字"为"白字"。)相与大笑。

余曰:"卿既知诗,亦当知赋之弃取。"

芸曰:"《楚辞》为赋之祖,妾学浅费解。就汉、晋人中,调高语炼,似觉相如为最。"

余戏曰:"当日文君之从长卿,或不在琴而在此乎?"复相与大笑而罢。

余性爽直,落拓不羁,芸若腐儒,迂拘多礼。偶为披衣整袖,必连声道"得罪";或递巾授扇,必起身来接。余始厌之,曰:"卿欲以礼缚我耶?语曰:'礼多必诈'。"芸两颊发赤,曰:"恭而有礼,何反言诈?"余曰:"恭敬在心,不在虚文。"芸曰:"至亲莫如父母,可内敬在心而外肆狂放耶?"余曰:"前言戏之耳。"芸曰:"世间反目多由戏起,后勿冤妾,令人郁死!"余乃挽之入怀,抚慰之,始解颜为笑。自此"岂敢"、"得罪"竟成语助词矣。鸿案相庄廿有三年,年愈久而情愈密。

家庭之内,或暗室相逢,窄途邂逅,必握手问曰:"何处去?"私心忐忑,如恐旁人见之者。实则同行并坐,初犹避人,久则不以为意。芸或与人坐谈,见余至,必起立,偏挪其身,余就而并焉。彼此皆不觉其所以然者,始以为惭,继成不期然而然。独怪老年夫妇相视如仇者,不知何意。或曰:"非如是,焉得白头偕老哉!"斯言诚然欤?

是年七夕,芸设香烛瓜果,同拜天孙于我取轩中。余镌"愿生生世世为夫妇"图章二方;余执朱文,芸执白文,以为往来书信之用。

是夜月色颇佳,俯视河中,波光如练,轻罗小扇,并坐水窗,仰见飞云过天,变态万状。芸曰:"宇宙之大,同此一月,不知今日世间,亦有如我两人之情兴否?"余曰:"纳凉玩月,到处有之;若品论云霞,或求之幽闺绣闼,慧心默证者固亦不少;若夫妇同观,所品论者恐不在此云霞耳。"未几,烛烬月沉,撤果归卧。

七月望,俗谓鬼节。芸备小酌,拟邀月畅饮。夜忽阴云如晦,芸愀然曰:"妾能与君白头偕老,月轮当出。"余亦索然。但见隔岸萤光,明灭万点,梳织于柳堤蓼渚间。

余与芸联句以遣闷怀,而两韵之后,逾联逾纵,想入非夷,随口乱道。芸已漱涎涕泪,笑倒余怀,不能成声矣。觉其鬓边茉莉浓香扑鼻,因拍其背,以他词解之曰:"想古人以茉莉形色如珠,故供助妆压鬓,不知此花必沾油头粉面之气,其香更可爱,所供佛手当退三舍矣。"芸乃止笑曰:"佛手乃香中君子,只在有意无意间;茉莉是香中小人,故须借人之势,其香也如胁肩谄笑。"余曰:"卿何远君子而近小人?"芸曰:"我笑君子爱小人耳。"

正话间,漏已三滴,渐见风扫云开,一轮涌出,乃大喜。倚窗对酌,酒未三杯,忽闻桥下哄然一声,如有人堕。就窗细瞩,波明如镜,不见一物,惟闻河滩有只鸭急奔声。余知沧浪亭畔素有溺鬼,恐芸胆怯,未敢即言。芸曰:"噫!此声也,胡为乎来哉?"不禁毛骨皆栗,急闭窗,携酒归房。一灯如豆,罗帐低垂,弓影杯蛇,惊神未定。剔灯入帐,芸已寒热大作。余亦继之,困顿两旬;真所谓乐极灾生,亦是白头不终之兆。

中秋日,余病初愈。以芸半年新妇,未尝一至间壁之沧浪亭,先令老仆约守者勿放闲人。于将晚时,偕芸及余幼妹,一妪一婢扶焉,老仆前导。过石桥,进门折东,曲径而入。叠石成山,林木葱翠,亭在土山之巅。循级至亭心,周望极目可数里,炊烟四起,晚霞灿然。隔岸名"近山林",为大宪行台宴集之地,时正谊书院犹未启也。携一毯设亭中,席地环坐,守者烹茶以进。少焉,一轮明月已上林梢,渐觉风生袖底,月到波心,俗虑尘怀,爽然顿释。芸曰:"今日之游乐矣!若驾一叶扁舟,往来亭下,不更快哉!"时已上灯,忆及七月十五夜之惊,相扶下亭而归。吴俗,妇女是晚不拘大家小户皆出,结队而游,名曰"走月亮"。沧浪亭幽雅清旷,反无一人至者。

吾父稼夫公喜认义子,以故余异姓弟兄有二十六人。吾母亦有义女九人,九人中王二姑、俞六姑与芸最和好。王痴憨善饮,俞豪爽善谈。每集,必逐余居外,而得三女同榻,此俞六姑一人计也。余笑曰:"俟妹于归后,我当邀妹丈来,一住必十日。"俞曰:"我亦来此,与嫂同榻,不大妙耶?"芸与王微笑而已。

时为吾弟启堂婆妇,迁居饮马桥之仓米巷。屋虽宏畅,非复沧浪亭之幽雅矣。吾母诞辰演剧,芸初以为奇观。吾父素无忌讳,点演《惨别》等剧,老伶刻画,见者情动。余窥帘见芸忽起去,良久不出,入内探之。俞与王亦继至。见芸一人支颐独坐镜奁之侧,余曰:"何不快乃尔?"芸曰:"观剧原以陶情,今日之戏徒令人断肠耳。"俞与王皆笑之。余曰:"此深于情者也。"俞曰:"嫂将竟日独坐于此耶?"芸曰:"俟有可观者再往耳。"王闻言先出,请吾母点《刺梁》、《后索》等剧,劝芸出观,始称快。

余堂伯父素存公早亡,无后,吾父以余嗣焉。墓在西跨塘福寿山祖茔之侧，每年春日必挈芸拜扫。王二姑闻其地有戈园之胜，请同往。芸见地下小乱石有苔纹，斑驳可观，指示余曰："以此叠盆山，较宣州白石为古致。"余曰："若此者恐难多得。"王曰："嫂果爱此，我为拾之。"即向守坟者借麻袋一，鹤步而拾之。每得一块，余"善"，即收之；余"否"，即去之。未几，粉汗盈盈，拽袋返曰："再拾则力不胜矣。"芸且拣且言曰："我闻山果收获，必借猴力，果然！"王愤撮十指作哈痒状，余横阻之，责芸曰："人劳汝逸，犹作此语，无怪妹之动愤也。"

归途游戈园，稚绿娇红，争妍竞媚。王素憨，逢花必折。芸叱曰："既无瓶养，又不簪戴，多折何为！"王曰："不知痛痒者，何害？"余笑曰："将来罚嫁麻面多须郎，为花泄忿。"王怒余以目，掷花于地，以莲钩拨入池中，曰："何欺侮我之甚也！"芸笑解之而罢。

芸初缄默，喜听余议论。余调其言，如蟋蟀之用纤草，渐能发议。其每日饭必用茶泡，喜食芥卤乳腐，吴俗呼为"臭乳腐"；又喜食虾卤瓜。此二物余生平所最恶者，因戏之曰："狗无胃而食粪，以其不知臭秽；蜣螂团粪而化蝉，以其欲修高举也。卿其狗耶，蝉耶？"芸曰："腐取其价廉而可粥可饭，幼时食惯。今至君家，已如蜣螂化蝉，犹喜食之者，不忘本出。至卤瓜之味，到此初尝耳。"

余曰："然则我家系狗窦耶？"芸窘而强解曰："夫粪，人家皆有之，要在食与不食之别耳。然君喜食蒜，妾亦强啖之。腐不敢强，瓜可掩鼻略尝，入咽当知其美，此犹无盐貌丑而德美也。"余笑曰："卿陷我作狗耶？"芸曰："妾作狗久矣，屈君试尝之。"以箸强塞余口，余掩鼻咀嚼之，似觉脆美，开鼻再嚼，竟成异味，从此亦喜食。芸以麻油加白糖少许拌卤腐，亦鲜美。以卤瓜捣烂拌卤腐，名之曰"双鲜酱"，有异味。余曰："始恶而终好之，理之不可解也。"芸曰："情之所钟，虽丑不嫌。"

余启堂弟妇，王虚舟先生孙女也，催妆时偶缺珠花。芸出其纳采所受者呈吾母，婢妪旁惜之。芸曰："凡为妇人，已属纯阴，珠乃纯阴之精，用为首饰，阳气全克矣，何贵焉？"而于破书残画，反极珍惜。书之残缺不全者，必搜集分门，汇订成帙，统名之曰"断简残编"；字画之破损者，必觅故纸粘补成幅，有破缺处，倩予全好而卷之，名曰"弃余集赏"。于女红、中馈之暇，终日琐琐，不惮烦倦。芸于破簏烂卷中，偶获片纸可观者，如得异宝。旧邻冯妪每收乱卷卖之。其癖好与余同，且能察眼意，懂眉语，一举一动，示之以色，无不头头是道。

余尝曰："惜卿雌而伏，苟能化女为男，相与访名山，搜胜迹，遨游天下，不亦快哉！"

芸曰："此何难。俟妾鬓斑之后，虽不能远游五岳，而近地之虎阜、灵岩，南至西湖，北至平山，尽可偕游。"

余曰："恐卿鬓斑之日，步履已艰。"

芸曰："今世不能，期以来世。"

余曰："来世卿当作男，我为女子相从。"

芸曰："必得不昧今生，方觉有情趣。"

余笑曰："幼时一粥犹谈不了；若来世不昧今生，合卺之夕，细谈隔世，更无合眼时矣。"

芸曰："世传月下老人专司人间婚姻事，今生夫妇已承牵合，来世姻缘亦须仰藉神力，盍绘一像祀之？"

时有苕溪戚柳堤，名遵，善写人物。倩绘一像，一手挽红丝，一手携杖悬姻缘簿，童颜鹤发，奔驰于非烟非雾中。此戚君得意笔也。友人石琢堂为题赞语于首，悬之内室。每逢朔望，余夫妇必焚香拜祷。后因家庭多故，此画竟失所在，不知落在谁家矣。"他生未卜此生休"，两人痴情，果邀神鉴耶？

迁仓米巷，余颜其卧楼曰"宾香阁"，盖以芸名而取如宾意也。院窄墙高，一无可取。后有厢楼，通藏书处，开窗对陆氏废园，但有荒凉之象。沧浪风景，时切芸怀。

有老妪居金母桥之东，埂巷之北。绕屋皆菜圃，编篱为门。门外有池约亩许，花光树影，错杂篱边。其地即元末张士诚王府废基也。屋西数武，瓦砾堆成土山，登其巅可远眺，地旷人稀，颇饶野趣。

妪偶言及，芸神往不置，谓余曰："自别沧浪，梦魂常绕，今不得已而思其次,其老妪之居乎?"余曰:"连朝秋暑灼人,正思得一清凉地以消长昼。卿若愿往,我先观其家,可居,即袱被而往,作一月盘桓何如?"芸曰:"恐堂上不许。"余曰:"我自请之。"越日至其地,屋仅二间,前后隔而为四,纸窗竹榻,颇有幽趣。老妪知余意,欣然出其卧室为赁,四壁糊以白纸,顿觉改观。于是禀知吾母,挈芸居焉。

邻仅老夫妇二人,灌园为业,知余夫妇避暑于此,先来通殷勤,并钓池鱼、摘园蔬为馈。偿其价,不受,芸作鞋报之,始谢而受。

时方七月,绿树阴浓,水面风来,蝉鸣聒耳。邻老又为制鱼竿,与芸垂钓于柳阴深处。日落时,登土山,观晚霞夕照,随意联吟,有"兽云吞落日,弓月弹流星"之句。少焉,月印池中,虫声四起,设竹榻于篱下。老妪报酒温饭熟,遂就月光对酌,微醺而饭。浴罢则凉鞋蕉扇,或坐或卧,听邻老谈因果报应事。三鼓归卧,周体清凉,几不知身居城市矣。

篱边倩邻老购菊,遍植之。九月花开,又与芸居十日。吾母亦欣然来观,持螯对菊,赏玩竟日。

芸喜曰:"他年当与君卜筑于此,买绕屋菜园十亩,课仆妪,植瓜蔬,以供薪水。君画我绣,以为诗酒之需。布衣菜饭,可乐终身,不必作远游计也。"余深然之。今即得有境地,而知己沦亡,可胜浩叹!

离余家半里许,醋库巷有洞庭君祠,俗呼水仙庙,回廊曲折,小有园亭。每逢神诞,众姓各认一落,密悬一式之玻璃灯,中设宝座,旁列瓶几,插花陈设,以较胜负。日惟演戏,夜则参差高下,插烛于瓶花间,名曰"花照"。花光灯影,宝鼎香浮,若龙宫夜宴。司事者或笙箫歌唱,或煮茗清谈,观者如蚁集,檐下皆设栏为限。

余为众友邀去插花布置,因得躬逢其盛。归家向芸艳称之,芸曰:"惜妾非男子,不能往。"余曰:"冠我冠,衣我衣,亦化女为男之法也。"于是易髻为辫,添扫蛾眉,加余冠,微露两鬓,尚可掩饰。服余衣,长一寸又半,于腰间折而缝之,外加马褂。芸曰:"脚下将奈何?"余曰:"坊间有蝴蝶履,大小由之,购亦极易,且早晚可代撒鞋之用,不亦善乎?"芸欣然。及晚餐后,装束既毕,效男子拱手阔步者良久,忽变卦曰:"妾不去矣,为人识出既不便，堂上闻之又不可。"余怂恿曰："庙中司事者谁不知我，即识出亦不过付之一笑耳。吾母现在九妹丈家，密去密来，焉得知之。"

芸揽镜自照，狂笑不已。余强挽之，悄然径去。遍游庙中，无识出为女子者，或问何人，以表弟对，拱手而已。最后至一处，有少妇幼女坐于所设宝座后，乃杨姓司事者之眷属也。芸忽趋彼通款曲，身一侧，而不觉一按少妇之肩。旁有婢媪怒而起曰："何物狂生，不法乃尔！"余欲为措词掩饰，芸见势恶，即脱帽翘足示之曰："我亦女子耳。"相与愕然，转怒为欢，留茶点，唤肩舆送归。

吴江钱师竹病故，吾父信归，命余往吊。芸私谓余曰："吴江必经太湖，妾欲偕往，一宽眼界。"余曰："正虑独行踽踽，得卿同行，固妙，但无可托词耳。"芸曰："托言归宁。君先登舟，妾当继至。"余曰："若然，归途当泊舟万年桥下，与卿待月乘凉，以续沧浪韵事。"

时六月十八日也。是日早凉，携一仆先至胥江渡口，登舟而待。芸果肩舆至，解维出虎啸桥，渐见风帆沙鸟，水天一色。芸曰："此即所谓太湖耶？今得见天地之宽，不虚此生矣！想闺中人有终身不能见此者。"闲话未几，风摇岸柳，已抵江城。

余登岸拜奠毕，归视舟中洞然，急询舟子。舟子指曰："不见长桥柳阴下观鱼鹰捕鱼者乎？"盖芸已与船家女登岸矣。余至其后，芸犹粉汗盈盈，倚女而出神焉。余拍其肩曰："罗衫汗透矣！"芸回首曰："恐钱家有人到舟，故暂避之。君何回来之速也？"余笑曰："欲捕逃耳。"

于是相挽登舟，返棹至万年桥下，阳乌犹未落山。舟窗尽落，清风徐来，纨扇罗衫，剖瓜解暑。少焉霞映桥红，烟笼柳暗，银蟾欲上，渔火满江矣。命仆至船梢与舟子同饮。

船家女名素云，与余有杯酒交，人颇不俗，招之与芸同坐。船头不张灯火，待月快酌，射覆为令。素云双目闪闪，听良久，曰："觞政侬颇娴习，从未闻有斯令，愿受教。"芸即譬其言而开导之，终茫然。

余笑曰："女先生且罢论，我有一言作譬，即了然矣。"芸曰："君若何譬之？"余曰："鹤善舞而不能耕，牛善耕而不能舞，物性然也。先生欲反而教之，无乃劳乎？"素云笑捶余肩曰："汝骂我耶！"芸出令曰："只许动口，不许动手！违者罚大觥。"素云量豪，满斟一觥，一吸而尽。余曰："动手但准摸索，不准捶人。"芸笑挽素云置余怀，曰："请君摸索畅怀。"余笑曰："卿非解人，摸索在有意无意间耳。拥而狂探，田舍郎之所为也。"时四鬓所簪茉莉，为酒气所蒸，杂以粉汗油香，芳馨透鼻。余戏曰："小人臭味充满船头，令人作恶。"素云不禁握拳连捶曰："谁教汝狂嗅耶？"

芸呼曰："违令，罚两大觥！"

素云曰："彼又以小人骂我，不应捶耶？"

芸曰："彼之所谓小人，益有故也。请干此，当告汝。"

素云乃连尽两觥，芸乃告以沧浪旧居乘凉事。

素云曰："若然，真错怪矣，当再罚。"又干一觥。

芸曰："久闻素娘善歌，可一聆妙音否？"素即以象箸击小碟而歌。芸欣然畅饮，不觉酩酊，乃乘舆先归。余又与素云茶话片刻，步月而回。

时余寄居友人鲁半舫家萧爽楼中。越数日，鲁夫人误有所闻，私告芸曰："前日闻若婿挟两妓饮于万年桥舟中，子知之否？"芸曰："有之，其一即我也。"因以偕游始末详告之。鲁大笑，释然而去。

乾隆甲寅七月，余自粤东归。有同伴携妾回者，曰徐秀峰，余之表妹婿也，艳称新人之美，邀芸往观。芸他日谓秀峰曰："美则美矣，韵犹未也。"秀峰曰："然则若郎纳妾，必美而韵者乎？"芸曰："然。"从此痴心物色，而短于资。

时有浙妓温冷香者，寓于吴，有咏柳絮四律，沸传吴下，好事者多和之。余友吴江张闲憨素赏冷香，携柳絮诗索和。芸微其人而置之，余技痒而和其韵，中有"触我春愁偏婉转，撩他离绪更缠绵"之句，芸甚击节。

明年乙卯秋八月五日，吾母将挈芸游虎丘，闲憨忽至，曰："余亦有虎丘之游，今日特邀君作探花使者。"因请吾母先行，期于虎丘半塘相晤。拉余至冷香寓，见冷香已半老，有女名憨园，瓜期未破，亭亭玉立，真"一泓秋水照人寒"者也。款接间，颇知文墨，有妹文园，尚雏。

余此时初无痴想，且念一杯之叙，非寒士所能酬，而既入个中，私心志忸,强为酬答。

因私谓闲憨曰:"余贫士也,子以尤物玩我乎?"

闲憨笑曰:"非也。今日有友人邀憨园答我,席主为尊客拉去,我代客转邀客,毋烦他虑也。"余始释然。至半塘,两舟相遇,令憨园过舟叩见吾母。芸、憨相见,欢同旧识,携手登山,备览名胜。芸独爱千顷云高旷,坐赏良久。返至野芳滨,畅饮甚欢,并舟而泊。

及解维,芸谓余曰:"子陪张君,留憨陪妾可乎?"余诺之。返棹至都中桥,始过船分袂。归家已三鼓。

芸曰:"今日得见美丽韵者矣。顷已约憨园,明日过我,当为子图之。"

余骇曰:"此非金屋不能贮,穷措大岂敢生此妄想哉!况我两人伉俪正笃,何必外求?"

芸笑曰:"我自爱之,子姑待之。"

明午,憨果至。芸殷勤款接,筵中以猜枚——赢吟输饮——为令,终席无一罗致语。及憨园归,芸曰:"顷又与密约,十八日来此结为姊妹,子宜备牲牢以待。"笑指臂上翡翠钏曰:"若见此钏属于憨,事必谐矣。顷已吐意,未深结其心也。"余姑听之。

十八日大雨,憨竟冒雨至。入室良久,始挽手出,见余有羞色,盖翡翠钏已在憨臂矣。焚香结盟后,拟再续前饮,适憨有石湖之游,即别去。

芸欣然告余曰:"丽人已得,君何以谢媒耶?"余询其详。

芸曰:"向之秘言,恐憨意另有所属也。顷探之无他,语之曰:'妹知今日之意否?'憨曰:'蒙夫人抬举,真蓬蒿倚玉树也。但吾母望我奢,恐难自主耳,愿彼此缓图之。'脱钏上臂时,又语之曰:'玉取其坚,且有团圞不断之意,妹试笼之,以为先兆。'憨曰:'聚合之权,总在夫人也。'即此观之,憨心已得,所难必者冷香耳,当再图之。"

余笑曰:"卿将效笠翁之《怜香伴》耶?"

芸曰:"然。"

自此无日不谈憨园矣。后憨为有力者夺去,不果。芸竟以之死。

Wedded Bliss

I was born in 1763, under the reign of Ch'ienlung, on the twenty-second day of the eleventh moon. The country was then in the heyday of peace and, moreover, I was born in a scholars' family, living by the side of the Ts'anglang Pavilion in Soochow. So altogether I may say the gods have been unusually kind to me. Su Tungp'o said, "Life is like a spring dream which vanishes without a trace." I should be ungrateful to the gods if I did not try to put my life down on record.

Since the *Book of Poems* begins with a poem on wedded love, I thought I would begin this book by speaking of my marital relations and then let other matters follow. My only regret is that I was not properly educated in childhood; all I know is a simple language and I shall try only to record the real facts and real sentiments. I hope the reader will be kind enough not to scrutinize my grammar, which would be like looking for brilliance in a tarnished mirror.

I was engaged in my childhood to one Miss Yü, of Chinsha, who died in her eighth year, and eventually I married a girl of the Ch'en clan. Her name was Yün and her literary name Suchen. She was my cousin, being the daughter of my maternal uncle, Hsinyü. Even in her childhood, she was a very clever girl, for while she was learning to speak, she was taught Po Chüyi's poem, "The *P'i P'a* Player", and could at once repeat it. Her father died when she was four years old, and in the family there were only her mother (of the Chin clan) and her younger brother K'ehch'ang and herself, being then practically destitute. When Yün grew up and had learnt needlework, she was providing for the family of three, and contrived always to pay K'ehch'ang's tuition fees punctually. One day, she picked up a copy of the poem "The *P'i P'a* Player" from a wastebasket, and from that, with the help of her memory of the lines, she learnt to read word by word. Between her needlework, she gradually learnt to write poetry. One of her poems contained the two lines:

"Touched by autumn, one's figure grows slender,

Soaked in frost, the chrysanthemum blooms full."

When I was thirteen years old, I went with my mother to her maiden home and there we met. As we were two young innocent children, she allowed me to read her poems. I was quite struck by her talent, but feared that she was too clever to be happy. Still I could not help thinking of her all the time, and once I told my mother, "If you were to choose a girl for me, I won't marry any one except Cousin Su." My mother also liked her being so gentle, and gave her her gold ring as a token for the betrothal.

This was on the sixteenth of the seventh moon in the year 1775. In the winter of that year, one of my girl cousins (the daughter of another maternal uncle of mine) was going to get married and I again accompanied my mother to her maiden home.

Yün was the same age as myself, but ten months older, and as we had been accustomed to calling each other "elder sister" and "younger brother" from childhood, I continued to call her "Sister Su."

At this time the guests in the house all wore bright dresses, but Yün alone was clad in a dress of quiet color, and had on a new pair of shoes. I noticed that the embroidery on her shoes was very fine, and learnt that it was her own work, so that I began to realize that she was gifted at other things, too, besides reading and writing.

Of a slender figure, she had drooping shoulders and a rather long neck, slim but not to the point of being skinny. Her eyebrows were arched and in her eyes there was a look of quick intelligence and soft refinement. The only defect was that her two front teeth were slightly inclined forward, which was not a mark of good omen. There was an air of tenderness about her which completely fascinated me.

I asked for the manuscripts of her poems and found that they consisted mainly of couplets and three or four lines, being unfinished poems, and I asked her the reason why. She smiled and said, "I have had no one to teach me poetry, and wish to have a good teacher-friend who could help me to finish these poems." I wrote playfully on the label of this book of poems the words: "Beautiful Lines in an Embroidered Case," and did not realize that in this case lay the cause of her short life.

That night, when I came back from outside the city, whither I had accompanied my girl cousin the bride, it was already midnight, and I felt very hungry and asked for something to eat. A maid-servant gave me some dried dates, which were too sweet for me. Yün secretly pulled me by the sleeve into her room, and I saw that she had hidden away a bowl of warm congee and some dishes to go with it. I was beginning to take up the chopsticks and eat it with great gusto when Yün's boy cousin Yüheng called out, "Sister Su, come quick!" Yün quickly shut the door and said, "I am very tired and going to bed." Yüheng forced the door open and, seeing the situation, he said with a malicious smile at Yün, "So, that's it! A while ago I asked for congee and you said there was no more, but you really meant to keep it for your future husband." Yün was greatly embarrassed and everybody laughed at her, including the servants. On my part, I rushed away home with an old servant in a state of excitement.

Since the affair of the congee happened, she always avoided me when I went to her home, and I knew that she was only trying to avoid being made a subject of ridicule.

Our wedding took place on the twenty-second of the first moon in 1780. When she came to my home on that night, I found that she had the same slender figure as before. When her bridal veil was lifted, we looked at each other and smiled. After the drinking of the customary twin cups between bride and groom, we sat down together at dinner and I secretly held her hand under the table, which was warm and small, and my heart was palpitating. I asked her to eat and learnt that she was in her vegetarian fast, which she had been keeping for several years already. I found that the time when she began her fast coincided with my small-pox illness, and said to her laughingly, "Now that my face is clean and smooth without pock-marks, my dear sister, will you break your fast?" Yün looked at me with a smile and nodded her head.

As my own sister is going to get married on the twenty-fourth, only two days later, and as there was to be a national mourning and no music was to be allowed on the twenty-third, my sister was given a send-off dinner on the night of the twenty-second, my wedding day, and Yün was present at table. I was playing the finger-guessing game with the bride's companion in the bridal chamber and, being a loser all the time, I fell asleep drunk like a fish. When I woke up the next morning, Yün had not quite finished her morning toilet.

That day, we were kept busy entertaining guests and towards evening, music was played. After midnight, on the morning of the twenty-fourth, I, as the bride's brother, sent my sister away and came back towards three o'clock. The room was then pervaded with quietness, bathed in the silent glow of the candle-lights. I went in and saw Yün's bride's companion was taking a nap down in front of our bed on the floor, while Yün had taken off her bridal costume, but had not yet gone to bed. She was bending her beautiful white neck before the bright candle, quite absorbed reading a book. I patted her on the shoulder and said, "Sister, why are you still working so hard? You must be quite tired with the full days we've had."

Quickly Yün turned her head and stood up saying, "I was going to bed when I opened the book-case and saw this book and have not been able to leave it since. Now my sleepiness is all gone. I have heard of the name of *Western Chamber* for a long time, but today I see it for the first time. It is really the work of a genius, only I feel that its style is a little bit biting."

"Only geniuses can write a biting style," I smiled and said.

The bride's companion asked us to go to bed, but we told her to shut the door and retire first. I began to sit down by Yün's side and we joked together like old friends after a long period of separation. I touched her breast in fun and felt that her heart was palpitating too. "Why is Sister's heart palpitating like that?" I bent down and whispered in her ear. Yün looked back at me with a smile and our souls were carried away in a mist of passion. Then we went to bed, when all too soon the dawn came.

As a bride, Yün was very quiet at first. She was never sullen or displeased, and when people spoke to her, she merely smiled. She was respectful towards her superiors and kindly towards those under her. Whatever she did was done well, and it was difficult to find fault with her. When she saw the grey dawn shining in through the window, she would get up and dress herself as if she had been commanded to do so. "Why?" I asked, "You don't have to be afraid of gossip, like the days when you gave me that warm congee." "I was made a laughing-stock on account of that bowl of congee," she replied, "but now I am not afraid of people's talk; I only fear that our parents might think their daughter-in-law lazy."

Although I wanted her to lie in bed longer, I could not help admiring her virtue, and so got up myself, too, at the same time with her. And so every day we rubbed shoulders together and clung to each other like an object and its shadow, and the love between us was something that surpassed the language of words.

So the time passed happily and the honeymoon was too soon over. At this time, my father Chiafu was in the service of the Kueich'i district government, and he sent a special messenger to bring me there, for, it should be noted that, during this time, I was under the tutorship of Chao Shengtsai of Wulin [Hangchow]. Chao was a very kindly teacher and today the fact that I can write at all is due entirely to his credit.

Now, when I came home for the wedding, it had been agreed that as soon as the ceremonies were over, I should go back at once to my father's place in order to resume my studies. So when I got this news, I did not know what to do. I was afraid Yün might break into tears, but on the other hand she tried to look cheerful and comforted me and urged me to go, and packed up things for me. Only that night I noticed that she did not look quite her usual self. At the time of parting, she whispered to me, "Take good care of yourself, for there will be no one to look after you."

When I went up on board the boat, I saw the peach and pear trees on the banks were in full bloom, but I felt like a lonely bird that had lost its companions and as if the world was going to collapse around me. As soon as I arrived, my father left the place and crossed the river for an eastward destination.

Thus three months passed, which seemed to me like ten insufferable long years. Although Yün wrote to me regularly, still for two letters that I sent her, I received only one in reply, and these letters contained only words of exhortation and the rest was filled with airy, conventional nothings, and I felt very unhappy. Whenever the breeze blew past my bamboo courtyard, or the moon shone upon my window behind the green banana leaves, I thought of her and was carried away into a region of dreams.

My teacher noticed this, and sent word to my father, saying that he would give me ten subjects for composition and let me go home. I felt like a garrison prisoner receiving his pardon.

Strange to say, when I got on to the boat and was on my way home, I felt that a quarter of an hour was like a long year. When I arrived home, I went to pay my respects to my mother and then entered my room. Yün stood up to welcome me, and we held each other's hands in silence, and it seemed then that our souls had melted away or evaporated like a mist. My ears tingled and I did not know where I was.

It was in the sixth moon, then, and the rooms were very hot. Luckily, we were next door to the Lotus Lover's Lodge of the Ts'anglang Pavilion on the east. Over the bridge, there was an open hall overlooking the water, called "After My Heart"—the reference was to an old poem: "When the water is clear, I will wash the tassels of my hat, and when the water is muddy, I will wash my feet." By the side of the eaves, there was an old tree which spread its green shade over the window, and made the people's faces look green with it; and across the creek, you could see people passing to and fro. This was where my father used to entertain his guests inside the bamboo-framed curtains. ① I asked for permission from my mother to bring Yün and stay there for the summer. She stopped embroidery during the summer months because of the heat, and the whole day long, we were either reading together or discussing the ancient things, or else enjoying the moon and passing judgments on the flowers. Yün could not drink, but could take at most three cups when compelled to. I taught her literary games in which the loser had to drink. We thought there could not be a more happy life on earth than this.

One day Yün asked me, "Of all the ancient authors, which one should we regard as the master?" And I replied: "*Chankuots'eh* and *Chuangtzŭ* are noted for their agility of thought and expressiveness of style, K'uang Heng and Liu Hsiang are known for their classic severity, Ssuma Ch'ien and Pan Ku are known for their breadth of knowledge, Han Yü is known for his mellow qualities, Liu Tsungyüan for his rugged beauty, Ouyang Hsiu for his romantic abandon, and the Su's, father and sons, are known for their sustained eloquence. There are, besides, writings like the political essays of Chia Yi and Tung Chungshu, the euphuistic prose of Yü Hsin and Hsü Ling, the memorandums of Loh Chih, and others more than one can enumerate. True appreciation, however, must come from the reader himself."

"The ancient literature," Yün said, "depends for its appeal on depth of thought and greatness of spirit, which I am afraid it is difficult for a woman to attain. I believe, however, that I do understand something of poetry."

---

① As there were no walls or lattices whatsoever round the pavilion, they used to hang down bamboo-framed curtains so that the dining party might not be seen by the people across the creek.

"Poetry was used," I said, "as a literary test in the imperial examinations of the T'ang Dynasty, and people acknowledge Li Po and Tu Fu as the master poets. Which of the two do you like better?"

"Tu's poems," she said, "are known for their workmanship and artistic refinement, while Li's poems are known for their freedom and naturalness of expression. I prefer the vivacity of Li Po to the severity of Tu Fu."

"Tu Fu is the acknowledged king of poets," said I, "and he is taken by most people as their model. Why do you prefer Li Po?"

"Of course," said she, "as for perfection of form and maturity of thought, Tu is the undisputed master, but Li Po's poems have the wayward charm of a nymph. His lines come naturally like dropping petals and flowing waters, and are so much lovelier for their spontaneity. I am not saying that Tu is second to Li; only personally I feel, not that I love Tu less, but that I love Li more."

"I say, I didn't know that you are a bosom friend of Li Po!"

"I have still in my heart another poet, Po Chüyi, who is my first tutor, as it were, and I have not been able to forget him."

"What do you mean?" I asked.

"Isn't he the one who wrote the poem on 'The *P'i P'a* Player'?"

"This is very strange," I laughed and said. "So Li *Po* is your bosom friend, *Po* Chüyi is your first tutor and your husband's literary name is San *Po*. It seems that your life is always bound up with the *Po*'s."

"It is all right," Yün smiled and replied, "to have one's life bound up with the *Po*'s, only I am afraid I shall be writing *Po* characters all my life." (For in Soochow we call misspelt words "*po* characters.") And we both laughed.

"Now that you know poetry," I said, "I should like also to know your taste for *fu* poems."

"The *Ch'u Tz'u* is, of course, the fountain head of *fu* poetry, but I find it difficult to understand. It seems to me that among the Han and Chin *fu* poets, Ssuma Hsiangju is the most sublime in point of style and diction."

"Perhaps," I said, "Wenchün was tempted to elope with Hsiangju not because of his *ch'in* music, but rather because of his *fu* poetry," and we laughed again.

I am by nature unconventional and straightforward, but Yün was a stickler for forms, like the Confucian schoolmasters. Whenever I put on a dress for her or tidied up her sleeves, she would say "So much obliged" again and again, and when I passed her a towel or a fan, she would always stand up to receive it. At first I disliked this and said to her, "Do you mean to tie me down with all this ceremony? There is a proverb which says, 'One who is overcourteous is crafty.'" Yün blushed all over and said, "I am merely trying to be polite and respectful, why do you charge me with craftiness?" "True respect is in the heart, and does not require such empty forms," said I, but Yün said, "There is no more intimate relationship than that between children and their parents. Do you mean to say that children should behave freely towards their parents and keep their respect only in their heart?" "Oh! I was only joking," I said. "The trouble is," said Yün, "most marital troubles begin with joking. Don't you accuse me of disrespect later, for then I shall die of grief without being able to defend myself." Then I held her close to my breast and caressed her until she smiled. From then on our conversations were full of "I'm sorry's" and "I beg your pardon's." And so we remained courteous to each other for twenty-three years of our married life like Liang Hung and Meng Kuang [of the East Han Dynasty], and the longer we stayed together, the more passionately attached we became to each other.

Whenever we met each other in the house, whether it be in a dark room or in a narrow corridor, we used to hold each other's hands and ask, "Where are you going?" and we did this on the sly as if afraid that people might see us. As a matter of fact, we tried at first to avoid being seen sitting or walking together, but after a while, we did not mind it any more. When Yün was sitting and talking with somebody and saw me come, she would rise and move sideways for me to sit down together with her. All this was done naturally almost without any consciousness, and although at first we felt uneasy about it, later on it became a matter of habit. I cannot understand why all old couples must hate each other like enemies. Some people say, "If they weren't enemies, they would not be able to live together until old age." Well, I wonder!

On the seventh night of the seventh moon of that year, Yün prepared incense, candles and some melons and other fruits, so that we might together worship the Grandson of Heaven① in the Hall called "After My Heart." I had carved two seals with the inscription "That we might remain husband and wife from incarnation to incarnation." I kept the seal with positive characters, while she kept the one with negative characters, to be used in our correspondence.

That night, the moon was shining beautifully and when I looked down at the creek, the ripples shone like silvery chains. We were

---

① The seventh day of the seventh moon is the only day in the year when the pair of heavenly lovers, the Cowherd ("Grandson of Heaven") and the Spinster, are allowed to meet each other across the Milky Way.

wearing light silk dresses and sitting together with a small fan in our hands, before the window overlooking the creek. Looking up at the sky, we saw the clouds sailing through the heavens, changing at every moment into a myriad forms, and Yün said, "This moon is common to the whole universe. I wonder if there is another pair of lovers quite as passionate as ourselves looking at the same moon tonight?" And I said, "Oh! There are plenty of people who will be sitting in the cool evening and looking at the moon, and perhaps also many women enjoying and appreciating the clouds in their chambers; but when a husband and wife are looking at the moon together, I hardly think that the clouds will form the subject of their conversation." By and by, the candle-lights went out, the moon sank in the sky, and we removed the fruits and went to bed.

The fifteenth of the seventh moon was All Souls' Day. Yün prepared a little dinner, so that we could drink together with the moon as our company, but when night came, the sky was suddenly overcast with dark clouds. Yün knitted her brow and said, "If it be the wish of God that we two should live together until there are silver threads in our hair, then the moon must come out again tonight." On my part I felt disheartened also. As we looked across the creek, we saw will-o'-the-wisps flitting in crowds hither and thither like ten thousand candle-lights, threading their way through the willows and smartweeds.

And then we began to compose a poem together, each saying two lines at a time, the first completing the couplet which the other had begun, and the second beginning another couplet for the other to finish, and after a few rhymes, the longer we kept on, the more nonsensical it became, until it was a jumble of slapdash doggerel. By this time, Yün was buried amidst tears and laughter and choking on my breast, while I felt the fragrance of the jasmine in her hair assail my nostrils. I patted her on the shoulder and said jokingly, "I thought that the jasmine was used for decoration in women's hair because it was clear and round like a pearl; I did not know that it is because its fragrance is so much finer when it is mixed with the smell of women's hair and powder. When it smells like that, even the citron cannot remotely compare with it." Then Yün stopped laughing and said, "The citron is the gentleman among the different fragrant plants because its fragrance is so slight that you can hardly detect it; on the other hand, the jasmine is a common fellow because it borrows its fragrance partly from others. Therefore, the fragrance of the jasmine is like that of a smiling sycophant." "Why, then," I said, "do you keep away from the gentleman and associate with the common fellow?" And Yün replied, "But I only laugh at that gentleman who loves a common fellow."

While we were thus bandying words about, it was already midnight, and we saw the wind had blown away the clouds in the sky and there appeared the full moon, round like a chariot wheel, and we were greatly delighted. And so we began to drink by the side of the window, but before we had tasted three cups, we heard suddenly the noise of a splash under the bridge, as if someone had fallen into the water. We looked out through the window and saw there was not a thing, for the water was as smooth as a mirror, except that we heard the noise of a duck scampering in the marshes. I knew that there was a ghost of someone who had been drowned by the side of the Ts'anglang Pavilion, but knowing that Yün was very timid, I dared not mention it to her. And Yün sighed and said, "Alas! Whence cometh this noise?" and we shuddered all over. Quickly we shut the window and carried the wine pot back into the room. The light of a rapeseed oil lamp was then burning as small as a pea, and the edges of the bed curtain hung low in the twilight, and we were shaking all over. We then made the lamplight a little brighter and went inside the bed curtain, and Yün already ran up a high fever. Soon I had a high temperature myself, and our illness dragged on for about twenty days. True it is that when the cup of happiness overflows, disaster follows, as the saying goes, and this was also an omen that we should not be able to live together until old age.

On the fifteenth of the eighth moon, or the Mid-Autumn Festival, I had just recovered from my illness. Yün had now been a bride in my home for over half a year, but still had never been to the Ts'anglang Pavilion itself next door. So I first ordered an old servant to tell the watchman not to let any visitors enter the place. Toward evening, I went with Yün and my younger sister, supported by an amah and a maid-servant and led by an old attendant. We passed a bridge, entered a gate, turned eastwards and followed a zigzag path into the place, where we saw huge grottoes and abundant green trees. The Pavilion stood on the top of a hill. Going up by the steps to the top, one could look around for miles, where in the distance chimney smoke arose from the cottages against the background of clouds of rainbow hues. Over the bank, there was a grove called the "Forest by the Hill" where the high officials used to entertain their guests. Later on, the Chengyi College was erected on this spot, but it wasn't there yet. We brought a blanket which we spread on the Pavilion floor, and then sat round together, while the watchman served us tea. After a while, the moon had already arisen from behind the forest, and the breeze was playing about our sleeves, while the moon's image sparkled in the rippling water, and all worldly cares were banished from our breasts. "This is the end of a perfect day," said Yün. "Wouldn't it be fine if we could get a boat and row around the Pavilion!" At this time, the lights were already shining from people's homes, and thinking of the incident on the fifteenth night of the seventh moon, we left the Pavilion and hurried home. According to the custom at Soochow, the women of all families, rich or poor, came out in groups on the Mid-Autumn night, a custom which was called "pacing the moonlight." Strange to say, no one came to such a beautiful neighborhood as the Ts'anglang Pavilion.

My father Chiafu was very fond of adopting children; hence I had twenty-six adopted brothers. My mother, too, had nine adopted daughters, among whom Miss Wang, the second, and Miss Yü, the sixth, were Yün's best friends. Wang was a kind of a tomboy and a great drinker, while Yü was straightforward and very fond of talking. When they came together, they used to chase me out, so that the three of them could sleep in the same bed. I knew Miss Yü was responsible for this, and once I said to her in fun, "When you get married, I am going to invite your husband to come and keep him for ten days at a stretch." "I'll come here, too, then," said Miss Yü, "and sleep in the same bed with Yün. Won't that be fun?" At this Yün and Wang merely smiled.

At this time, my younger brother Ch'it'ang was going to get married, and we moved to Ts'angmi Alley by the Bridge of Drinking Horses. The house was quite big, but not so nice and secluded as the one by the Ts'anglang Pavilion. On the birthday of my mother, we had theatrical performances at home, and Yün at first thought them quite wonderful. Scorning all taboos, my father asked for the performance of a scene called "Sad Parting," and the actors played so realistically that the audience were quite touched. I noticed across the screen that

Yün suddenly got up and disappeared inside for a long time. I went in to see her and the Misses Yü and Wang also followed suit. There I saw Yün sitting alone before her dressing table, resting her head on an arm. "Why are you so sad?" I asked. "One sees a play for diversion," Yün said, "but today's play only breaks my heart." Both Wang and Yü were laughing at her, but I defended her. "She is touched because hers is a profoundly emotional soul." "Are you going to sit here all day long?" asked Miss Yü. "I'll stay here until some better selection is being played," Yün replied. Hearing this, Miss Wang left first and asked my mother to select more cheerful plays like *Ch'ihliang* and *Househ*. Then Yün was persuaded to come out and watch the play, which made her happy again.

My uncle Such'ün died early without an heir, and my father made me succeed his line. His tomb was situated on the Hill of Good Fortune and Longevity in Hsikuat'ang by the side of our ancestral tombs, and I was accustomed to go there with Yün and visit the grave every spring. As there was a beautiful garden called Koyüan in its neighborhood, Miss Wang begged to come with us. Yün saw that the pebbles on this hill had beautiful grains of different colors, and said to me, "If we were to collect these pebbles and make them into a grotto, it would be even more artistic than one made of Hsüanchow stones." I expressed the fear that there might not be enough of this kind. "If Yün really likes them, I'll pick them for her," said Miss Wang. So she borrowed a bag from the watchman, and went along with a stork's strides collecting them. Whenever she picked up one, she would ask for my opinion. If I said "good," she would put it into the bag; and if I said "no," she would throw it away. She stood up before long and came back to us with the bag, perspiring all over. "My strength will fail me

if I am going to pick any more," she said. "I have been told," said
Yün, as she was selecting the good ones in the bag, "that mountain
fruits must be gathered with the help of monkeys, which seems quite
true." Miss Wang was furious and stretched both her hands as if to
tease her. I stopped her and said to Yün by way of reproof, "You
cannot blame her for being angry, because she is doing all the work and
you stand by and say such unkind things."

Then on our way back, we visited the Koyüan Garden, in which
we saw a profusion of flowers of all colors. Wang was very childish;
she would now and then pick a flower for no reason, and Yün scolded
her, saying, "What do you pick so many flowers for, since you are not
going to put them in a vase or in your hair?" "Oh! What's the harm?
These flowers don't feel anything." "All right," I said, "you will be
punished for this one day by marrying a pock-marked bearded fellow
for your husband to avenge the flowers." Wang looked at me in anger,
threw the flowers to the ground and kicked them into the pond. "Why
do you all bully me?" she said. However, Yün made it up with her,
and she was finally pacified.

Yün was at first very quiet and loved to hear me talk, but I
gradually taught her the art of conversation as one leads a cricket with
a blade of grass. She then gradually learnt the art of conversation. For
instance, at meals, she always mixed her rice with tea, and loved to eat
stale pickled bean-curd, called "stinking bean-curd" in Soochow.
Another thing she liked to eat was a kind of small pickled cucumber. I
hated both of these things, and said to her in fun one day, "The dog,
which has no stomach, eats human refuse because it doesn't know that
refuse stinks, while the beetle rolls in dunghills and is changed into a
cicada because it wants to fly up to heaven. Now are you a dog or a

beetle?" To this Yün replied, "One eats bean-curd because it is so cheap and it goes with dry rice as well as with congee. I am used to this from childhood. Now I am married into your home, like a beetle that has been transformed into a cicada, but I am still eating it because one should not forget old friends. As for pickled cucumber, I tasted it for the first time in your home."

"Oh, then, my home is a dog's kennel, isn't it?" Yün was embarrassed and tried to explain it away by saying, "Of course there is refuse in every home; the only difference is whether one eats it or not. You yourself eat garlic, for instance, and I have tried to eat it with you. I won't compel you to eat stinking bean-curd, but cucumber is really very nice, if you hold your breath while eating. You will see when you have tasted it yourself. It is like Wuyien, an ugly but virtuous woman of old." "Are you going to make me a dog?" I asked. "Well, I have been a dog for a long time, why don't you try to be one?" So she picked a piece of cucumber with her chopsticks and stuck it into my mouth. I held my breath and ate it and found it indeed delicious. Then I ate it in the usual way and found it to have a marvellous flavor. And from that time on, I loved the cucumber also. Yün also prepared pickled bean-curd mixed with sesame seed oil and sugar, which I found also to be a delicacy. We then mixed pickled cucumber with pickled bean-curd and called the mixture "the double-flavored gravy." I said I could not understand why I disliked it at first and began to love it so now. "If you are in love with a thing, you will forget its ugliness," said Yün.

My younger brother Ch'it'ang married the grand-daughter of Wang Hsüchou. It happened that on the wedding day, she wanted some pearls. Yün took her own pearls, which she had received as her bridal gift, and gave them to my mother. The maid-servant thought it a pity, but Yün said, "A woman is an incarnation of the female principle, and so are pearls. For a woman to wear pearls would be to leave no room for the male principle. For that reason I don't prize them." She had, however, a peculiar fondness for old books and broken slips of painting. Whenever she saw odd volumes of books, she would try to sort them out, arrange them in order, and have them rebound properly. These were collected and labelled "Ancient Relics." When she saw scrolls of calligraphy or painting that were partly spoilt, she would find some old paper and paste them up nicely, and ask me to fill up the broken spaces. [1] These were kept rolled up properly and called "Beautiful Gleanings." This was what she was busy about the whole day when she was not attending to the kitchen or needlework. When she found in old trunks or piles of musty volumes any writing or painting that pleased her, she felt as if she had discovered some precious relic, and an old woman neighbor of ours, by the name of Feng, used to buy up old scraps and sell them to her. She had the same tastes and habits as myself, and besides had the talent of reading my wishes by a mere glance or movement of the eyebrow, doing things without being told and doing them to my perfect satisfaction.

Once I said to her, "It is a pity that you were born a woman. If you were a man, we could travel together and visit all the great mountains and the famous places throughout the country."

"Oh! This is not so very difficult," said Yün. "Wait till I have got

---

[1] The author was a painter, and for a time painted for his living.

my grey hairs. Even if I cannot accompany you to the Five Sacred Mountains① then, we can travel to the nearer places, like Huch'iu and Lingyen, as far south as the West Lake and as far north as P'ingshan [in Yangchow]."

"Of course this is all right, except that I am afraid when you are grey-haired, you will be too old to travel."

"If I can't do it in this life, then I shall do it in the next."

"In the next life, you must be born a man and I will be your wife."

"It will be quite beautiful if we can then still remember what has happened in this life."

"That's all very well, but even a bowl of congee has provided material for so much conversation. We shan't be able to sleep a wink the whole wedding night, but shall be discussing what we have done in the previous existence, if we can still remember what's happened in this life then."

"It is said that the Old Man under the Moon is in charge of matrimony," said Yün. "He was good enough to make us husband and wife in this life, and we shall still depend on his favor in the affair of marriage in the next incarnation. Why don't we make a painting of him and worship him in our home?"

So we asked a Mr. Ch'i Liut'i of T'iaoch'i who specialized in portraiture, to make a painting of the Old Man under the Moon, which he did. It was a picture of the Old Man holding, in one hand, a red silk

---

① The Five Sacred Mountains are: (1) Taishan, the East Sacred Mountain (in Shantung), (2) Huashan, the West Sacred Mountain (in Shensi), (3) Hengshan, the North Sacred Mountain (in Shansi), (4) Hengshan, the South Sacred Mountain (in Hunan) and (5) Sungshan, the Central Sacred Mountain (in Honan).

thread [for the purpose of binding together the hearts of all couples] and, in the other, a walking-stick with the Book of Matrimony suspended from it. He had white hair and a ruddy complexion, apparently bustling about in a cloudy region. Altogether it was a very excellent painting of Ch'i's. My friend Shih Chot'ang wrote some words of praise on it and we hung the picture in our chamber. On the first and fifteenth of every month, we burnt incense and prayed together before him. I do not know where this picture is now, as we have lost it after all the changes and upsets in our family life. "Ended is the present life and uncertain the next," as the poet says. I wonder if God will listen to the prayer of us two silly lovers.

After we had moved to Ts'angmi Alley, I called our bedroom the "Tower of My Guest's Fragrance," with a reference to Yün's name①, and to the story of Liang Hung and Meng Kuang who, as husband and wife, were always courteous to each other "like guests." We rather disliked the house because the walls were too high and the courtyard was too small. At the back, there was another house, leading to the library. Looking out of the window at the back, one could see the old garden of Mr. Loh then in a dilapidated condition, Yün's thoughts still hovered about the beautiful scenery of the T'sanglang Pavilion.

At this time, there was an old peasant woman living on the east of Mother Gold's Bridge and the north of Kenghsiang. Her little cottage was surrounded on all sides by vegetable fields and had a wicker gate. Outside the gate, there was a pond about thirty yards across, and a wilderness of flowers and trees covered the sides of the hedgerow. This was the old site of the home of Chang Ssǔch'eng at the end of the Yüan

---

① "Yün" in Chinese means a fragrant weed.

Dynasty. A few paces to the west of the cottage, there was a mound filled with broken bricks, from the top of which one could command a view of the surrounding territory, which was an open country with a stretch of wild vegetation.

Once the old woman happened to mention the place, and Yün kept on thinking about it. So she said to me one day, "Since leaving the Ts'anglang Pavilion, I have been dreaming about it all the time. As we cannot live there, we must put up with the second best. I have a great idea to go and live in the old woman's cottage." "I have been thinking, too," I said, "of a place to go to and spend the long summer days. If you think you'll like the place, I'll go ahead and take a look. If it is satisfactory, we can carry our beddings along and go and stay there for a month. How about it?" "I'm afraid mother won't allow us." "Oh! I'll see to that," I told her. So the next day, I went there and found that the cottage consisted only of two rooms, which were partitioned into four. With paper windows and bamboo beds, the house would be quite a delightfully cool place to stay in. The old woman knew what I wanted and gladly rented me her bedroom, which then looked quite new, when I had repapered the walls. I then informed my mother of it and went to stay there with Yün.

Our only neighbors were an old couple who raised vegetables for the market. They knew that we were going to stay there for the summer, and came and called on us, bringing us some fish from the pond and vegetables from their own fields. We offered to pay for them, but they wouldn't take any money, and afterwards Yün made a pair of shoes for each of them, which they were finally persuaded to accept.

This was in the seventh moon when the trees cast a green shade over the place. The summer breeze blew over the water of the pond, and cicadas filled the air with their singing the whole day. Our old neighbor also made a fishing rod for us, and we used to angle together under the shade of the willow trees. Late in the afternoons, we would go up on the mound to have a look at the evening glow and compose lines of poetry, when we felt so inclined. Two of the best lines were:

"*Beast-clouds swallow the sinking sun,*

And the bow-moon shoots the falling stars."

After a while, the moon cut her image in the water, insects began to chirp all round, and we placed a bamboo bed near the hedgerow to sit or lie upon. The old woman then would inform us that wine had been warmed up and dinner prepared, and we would sit down to have a little drink under the moon before our meal. Then after bath, we would put on our slippers and carry a fan, and lie or sit there, listening to old tales of retribution told by our neighbor. When we came in to sleep about midnight, we felt nice and cool all over the body, almost forgetting that we were living in a city.

There along the hedgerow, we asked the gardener to plant chrysanthemums. The flowers bloomed in the ninth moon, and we continued to stay there for another ten days. My mother was also quite delighted and came to see us there. So we ate crabs in the midst of chrysanthemums and whiled away the whole day.

Yün was quite enchanted with all this and said, "Some day we must build a cottage here. We'll buy ten *mow* of ground around the cottage, and see to our servants planting in the fields vegetables and melons to be sold for the expenses of our daily meals. You will paint and I will do embroidery, from which we could make enough money to buy wine for entertaining our friends who will gather here together to compose poems. Thus, clad in simple gowns and eating simple meals, we could live a very happy life together without going anywhere." I fully agreed with her. Now the place is still there, while my bosom friend is dead. Alas! Such is life!

About half a *li* from my home, there was a temple to the God of the Tungt'ing Lake, popularly known as the Narcissus Temple, situated in the Ch'uk'u Alley. It had many winding corridors and something of a garden with pavilions. On the birthday of the God, every clan would be assigned a corner in the Temple, where they would hang beautiful glass lanterns of a kind, with a chair in the center, on the either side of which were placed vases on wooden stands. These vases were decorated with flowers for competition. In the daytime, there would be theatrical performances, while at night the flower-vases were brilliantly illuminated with candlelights in their midst, a custom which was called "Illuminated Flowers." With the flowers and the lanterns and the smell of incense, the whole show resembled a night feast in the Palace of the Dragon King. The people there would sing or play music, or gossip over their tea-cups. The audience stood around in crowds to look at the show and there was a railing at the curb to keep them within a certain limit.

I was asked by my friends to help in the decorations and so had the pleasure of taking part in it. When Yün heard me speaking about it at home, she remarked, "It is a pity that I am not a man and cannot go to see it." "Why, you could put on my cap and gown and disguise yourself as a man," I suggested. Accordingly she changed her coiffure into a queue, painted her eyebrows, and put on my cap. Although her hair showed slightly round the temples, it passed off tolerably well. As my gown was found to be an inch and a half too long, she tucked it round the waist and put on a *makua* on top. "What am I going to do about my feet?" she asked. I told her there was a kind of shoes called "butterfly shoes," which could fit any size of feet and were very easy to obtain at the shops, and suggested buying a pair for her, which she could also use as slippers later on at home. Yün was delighted with the idea, and after supper, when she had finished her make-up, she paced about the room, imitating the gestures and gait of a man for a long time, when all of a sudden she changed her mind and said, "I am not going! It would be so embarrassing if somebody should discover it, and besides, our parents would object." Still I urged her to go. "Who doesn't know me at the Temple?" I said. "Even if they should find it out, they would laugh it off as a joke. Mother is at present in the home of the ninth sister. We could steal away and back without letting anyone know about it."

Yün then had such fun looking at herself in the mirror. I dragged her along and we stole away together to the Temple. For a long time nobody in the Temple could detect it. When people asked, I simply said she was my boy cousin, and people would merely curtsy with their hands together and pass on. Finally, we came to a place where there were some young women and girls sitting behind the flower show. They were the family of the owner of that show, by the name of Yang. Yün suddenly went over to talk with them, and while talking, she casually leant over and touched the shoulder of a young woman. The maid-servants nearby shouted angrily, "How dare the rascal!" I attempted to explain and smooth the matter over, but the servants still scowled ominously on us, and seeing that the situation was desperate, Yün took off her cap and showed her feet, saying "Look here, I am a woman, too!" They all stared at each other in surprise, and then, instead of being angry, began to laugh. We were then asked to sit down and have some tea. Soon afterwards we got sedan-chairs and came home.

When Mr. Ch'ien Shihchu of Wukiang died of an illness, my father wrote a letter to me, asking me to go and attend the funeral. Yün secretly expressed her desire to come along since on our way to Wukiang, we would pass the Taihu Lake, which she wished very much to see. I told her that I was just thinking it would be too lonely for me to go alone, and that it would be excellent, indeed, if she could come along, except that I could not think of a pretext for her going.

"Oh, I could say that I am going to see my mother," Yün said. "You can go ahead, and I shall come along to meet you." "If so," I said, "we can tie up our boat beneath the Bridge of Ten Thousand Years on our way home, where we shall be able to look at the moon again as we did at the Ts'anglang Pavilion."

This was on the eighteenth day of the sixth moon. That day, I brought a servant and arrived first at Hsükiang Ferry, where I waited for her in the boat. By and by, Yün arrived in a sedan-chair, and we started off, passing by the Tiger's Roar Bridge, where the view opened up and we saw sailing boats and sand-birds flitting over the lake. The water was a white stretch, joining the sky at the horizon. "So this is Taihu!" Yün exclaimed. "I know now how big the universe is, and I have not lived in vain! I think a good many ladies never see such a view in their whole lifetime." As we were occupied in conversation, it wasn't very long before we saw swaying willows on the banks, and we knew we had arrived at Wukiang.

I went up to attend the funeral ceremony, but when I came back, Yün was not in the boat. I asked the boatman and he said, "Don't you see someone under the willow trees by the bridge, watching the cormorants catching fish?" Yün, then, had gone up with the boatman's daughter. When I got behind her, I saw that she was perspiring all over, still leaning on the boatman's daughter and standing there absorbed looking at the cormorants. I patted her shoulder and said, "You are wet through." Yün turned her head and said, "I was afraid that your friend Ch'ien might come to the boat, so I left to avoid him. Why did you come back so early?" "In order to catch the renegade!" I replied.

We then came back hand-in-hand to the boat, and when we stopped at the Bridge of Ten Thousand Years, the sun had not yet gone down. And we let down all the windows to allow the river breeze to come in, and there, dressed in light silk and holding a silk fan, we sliced a melon to cool ourselves. Soon the evening glow was casting a red hue over the bridge, and the distant haze enveloped the willow trees in twilight. The moon was then coming up, and all along the river we saw a stretch of lights coming from the fishing boats. I asked my servant to go astern and have a drink with the boatman.

The boatman's daughter was called Suyün. She was quite a likeable girl, and I had known her before. I beckoned her to come and sit together with Yün on the bow of the boat. We did not put on any light, so that we could better enjoy the moon, and there we sat drinking heartily and playing literary games with wine as forfeit. Suyün just stared at us, listening for a long time before she said, "Now I am quite familiar with all sorts of wine-games, but have never heard of this one. Will you explain it to me?" Yün tried to explain it by all sorts of analogies to her, but still she failed to understand.

Then I laughed and said, "Will the lady teacher please stop a moment? I have a parable for explaining it, and she will understand at once." "You try it, then!" "The stork," I said, "can dance, but cannot plow, while the buffalo can plow, but cannot dance. That lies in the nature of things. You are making a fool of yourself by trying to teach the impossible to her." Suyün pummelled my shoulder playfully, saying, "You are speaking of me as a buffalo, aren't you?" Then Yün said, "Hereafter let's make a rule: let's have it out with our mouths, but no hands! One who breaks the rule will have to drink a big cup." As Suyün was a great drinker, she filled a cup full and drank it up at a draught. "I suggest that one may be allowed to use one's hands for caressing, but not for striking," I said. Yün then playfully pushed Suyün into my lap, saying, "Now you can caress her to your full." "How stupid of you!" I laughed in reply. "The beauty of caressing lies in doing it naturally and half unconsciously. Only a country bumpkin will hug and caress a woman roughly." I noticed that the jasmine in the hair of both of them gave out a strange fragrance, mixed with the flavor of wine, powder and hair lotion and remarked to Yün, "The 'common little fellow' stinks all over the place. It makes me sick." Hearing this, Suyün struck me blow after blow with her fist in a rage, saying, "Who told you to smell it?"

"She breaks the rule! Two big cups!" Yün shouted.

"He called me 'common little fellow.' Why shouldn't I strike him?" protested Suyün.

"He really means by the 'common little fellow' something which you don't understand. You finish these two cups first and I'll tell you."

When Suyün had finished the two cups, Yün told her of our discussion about the jasmine at the Ts'anglang Pavilion.

"Then the mistake is mine. I must be penalized again," said Suyün. And she drank a third cup.

Yün said then that she had long heard of her reputation as a singer and would like to hear her sing. This Suyün did beautifully, beating time with her ivory chopsticks on a little plate. Yün drank merrily until she was quite drunk, when she took a sedan-chair and went home first, while I remained chatting with Suyün for a moment, and then walked home under the moonlight.

At this time, we were staying in the home of our friend Lu Panfang, in a house called Hsiaoshuanglou. A few days afterwards, Mrs. Lu heard of the story from someone, and secretly told Yün, "Do you know that your husband was drinking a few days ago at the Bridge of Ten Thousand Years with two sing-song girls?" "Yes, I do," replied Yün, "and one of the sing-song girls was myself." Then she told her the whole story and Mrs. Lu had a good laugh at herself.

When I came back from Eastern Kwangtung in the seventh moon, 1794, there was a boy cousin-in-law of mine, by the name of Hsü Hsiufeng, who had brought home with him a concubine. He was crazy about her beauty and asked Yün to go and see her. After seeing her, Yün remarked to Hsiufeng one day. "She has beauty but no charm." "Do you mean to say that when your husband takes a concubine, she must have both beauty and charm?" answered Hsiufeng. Yün replied in the affirmative. So from that time on, she was quite bent on finding a concubine for me, but was short of cash.

At this time there was a Chekiang sing-song girl by the name of Wen Lenghsiang, who was staying at Soochow. She had composed four poems on the Willow Catkins which were talked about all over the city, and many scholars wrote poems in reply, using the same rhyme-words as her originals, as was the custom. There was a friend of mine, Chang Hsienhan of Wukiang, who was a good friend of Lenghsiang and brought her poems to me, asking us to write some in reply. Yün wasn't interested because she did not think much of her, but I was intrigued and composed one on the flying willow catkins which filled the air in May. Two lines which Yün liked very much were:

"*They softly touch the spring sorrow in my bosom,*
And gently stir the longings in her heart."

On the fifth day of the eighth moon in the following year, my mother was going to see Huch'iu with Yün, when Hsienhan suddenly appeared and said, "I am going to Huch'iu, too. Will you come along with me and see a beautiful sing-song girl?" I told my mother to go ahead and agreed to meet her at Pant'ang near Huch'iu. My friend then dragged me to Lenghsiang's place. I saw that Lenghsiang was already in her middle-age, but she had a girl by the name of Hanyüan, who was a very sweet young maiden, still in her teens. Her eyes looked "like an autumn lake that cooled one by its cold splendor." After talking with her for a while, I learnt that she knew very well how to read and write. There was also a younger sister of hers, by the name of Wenyüan, who was still a mere child.

I had then no thought of going about with a sing-song girl, fully realizing that, as a poor scholar, I could not afford to take part in the feast in such a place. But since I was there already, I tried to get along as best as I could.

"Are you trying to seduce me?" I said to Hsienhan secretly.

"No," he replied, "someone had invited me today to a dinner in Hanyüan's place in return for a previous dinner. It happened that the host himself was invited by an important person, and I am acting in his place. Don't you worry!"

I felt then quite relieved. Arriving at Pant'ang, we met my

mother's boat, and I asked Hanyüan to go over to her boat and meet her. When Yün and Han met each other, they instinctively took to each other like old friends, and later they went hand-in-hand all over the famous places on the hill. Yün was especially fond of a place called "A Thousand Acres of Clouds" for its loftiness, and she remained there for a long time, lost in admiration of the scenery. We returned to the Waterside of Rural Fragrance where we tied up the boats and had a jolly drinking party together.

When we started on our way home, Yün said, "Will you please go over to the other boat with your friend, while I share this one with Han?" We did as she suggested, and I did not return to my boat until we had passed the Tut'ing Bridge, where we parted from my friend and Hanyüan. It was midnight by the time we returned home.

"Now I have found a girl who has both beauty and charm," Yün said to me. "I have already asked Hanyüan to come and see us tomorrow, and I'll arrange it for you." I was taken by surprise.

"You know we are not a wealthy family. We can't afford to keep a girl like that, and we are so happily married. Why do you want to find somebody else?"

"But I love her," said Yün smilingly. "You just leave it to me."

The following afternoon, Hanyüan actually came. Yün was very cordial to her and prepared a feast, and we played the finger-guessing game and drank, but during the whole dinner, not a word was mentioned about securing her for me. When Hanyüan had gone, Yün said, "I have secretly made another appointment with her to come on the eighteenth, when we will pledge ourselves as sisters. You must prepare a sacrificial offering for the occasion"; and pointing to the emerald bracelet on her arm, she continued, "if you see this bracelet appear on Hanyüan's arm, you'll understand that she has consented. I have already hinted at it to her, but we haven't got to know each other as thoroughly as I should like to yet." I had to let her have her own way.

On the eighteenth, Hanyüan turned up in spite of a pouring rain. She disappeared in the bedroom for a long time before she came out hand-in-hand with Yün. When she saw me, she felt a little shy, for the bracelet was already on her arm. After they had burnt incense and pledged an oath, Yün wanted to have another drink together with her that day. But it happened that Hanyüan had an engagement to go and visit the Shih-hu Lake, and soon she left.

Yün came to me all smiles and said, "Now that I have found a beauty for you, how are you going to reward the go-between?" I asked her for the details.

"I had to broach the topic delicately to her," she said, "because I was afraid that she might have someone else in mind. Now I have learnt that there isn't anyone, and I asked her, 'Do you understand why we have this pledge today?' 'I should feel greatly honored if I could come to your home, but my mother is expecting a lot of me and I can't decide by myself. We will watch and see,' she replied. As I was putting on the bracelet, I told her again, 'The jade is chosen for its hardness as a token of fidelity and the bracelet's roundness is a symbol of everlasting faithfulness. Meanwhile, please put it on as a token of our pledge. She replied that everything depends on me. So it seems that she is willing herself. The only difficulty is her mother, Lenghsiang. We will wait and see how it turns out."

"Are you going to enact the comedy *Lianhsiangpan* of Li Liweng right in our home?"

"Yes!" Yün replied.

From that time on, not a day passed without her mentioning Hanyüan's name. Eventually Hanyüan was married by force to some influential person, and our arrangements did not come off. And Yün actually died of grief on this account.

林语堂译事年表①

1895 年

出生在福建省龙溪县(今属漳州市)。

1914 年

所译《卜舫济先生论欧战之影响于中国》载《约翰声》第 25 卷第 8 期中文版。

所撰英文文章"A Mission to Heaven"(《评李提摩太〈长春真人西游记〉英译本》)载《约翰声》第 25 卷第 3 期英文版。

1923 年

所译《海呐选译》(海呐,即海涅)在《晨报副刊》连载,从第 297 号开始持续刊登十余次。

所译《海呐歌谣第二》载《晨报副刊》第 332 号。

1924 年

所译《德文"古诗无名氏"一首》载《晨报副刊》第 78 号。

所译《戏论伯拉多式的恋爱》载《晨报副刊》第 90 号,作者为海涅。

---

① 本年表的整理主要参考了以下著作:郑锦怀.林语堂学术年谱.厦门:厦门大学出版社,2018.

所译《海呐春醒集第十七》载《晨报副刊》第 91 号。

所译《春醒集第三十六》载《晨报副刊》第 124 号。

1925 年

所译《海呐除夕歌》载《语丝》第 11 期。

所译《劝文豪歌》载《语丝》第 31 期。

所译《北大教授上段执政书》(英译)载《京报副刊》"沪汉后援专刊
(二)"。

1926 年

所译《莪默五首》载《语丝》第 66 期,作者为莪默。

1927 年

翻译尼采的《走过去》(选自尼采《查拉图斯特拉如是说》第七章
"Passing By"),借以送鲁迅离开厦门大学。

所译《西汉方音区域考上》载《贡献》第 2 期;所译《西汉方音区域考
下》载《贡献》第 3 期。

1928 年

所译《哈第论死生与上帝》(哈第,即哈代)载《语丝》第 11 期。

所译《论静思与空谈——〈艺术的批评家〉节译之一》载《语丝》第 13
期,作者为王尔德。所译《论创作与批评——〈艺术的批评家〉节译之二》
载《语丝》第 18 期。

所译《批评家与少年美国》载《奔流》第 1 卷第 1 期,作者为布鲁克斯。

1929 年

所译《易卜生评传及其情书》由上海春潮书局出版,作者为勃兰兑斯,
该书被列为林语堂主编的"现代读者丛书"第一种。

所译《女子与知识》由北新书局出版,作者为罗素夫人。

所译《新俄学生日记》由上海春潮书局出版,与张友松合译,作者为奥格涅夫,该译本转译自沃斯的英译本。

所译《美学:表现的科学》载《语丝》第 36 期,并续载于第 37 期,作者为克罗齐。

所译《国民革命外纪》由上海北新书局出版,作者为蓝孙姆。

1930 年

自译"The Function of Criticism at the Present Time"(《论现代批评的职务》)载《中国评论周报》第 3 卷第 4 期《专论》栏目。林语堂有很多自译作品,尤其是小品文,原文多为英语写作,汉语为翻译,原文频见于《中国评论周报》的《小评论》专栏。

辑译《新的批评》由上海北新书局出版,列为"文艺论述"丛书第一种。

1931 年

所译"The Nun's Soliloquy"(《尼姑思凡》)载《中国评论周报》第 4 卷第 15 期《小评论》专栏。(该文标题此后还有其他译法。)

所译《卖花女》由开明书店出版,为英汉对译版本,作者为萧伯纳。

1932 年

所撰《翻译之难》载《申报》12 月 18 日第 18 版《自由谈》栏目。

1933 年

所译"Talking Pictures"(《有声电影》)载《中国评论周报》第 6 卷第 49 期《小评论》专栏,作者为老舍。

所撰《语言学论丛》由上海开明书店出版,内有《论翻译》一文,此系林语堂探讨翻译最为系统、最为全面的理论性文章。

1934 年

所撰英文书评"*All Men Are Brothers*"(《评赛珍珠〈水浒传〉英译本》)载《中国评论周报》第 7 卷第 1 期《小评论》专栏。

所译"A Cock-Fight in Old China"(《山居斗鸡记》)载《中国评论周报》第 7 卷第 47 期《小评论》专栏,作者为明代袁中郎。

1935 年

所译《人生七计》载《论语》第 56 期("西洋幽默专号")《我的话》栏目,作者为莎士比亚。

辑译"The Humor of Mencius"(《孟子的幽默》)载《中国评论周报》第 8 卷第 1 期《小评论》专栏,分别译自《孟子·离娄》和《孟子·梁惠王》。

辑译"The Humor of Liehtse"(《列子的幽默》)载《中国评论周报》第 8 卷第 3 期《小评论》专栏。

所译"Ah Chen's Death"(《祭震女文》)载《中国评论周报》第 8 卷第 12 期《小评论》专栏,作者为明代沈君烈。(该文标题此后还有其他译法。)

所译"The Epigrams of Chang Ch'ao"(《张潮的〈幽梦影〉》)载《中国评论周报》第 9 卷第 4 期《小评论》专栏。(该文标题此后还有其他译法。)

所译"A Chinese Ventriloquist"(《一位中国口技表演者》)载《中国评论周报》第 9 卷第 7 期《小评论》专栏,原文为明代林嗣环的《秋声诗自序》,也常被称为《口技》。

所译 *Six Chapters of a Floating Life*(《浮生六记》)第一记《闺房记乐》载《天下》(*T'ien Hsia Monthly*)第 1 卷第 1 期《译文》("Translations")栏目,作者为清代沈复。第二记《闲情记趣》载《天下》第 1 卷第 2 期,第三记《坎坷记愁》载《天下》第 1 卷第 3 期,第四记《浪游记快》载《天下》第 1 卷第 4 期。

所著 *My Country and My People*(《吾国与吾民》)由美国纽约的雷纳

尔和希区柯克公司出版,内有部分译文,后多次重印与再版。

所撰《〈浮生六记〉英译自序》载《人间世》第 40 期。

1936 年

所译"On Charm in Women"(《论女性魅力》,后又译为《说韵》)载《中国评论周报》第 12 卷第 10 期《小评论》专栏,原文为清代李笠翁的《闲情偶寄·态度》。

所译"Homeward Bound I Go!"载《中国评论周报》第 13 卷第 2 期《小评论》专栏,原文为陶渊明的《归去来辞》。

所译 *A Nun of Taishan and Other Translations* 由上海商务印书馆出版,中文书名为《英译〈老残游记〉第二集及其他选译》。

1937 年

所著 *The Importance of Living*(《生活的艺术》)由美国纽约的雷纳尔和希区柯克公司出版,内有很多译文,后多次重印与再版。

1938 年

所著 *The Wisdom of Confucius*(《孔子的智慧》)由美国纽约的兰登书屋出版,列入"现代文库",其中的译文也有少许取自国内外其他翻译家的译文,如辜鸿铭等。

1939 年

所译《有不为斋:归去来辞·兰亭集序》载《西风》第 30 期;所译《有不为斋:三十三不亦快哉》载《西风》第 31 期;所译《有不为斋(三):金圣叹〈论游〉》载《西风》第 32 期;所译《有不为斋(四):张潮〈幽梦影〉》载《西风》第 33 期;所译《有不为斋(五):张潮〈幽梦影〉(二)》载《西风》第 34 期;所译《有不为斋(六):张潮〈幽梦影〉(三)》载《西风》第 35 期;所译《有不为斋(七):张潮〈幽梦影〉(四)》载《西风》第 36 期;所译《有不为斋(八):蒋坦

〈秋灯琐忆〉(三)》载《西风》第 37 期;所译《有不为斋(九)》载《西风》第 38 期,原文为李笠翁的《论居室》;所译《有不为斋(十):半半歌及其他》载《西风》第 39 期;所译《有不为斋(十一):陈眉公〈小窗幽记〉》载《西风》第 40 期。(以上作品均以汉英对照形式发表。)

所译《成功之路》由中国杂志公司增订再版,作者为马尔腾,林语堂把作者的两本书合为一本。

所译《心理漫谈》由上海东方图书公司出版,作者为笳斯特娄。

所著英文长篇小说 *Moment in Peking*(《京华烟云》)由美国纽约的庄台公司出版,后多次重版。

1940 年

所译《冥寥子游(一)》载《西风》第 41 期;所译《冥寥子游(一续)》载《西风》第 42 期;所译《冥寥子游(三)》载《西风》第 43 期;所译《冥寥子游(四)》载《西风》第 44 期;所译《冥寥子游(五)》载《西风》第 45 期;所译《冥寥子游(六)》载《西风》第 46 期;所译《冥寥子游(七)》载《西风》第 47 期;所译《冥寥子游(八)》载《西风》第 48 期。(以上作品均以汉英对照形式发表。)

所译《有不为斋古文小品》由上海的西风社以汉英对照形式出版。

所译《有不为斋冥寥子游》由上海的西风社以汉英对照形式出版,列为"西风丛书"第八种,作者为屠纬真。

1941 年

所译《老残游记(卷上)》由上海朔风书店以英汉对照形式出版。

所著英文长篇小说 *A Leaf in the Storm: A Novel of War-Swept China*(《风声鹤唳》)由美国纽约的庄台公司出版。

1942 年

所著 *The Wisdom of China and India*(《中国与印度的智慧》)由美国

纽约的兰登书屋出版,列入"现代文库",后多次重印。

1943 年

所著 *Between Tears and Laughter*(《啼笑皆非》)由美国纽约的庄台公司出版。

所译 *Tales and Parables of Old China*(《古代中国故事与寓言》)由美国旧金山的加州图书俱乐部出版。

1944 年

所著英文小说 *The Vigil of a Nation*(《枕戈待旦》)由美国纽约的庄台公司出版。

1947 年

所著 *The Gay Genius: The Life and Times of Su Tungpo*(《苏东坡传》)由美国纽约的庄台公司出版。

1948 年

编译 *Famous Chinese Short Stories*(《英译重编传奇小说》,又译为《中国传奇小说》)由美国纽约的庄台公司出版。

所著 *The Wisdom of Laotse*(《老子的智慧》)由美国纽约的庄台公司出版。

1950 年

所译 *Miss Du*(《杜十娘》)由英国伦敦的威廉·海涅曼公司出版。

1951 年

所译 *Widow, Nun and Courtesan: Three Novelettes from the Chinese*(《寡妇、尼姑与歌妓:英译三篇小说集》)由美国纽约的庄台公司出

版,其中包括《杜十娘》等原文。

1953 年

所著 *The Vermilion Gate*(《朱门》)由美国纽约的庄台公司出版。

1957 年

所译 *Chuangtse*(《庄子》)由台北的世界书局出版。

所著 *Lady Wu: A True Story*(《武则天传》)由英国伦敦的威廉·海涅曼公司出版。

1960 年

所译 *The Importance of Understanding: Translations from the Chinese*(《古文小品译英》)由美国克利夫兰与纽约的世界出版公司出版。

1961 年

所著英文小说 *The Red Peony*(《红牡丹》)由美国克利夫兰与纽约的世界出版公司出版,后多次重印。

1965 年

所撰《论译诗》载台湾"中央日报"8 月 2 日第 10 版与当日《联合报》。

1967 年

所撰《英译黛玉葬花诗》载台湾"中央日报"6 月 19 日第 10 版。

所译 *The Chinese Theory of Art: Translations from the Masters of China*(《中国画论》)由美国纽约的 G. P. 普特南公司出版。

1973 年

完成其《红楼梦》英译书稿(编译,至今未正式出版),并将其寄给日本翻译家佐藤亮一,数月之后又将修订稿寄给佐藤亮一,后者据此完成了《红楼梦》日译本。

1976 年

病逝于香港。

中華譯學館 · 中华翻译家代表性译文库

许　钧　郭国良 / 总主编

第一辑   第二辑

图书在版编目(CIP)数据

中华翻译家代表性译文库. 林语堂卷 / 冯全功编
. —杭州:浙江大学出版社,2022.6
 ISBN 978-7-308-21377-6

Ⅰ.①中… Ⅱ.①冯… Ⅲ.①林语堂(1895—1976)
—译文—文集 Ⅳ.①I11

中国版本图书馆 CIP 数据核字(2021)第 095200 号

中华翻译家代表性译文库·林语堂卷
冯全功 编

出 品 人	褚超孚
丛书策划	张 琛 包灵灵
责任编辑	董 唯
责任校对	祁 潇
封面设计	闰江文化
出版发行	浙江大学出版社
	(杭州市天目山路 148 号 邮政编码 310007)
	(网址:http://www.zjupress.com)
排 版	浙江时代出版服务有限公司
印 刷	杭州高腾印务有限公司
开 本	710mm×1000mm 1/16
印 张	28
字 数	479 千
版 印 次	2022 年 6 月第 1 版 2022 年 6 月第 1 次印刷
书 号	ISBN 978-7-308-21377-6
定 价	88.00 元